MANAGER'S SCRIPT BOOK

MANAGER'S SCRIPT BOOK

by W. H. Weiss

PRENTICE HALL
Englewood Cliffs, New Jersey 07632

Prentice-Hall International (UK) Limited, *London*
Prentice-Hall of Australia Pty. Limited, *Sydney*
Prentice-Hall Canada, Inc., *Toronto*
Prentice-Hall Hispanoamericana, S.A., *Mexico*
Prentice-Hall of India Private Limited, *New Delhi*
Prentice-Hall of Japan, Inc., *Tokyo*
Simon & Schuster Asia Pte. Ltd., *Singapore*
Editora Prentice-Hall do Brasil, Ltda., *Rio de Janeiro*

© 1990 *by*
PRENTICE-HALL, Inc.
Englewood Cliffs, NJ

10

Library of Congress Cataloging-in-Publication Data

Weiss, W. H., 1918–
   Manager's script book / by W. H. Weiss.
     p.   cm.
   Includes index.
   ISBN 0-13-551839-3 : $39.95
    1. Communication in personnel management—Handbooks, manuals, etc.
   2. Supervisors—Handbooks, manuals, etc.   I. Title.
HF5549.5.C6W45   1990
658.4′52—dc20
                                            89-34715
                                          CIP

ISBN 0-13-551839-3

PRENTICE HALL
Englewood Cliffs, NJ 07632

A Simon & Schuster Company

Printed in the United States of America

Other Books by Author

SUPERVISOR'S STANDARD REFERENCE HANDBOOK

THE ART AND SKILL OF MANAGING PEOPLE

How This Book Will Help You

What words do you use in telling an employee you are going to suspend him or her a few days because of low productivity? What do you say to someone who has shown disloyalty to the company in public? How do you tell a faithful employee that he or she should consider retiring or a change in responsibilities is a likelihood?

This book tells you the words to use and how to say them when you find yourself in difficult personnel situations. In addition, you'll learn the probable responses and range of rebuttals you may get, and how you can counter them. Moreover, you are given the reasoning and logic for what you should say.

This book was written because of the widespread need of management people to know what to say to subordinates in order to help them with their problems. While managers knew and understood the basic principles of successful managing, they wanted help in finding the best and most appropriate words to use in specific situations.

While intended primarily for first-line managers in supervisional positions, many situations involving managers talking to supervisors are also covered. All levels of management in business and industry need to be adept in handling subordinates. THE MANAGER'S SCRIPT BOOK contains the most appropriate and effective words to say to motivate people, straighten them out, and have them perform to your desires and expectations.

THE MANAGER'S SCRIPT BOOK will benefit you in many ways:

- It will provide you insight to the many personnel problems that supervisors and managers encounter daily.
- It will make it easy for you to relate the situations which are presented to your own specific problems.
- It will give you an opportunity to evaluate the words which you might have said if you hadn't read the book.
- It will refresh your memory of the sound principles of management you already know but have not yet needed to implement.

- It will enable you to suggest to your fellow managers what they should say to their subordinates when handling difficult personnel problems.

This book is intended to be kept on your desk, ready for use. The contents are arranged so that you can quickly find a script covering a personnel problem which you must handle by talking to an individual. For example, if you want to know what to say to a person who wants to be a supervisor but doesn't have the qualifications, you simply turn to Chapter VIII titled "Interviewing and Job Suitability." In that chapter you will find several scripts appropriate for talking to people about the jobs in your department.

To present scripts in the clearest yet most encompassing way, THE MANAGER'S SCRIPT BOOK offers you over 150 situations covering the following 24 problem areas: Work Performance; Costs and Productivity; Communication; Rules and Regulations; Discipline; Motivation; Developing People; Interviewing and Job Suitability; Personal Qualities; Safety and Health; Assigning and Delegating; Problem People; Cooperation; Creativity and Innovation; Loyalty; Authority and Responsibility; Honesty; Pay and Promotions; Decision-Making; Standards; Gripes and Grievances; Instructing and Training; Drugs and Alcoholism; Change.

Every effort has been made to fill this book with logical, practical and straight-shooting scripts. There's no beating-around-the bush or weak attempts to make a point. Here are just a few of the wide range of personnel problems covered:

Chapter 2	What to say to an employee whose productivity isn't good enough.
Chapter 6	What to say to an employee who complains of the work being too boring.
Chapter 7	What to say to a supervisor who is insensitive to people's problems and needs.
Chapter 8	What to say to one of your people when he or she is not suited to a job opening.
Chapter 9	What to say to an employee who refuses to dress appropriately for the job.
Chapter 10	What to say to an employee who ignores the company's safety regulations.
Chapter 12	What to say to an employee who likes to play practical jokes.

As you can see, THE MANAGER'S SCRIPT BOOK is written to tell you what to say when you face a difficult personnel problem. Since it covers the full range of managerial responsibilities and duties, in almost any type of business—in the office, the plant, or out in the field—all people who lead and direct others can benefit from using it regularly.

W. H. Weiss

Table of Contents

CHAPTER 3   COMMUNICATION

CHAPTER 4   RULES AND REGULATIONS

CHAPTER 5   DISCIPLINE

CHAPTER 6   MOTIVATION

CHAPTER 7   DEVELOPING PEOPLE

CHAPTER 17   HONESTY

CHAPTER 18   PAY AND PROMOTION

CHAPTER 19   DECISION MAKING

CHAPTER 20   STANDARDS

CHAPTER 21   COMPLAINTS AND GRIEVANCES

CHAPTER 24   CHANGE

Chapter 1

WORK PERFORMANCE

In the following situations, note how the manager puts across the importance of work standards, what kind of performance management is looking for, and why inefficiency cannot be tolerated. Notice, also, how cooperation and showing of responsibility are expected of all subordinates.

PROBLEM NUMBER 1

What to say to subordinates to encourage them to volunteer for a job.

The Situation

You've had a meeting with your superior at which he gave you some assignments, one of which he said you should give top priority. It is apparent that you will have to delegate most, if not all of these assignments. However, since two of your people, Bob and John, are capable of handling the top priority job without much training or instruction, you decide to present it to them and ask for a volunteer.

What You Should Say and Some Responses

"Our department has been asked to work up a new monthly report and submit it to the Controller of the company. This report will contain cost, selling price, quantities shipped, and tax information on selected products we send to our distributors.

"I know that both of you have plenty of work to do, so I thought I'd throw it up for grabs to see if either of you wanted to take on this additional work."

1

You pause here to see if you get any immediate reaction or comment from either of your people, but there is none. Realizing that they really don't know all that the job entails, you go on.

"To prepare this report, you will have to work with some other departments including Purchasing and Accounting. This means you will have to ask certain people in those departments for the data and information you need, and get it each month. Once you set up the procedure, writing the report should be pretty routine."

Both of your people remain quiet. While you had hoped they would show some interest, neither has.

"You know, by taking on this project and doing a good job, you would be impressing an important executive in the company. At the same time, you would bring yourself to the attention of top management. By sidestepping this job and avoiding the extra work, you would be also sidestepping opportunity.

"It might make sense to avoid volunteering when you don't have anything to gain, or might even make a poor showing, but that isn't the case here. I'm sure that both of you are quite capable of handling this."

"I'll take it," Bob responded with a slight smile on his face.

"Thanks, Bob. Right after lunch I'll give you some suggestions on how to get started and who to see in those other departments."

Reasoning and Principle Involved

It's a good idea to occasionally ask for volunteers to take on projects instead of always assigning them. This way, you can learn which of your people is ambitious and would like to move up in the company.

What a lot of people on the job don't seem to realize is that extra work and opportunity are virtually synonymous. Yet some people prefer to look for reasons why they couldn't take on an extra assignment, rather than recognize the value of that opportunity.

Always thank or congratulate an individual when he or she volunteers to do a job. Your recognition provides a lift, confirms that the volunteer's decision was a good one, and shows that you appreciate the help.

PROBLEM NUMBER 2

What to say to employees when you must persuade them to work additional overtime.

The Situation

You've been told that executives from corporate headquarters will be visiting your plant in about two weeks. Your superior is anxious about the visit and wants to make a good impression on the executives. While the plant has been operating efficiently, some of the facilities and equipment need cleaning and attention. In addition, there are several rooms that should be painted. You realize that if this general cleanup is to be accomplished without interrupting production schedules, your people are going to have to work a lot of overtime. You see that the sooner you inform your people of this, the better.

What You Should Say and Some Responses

"This morning I was told that the President and one or more Vice Presidents will be visiting us in about two weeks. We've got a lot of work to do to clean up the place and make it as neat as possible. Most of this work is going to have to be done on overtime because we don't want to get behind on our production. So starting tomorrow we are going to schedule you to work a lot of overtime. Anybody have any questions?"

Expect that there will be none at this time. Consequently, you plan and line up the work. Your people then work overtime for the rest of the week and into the following week. However, there is still quite a bit of work to do at the end of the day on Friday. When you assign five of your people to work Saturday, three of them refuse. One of the three speaks for them.

"We've been knocking ourselves out for more than a week working all kinds of hours. How about giving us a break? We don't feel that we should have to work on Saturday too."

"I'm sorry, guys, but it can't be helped. You've really done a good job up to now, and I appreciate it. However, our visitors will be here on Monday and there's still a lot to be done. All I'm asking of you is just one more day of work."

"Yeah, but we don't think all this work is necessary. It's not like we aren't getting the production orders out. The plant's right on schedule. Also, we checked with the Union President, and he said that even though overtime is compulsory according to the contract, there has to be a good reason for it."

"According to the plant manager, there is a good reason."

"Well, we don't agree. We're not coming in tomorrow. It's not right for the company to make us work when there's no good reason for it."

"If you don't come in, you can expect a suspension without pay. It's up to you. That's all I have to say, except that I hope you change your minds."

Reasoning and Principle Involved

While some employees may feel that the company is being unreasonable, if the contract reads that overtime isn't voluntary, they don't have an argument. Also, it's management's function to decide what is a good reason for working overtime and what isn't.

Managers can't afford to put themselves in the position where one or more employees decide whether work is needed or not.

PROBLEM NUMBER 3

What to say to an employee when you must request overtime at the last minute.

The Situation

A power failure in the packaging department of your company has shut down operations for more than two hours. Your electrician, Paul, has been working on the problem, but has been unable to find the source of the trouble. The Production Department has been trying to fill an urgent order and get it shipped. You decide to talk to Paul to learn the status of the job and to ask him to work overtime if it is necessary.

What You Should Say and Some Responses

"How are you doing, Paul?"

"Not so good. This one's really tough."

"I don't know whether you heard or not, but the Production Department is trying to get an order shipped today. They have men waiting for the power to be turned on so they can get the stuff packaged and loaded on a trailer. Sales says that if we don't make the shipment today, we could lose the customer."

"I'm doing the best I can."

"I know that Paul, but I'm going to have to ask you to work overtime until you can get the power back on. This is an emergency."

"Gosh, I can't stay today. Why don't you ask Smitty to stay over?"

"Smitty doesn't know this system like you do. He wouldn't be of much help. I wouldn't ask you if it could be avoided. I have no other choice."

"I'm sorry. Neither have I. I've got to be at the airport at 6:00 to pick up some people visiting us, and I can't let those people down."

"The job is more important, Paul."

"Maybe. But this is a special occasion. Besides, you didn't give me any notice. You can't ask me to stay over half an hour before quitting time and expect me to work when I've got plans. I don't even have time to ask someone else to meet those people. It would be hard to do."

"I'm sorry, but like I said, it can't be helped."

"Well, I'm sorry too, but the answer's 'no'."

"Paul, this is a serious matter. I'm going to have to suspend you without pay if you don't work overtime."

"We'll see about that," Paul angrily replies.

Assuming Paul leaves the job at his regular quitting time without correcting the electrical problem, you must follow through with the suspension when he shows up for work the next morning.

Reasoning and Principle Involved

Paul should be suspended even though he and the Union say they will fight it. Whether Paul has a valid complaint because of not being notified earlier about the overtime is immaterial. He is obliged to comply with your request and then can turn in a grievance if he wants to. Employees are relieved of their obligation to comply with an order only if what they are told to do appears to be a health or safety hazard, is against the law, or is prohibited by the labor agreement.

PROBLEM NUMBER 4

What to say to a supervisor who needs to do something about inefficiency in the department.

The Situation

You've noticed that the operating costs of one of your production departments are much higher than those of your other departments. It doesn't take you long to investigate the operation and learn what is seemingly wrong. Now you must talk to the supervisor of the inefficient department and try to get the situation corrected.

What You Should Say and Some Responses

"Sam, I've noticed that the operating costs of your department are much higher than those of Dept. B and C which do similar work. Do you know why?"

Sam looks thoughtful, and then shakes his head. "Beats me. All I do is follow instructions."

"And you do that like a pro. But that isn't the problem. We've got to find out why these costs are so high, and do something about it. Our company is no different from most other manufacturing companies these days. The cost of labor and materials keeps rising. Yet we've got to keep the prices of our products down to stay ahead of the competition. I don't think I have to tell you there's only one way to do that."

"Better productivity," Sam says.

"Right! How do you think we can get it, Sam? Any ideas?"

At this point, you've got to give Sam time to think and to make some suggestions. Recognize that conscientious supervisors are usually aware of where the inefficiencies are in their operations. However, they may hesitate to bring these matters to the attention of their superiors for any of several reasons. Now you are giving Sam an opportunity to do so.

Whatever Sam suggests, be sure to give it considerable thought. Be slow to reject an idea even though it may appear illogical or impractical at the moment. Instead, say something like, "That's a possibility," or "I'll look into that," or "You might have something there." Then, make sure you follow up as quickly as possible.

In the event that Sam doesn't have any suggestions or if he makes any comments, bring up what you have learned or observed in the department's operations. If Sam does offer something, say, "I think you may be right, Sam, but I've noticed something else that is running up your costs." Then proceed to talk to Sam about it.

Reasoning and Principle Involved

Management hopes that supervisors will examine and analyze every aspect of their operations periodically for inefficiency. There is no better way to multiply productivity and profitability, departmental success, and personal success. But not all supervisors do this. When they don't, it behooves their superiors to pick up the slack.

PROBLEM NUMBER 5

What to say to the manager who lets subordinates set goals without recognizing basic standards.

The Situation

Bob White recently was promoted to manager of a group of engineers. Since he had no previous supervisory experience, he was very cautious in carrying out his responsibilities. Within three months, Bob's group was behind in its work. While he tried working some of the engineers overtime, it was not enough. Today, Bob came to you to request that another engineer be added to his staff.

What You Should Say and Some Responses

"Bob, I can't see why the work can't be handled by the people you now have. You're getting no more projects assigned to your group than you normally receive, and that hasn't changed in the last year."

Bob doesn't seem surprised by your comments. "I really don't know why they can't either. All I know is that we're getting too far behind."

"When you assign a project to an engineer, do you set a deadline for when it should be done?"

Bob replies, "A goal is set for every project."

"But how is that done?" you ask.

"Mostly by the men themselves. They've done the work in the past. They know how long a job should take."

You nod your head and reply slowly, "I think that this may be the problem. Setting goals is a tricky job. Setting them too high causes bitterness and also discourages some people. Setting them too low takes the challenge out of it.

"I think it's a good idea to have your people participate in setting goals instead of you doing it alone. But management must establish and adhere to certain standards regarding goals and objectives. They should be challenging, yet realistic and achievable. If you give some employees too much leeway, they may set their goals too low, even as much as 10 to 20 percent lower than they are capable of achieving, instead of the other way around."

Bob responds, "Well, you may have something there, but I'm not sure."

"I suggest you take a bigger part in setting due dates on the assignments you make from now on, even to the extent that you tell an engineer how long a job should take, and that you expect him or her to do it in that time or less."

Reasoning and Principle Involved

While it is poor management practice not to permit employees to have a say on how long it should take them to do a job, human nature should not be overlooked. Most people underestimate what they are capable of doing in a period of time. Managers should recognize this when looking for ways to raise the productivity of their people. There's nothing wrong with saying to a subordinate, "Why don't you shoot for three days on this project? I know you can do it!"

PROBLEM NUMBER 6

What to say to a foreman whom you want to dissuade from acting impulsively in handling an employee.

The Situation

One of the employees of your company recently spent a day in jail. He also has been known to drink quite a bit and occasionally gets into fights. His foreman, Art Thompson, is greatly bothered by such behavior and wants to have him discharged. To be sure such action is justified, you arrange to discuss the problem worker with the foreman.

What You Should Say and Some Responses

"I see that Barnes is in trouble."

"Yeah, he did some damage in a bar and wound up in jail. You know, I've just about had enough of that guy. I have a tough enough time running the department and keeping people in line. When you've got to deal with fellows who break the law, that gets to be a little too much. I'd like to get rid of him."

"That's always a last resort move Art, if the situation requires it. But let's talk about Barnes so we can be sure we don't make a mistake. Does he have a poor attendance record? What about his work in general?"

"Oh, he misses a couple days now and then. His work's no better or worse than the rest of the fellows. But the guy's unreliable, a loser. If there's one thing I don't need it's people who can't control their temper."

You nod. "You make a good point, but tell me, as far as you know, does Barnes ever drink on the job?"

"Not that I know of, but that doesn't mean . . . "

"Get into fights?"

"On the job? Not since I've been foreman. But I heard that a couple years ago, he got into an argument over a tool that was missing, and hit a guy. You know, the more I think about it, the more I'm inclined to try to get him out of here. I certainly would feel more at ease, if nothing else."

"I can understand how you feel. We could talk about Barnes and his behavior for a long time. But let's face it, Art, in the end there's only one thing that really matters: How does his behavior affect his work and that of his co-workers?

"Of course, we don't know what causes Barnes to act as he does, drink, fight, and lose his temper. Maybe he came from a bad home, or his parents did a poor job of raising him. Whatever, there are others with worse records than his who are still working for the company.

"My recommendation is that we take no action at all unless, or until, his behavior starts affecting his work or the work of your department. Also, there's another matter that shouldn't be overlooked. Because there are worse performers in the company, we might have trouble making his dismissal stick."

Reasoning and Principle Involved

Managers must constantly be on guard not to act impulsively on matters involving performance of their employees, especially when a dismissal is being considered. Firing an employee is a serious matter. Most companies, particularly the large ones, spend a large amount of time and money in training an employee to be productive and an asset to the company. A dismissal means that a new employee must be hired, and there is no assurance that he or she will perform any better than the person dismissed.

PROBLEM NUMBER 7

What to say to an employee who has just recently been performing below standard.

The Situation

In going over the piecework earnings of your department people, you notice that one of your top performers has failed to turn in a high production figure for three consecutive months. In fact, his earnings for all three months were considerably below his previous year's monthly average. Sensing that something is wrong, you arrange to take the fellow aside and talk to him.

What You Should Say and Some Responses

"Pete, I've noticed that your piecework earnings have dropped off considerably in the last few months. What's the problem?"

Pete shrugs and doesn't say anything.

"I know you're capable of turning out a lot more work. I like you personally, and I'd like to help you get your production rate back up. But you've been below just about everybody doing your type of work for several months now. What's the matter? Are you having trouble at home?"

"No. Nothing like that."

"How about the work? Have you lost interest in it or has it become boring?"

"No, I still like this work—I just don't seem to be able to turn out as much as I used to."

"Are you getting along OK with the other people in the department?"

"Yep." However, he gave you the impression that he wished you would stop the questions and leave him alone.

"How about Mary Smith? Do you get along OK with her? Does it bother you to take orders from a woman?"

Pete's answer to your last question was also negative, but he hesitated in replying. Also, he suddenly appeared self-conscious and nervous, tipping you off that you probably had the answer to his low productivity. It all added up when you realized that Pete was almost 60 years old and set in his ways. Mary had become supervisor of the department about four months ago when her boss, an older fellow, had retired. Now that you know why Pete's productivity has fallen off, you start thinking about what you should say to him to get him to accept Mary as his supervisor.

An Alternate Approach

"Pete, when did you last get your glasses changed?"

Pete scratches his head. "Oh, I'd say about four years ago."

But he was simply guessing. After you suggested that he see his eye doctor, he did so. He soon was wearing new glasses, and his piecework earnings immediately began to climb.

Reasoning and Principle Involved

Asking questions is an excellent way to get information and to attack a problem. Although some skill is involved in asking the right ones, you can easily learn this. Good questions are as important when you want information as a bat and ball when you go out to play baseball.

Most of your questions should be ones which cannot be answered with a yes or no. Not only do such questions gain you more information, but they also minimize the number you must ask.

PROBLEM NUMBER 8

What to say to a supervisor who is spending too much time doing work which subordinates could do.

The Situation

While you work overtime only occasionally, every time you do, you see one of your supervisors, Bill Jones, also working. You've noticed, too, that he usually is on the job before you arrive in the morning, and seldom leaves before you at quitting time. While you admire your supervisor's loyalty to the company and his conscientious approach to his job, you know that too much dedication to one's work can be harmful. You decide to talk to Bill about this.

What You Should Say and Some Responses

"Bill, the hours you're putting on the job indicate to me that we have a problem."

Bill frowns. "What's the problem?"

"That's what I'd like to find out—for the good of the company, your department, and most of all for your own good. Tell me, Bill, how do your wife and kids feel about all that overtime you're working?"

"Well," Bill hesitates, "I guess they hate it, but I figure it's part of the job, and I need to do it to carry out all my responsibilities."

"But do you honestly feel that you must spend more than 60 hours a week, every week, working?"

"Well. . . . " Bill smiles, but doesn't know what to say.

"How about doing something for me, Bill. Make a list of the jobs and reports on which you spend most of your time on this paper. Put down the number of hours you estimate you're spending on each one. Write them down in any order as they come to you. While you're doing that, I'll get us some coffee."

Bill starts to think and write while you go for the coffee. Don't rush or push him when you return. Give him at least 10 minutes or longer until you sense he is about finished or has run out of jobs to be listed.

"That's enough for now, Bill. Let's see what you've got. What's this—Cost Analysis of Operations? I see that it takes about six hours per week. Is there any reason why you have to do it yourself?"

"I've to to be sure it's right. It's an important report."

"No one else in your department could handle it if properly trained?" you ask.

"Well. . . ."

You go on reading. "Work Order Status Report, a monthly report that averages out to four hours per week. Is there any reason why one of your people couldn't do that?"

"No, I guess not. But I like to handle that job. I see what work we have to do and where we stand."

"Here's another one—Development Projects and Programs—ten hours a week. Why do you work on this?"

"It's complicated. I do the job faster and better than anyone else."

You nod and continue to read off other items on the list. Bill gives you pretty much the same answers on each. Finally, you lay the list down.

"Bill, a supervisor's job is to lead people and manage, not do what others could do if properly trained. You're functioning as a subordinate, even a clerk, not as a supervisor.

"You'd make me, your wife and kids, and especially yourself, happy if you'd train and qualify your people to take over many of these jobs you've been doing. Everyone holding a responsible job should take some time for relaxation, recreation and enjoying one's family.

"Delegation is the answer to getting work done and also carrying out all your responsibilities. You must practice it if you have hopes of moving up in the company. Your skill in delegating could be the deciding factor in whether you can handle greater responsibilities and a bigger job. Successful managers get things done through others."

Reasoning and Principle Involved

Most successful supervisors are skilled in the art of delegating. In case you're undecided about your need to do it, be convinced when you frequently find yourself taking work home at night or working a lot of overtime.

If supervisors feel that subordinates can't do certain jobs as well as they can, consideration should be given to whether it's really necessary to do those jobs that well. For several reasons, all supervisors have much more to gain than to lose by delegating.

Chapter 2

COSTS AND PRODUCTIVITY

In the following situations, note how the manager promotes productivity, what kinds of performance make for desirable productivity, and what needs to be done to improve it. Notice, also, how the manager sells cost-cutting procedures to employees.

PROBLEM NUMBER 1

What to say to a long-time employee who recently developed an attendance problem.

The Situation

Aware that absenteeism is costing your company large amounts of money, you are dismayed when a report put out by the Personnel Dept. shows that one of the worst offenders is Bob Smith, one of your people. Smith is a quiet fellow with many years of service over which he has a better than average attendance record. You recall, however having said, "I missed you yesterday, Bob," after one of his recent absences on a Monday, and receiving no response from him. You feel that it's time to have a talk with him.

What You Should Say and Some Responses

"Are you feeling OK, Bob? I've noticed that you missed quite a few days of work the last couple months."

"Yes, I'm feeling good. Those absences are a thing of the past. I'm on the job every day now."

While you expected Bob to say more, he turned away from you and got busy with his work. Sensing that he was not in the mood to talk, you withdraw, making a mental note to watch his attendance from that point on.

Two days later, Bob called to say he would not be coming to work that day. Now you had to have an explanation. You approach him on the job the next day suggesting that you have a cup of coffee together and talk. Reluctantly he agrees and the two of you go to a far-off corner of the cafeteria where you will not be disturbed.

"What happened, Bob? You were absent again yesterday."

Bob lowers his eyes and says nothing. After a few seconds, he speaks, "I'll take care of it. Just give me a chance."

After waiting a bit for him to continue without that happening, you softly say, "Bob, that's what you told me two days ago." No response from Bob.

"You know, Bob, management recognizes that excessive absence of an employee can be caused by a number of reasons. The employee may have personal problems he's unable to solve; he may be chronically ill; he may be lazy and irresponsible, indifferent to the company's cost involved, and not concerned about the deterioration of his reputation as a reliable individual.

"I'm particularly concerned about you, Bob, because I know you're not lazy or irresponsible, and you've had a good record over your many years with the company."

You pause a bit, waiting to see if Bob will say something, but he doesn't. Instead, he looks away from you, giving you the impression he's uncomfortable. You go on.

"If the employee's absence is beyond his personal control, then his background, record and number of years of service are carefully considered. Sometimes a switch in hours or shift can be helpful, or, if health is a problem, a suggested leave of absence. Other times, if an employee with a good record of attendance suddenly starts taking "sick" days where his illness looks suspicious, the problem could be with his job. Conflicts and friction may have developed or his work may have become boring and dull. In this case, a different job may be in order, or the start of a training program for a new job."

Again you wait for a response, but there is none. However, there are signs of emotion now on Bob's face.

"Bob, I'd like to help you. Tell me the problem."

"OK, OK, my wife is an alcoholic and I've been trying to break her of the habit. Maybe you've noticed that I've been reporting off frequently on Monday. I watch her very closely on weekends and don't let her out of my sight. I figure if I can string three days in a row without giving her a chance to have a drink, maybe I can break it. But usually when I come home from work on Tuesday, I can tell that she's been drinking again. Also, there are other days during the week when she is unable to get up, so I stay home then, too."

"Bob, I'm glad you told me about this. I'm not qualified to give advice on such problems, and I'm not going to try to do so. There's a fellow in our Personnel Department who may be able to help you. Everything you tell him will be held in strict confidence. I'd like to make an appointment for you to see Paul Murphy some day after work. May I do that for you?"

"Well, OK, but I don't want this known around the department."

"I can assure you that won't happen. I will let you know as soon as I can set the date. Perhaps even today."

Reasoning and Principle Involved

Whatever the case, studies have shown that where poor attendance of employees is a problem, any action on the supervisor's part is better than no action at all. It indicates to employees that the boss is aware of the situation, is concerned about it, and refuses to put up with it.

PROBLEM NUMBER 2

What to say to workers when the company is faced with high costs and must respond to them.

The Situation

You have called together the people working for you to talk to them about the serious problem of high costs the company is experiencing. You want to explain to them what the company can do about these costs, and what course of action it has decided to take.

What You Should Say and Some Responses

"The reason I called this meeting is because, like many other companies these days, we are caught up in a cost-price squeeze, and we have to make some decisions on how to respond to it. I could give you all kinds of figures from studies and reports the company has made on how labor, equipment, and material costs have been constantly rising. I could talk about the high cost of bank loans and what a company must go through to get financing today. But I wouldn't be telling you anything you don't already know, and I'd probably bore you to death in the process. What I'll do instead is to give you the facts as plainly and as bluntly as possible.

"The decision facing our company's management concerns the price of our products and services. We've been doing the best we can to hold the price line, to withstand price-boosting pressures, for quite some time. As a result, profits have been gradually diminishing and we've reached the point where we can't take further decreases. The company has to act, one way or another. If we continued on our present course, we'd soon be in the red. I don't have to tell you what this would mean for the company and for each and every one of us.

"There are two alternate courses of action open to us. The first looks like the simplest and would be the easiest to follow. We could simply raise the price of our product line (or service) or selected key items to the point where we would be assured of a reasonable profit, but there are disadvantages to this.

"Some of our customers are already complaining about our prices. There's no telling how they might react to another price increase at this time. They might look for other suppliers, place orders with our competitors, or look for alternative methods of production that would eliminate the need for our products. Either way, we'd lose some customers. How many would be impossible to determine. But if we lose too many . . . ."

At this point, don't finish the sentence. Just pause for a moment.

"The only other alternative is to get back to normal and reasonable profits by means of cost reduction, greater productivity, and elimination of waste. But, as you know, achieving these objectives requires hard work and a lot of thought and determination. What it means for each one of you is looking at your job, studying each and every aspect of it, and coming up with ideas and changes to make our operations more productive and efficient. I won't soft-soap you by pretending it will be easy.

"On the other hand, I can assure you that management feels there is not a department in the company that couldn't be made substantially more efficient and productive were the right approach taken. Management has asked me to get you people together and work up a program designed to cut costs, eliminate waste, streamline processing, and make any changes needed to make our operations more efficient and productive. Good intentions are important, but they're only a start. The important thing is commitment and action.

"I imagine you might have some questions at this point, so let's have them."

Expect to have silence for awhile, but give your listeners some time to absorb what you said. Eventually some one will speak up. If nobody does, get into the following subjects yourself.

"What kind of waste do you mean?" someone may ask.

"How about material waste for a starter? Perhaps we should set limits for each operation. This would set up definite targets to shoot for. While we're on the subject of materials, maybe we should watch the amount of material we withdraw from the storeroom; we might set up some controls that would discourage people from requisitioning more than they need."

Another person may comment on time waste. Wholeheartedly agree with this by saying, "You make a good point. I can't think of anything that is more destructive to productivity and profits than wasting time. We could break that down further into the different kinds of time waste, such as long lunch and break periods, and late starts on the job.

"Don't overlook long telephone conversations and people leaving their work stations to gab with other workers. Then, there are a few people who don't tell their supervisors when they've completed a job, or who don't keep busy while waiting for machines to be set up and made available.

"I'd like to encourage you to come up with timesaving and money-making ideas on your own. You can do this by turning in suggestions. All we need is some ideas—the form and wording of your suggestions aren't important. I can work with you to develop an idea and put it into presentable form.

"If we all put our minds on cutting costs and working together on this effort, I'm sure we can keep our company in the black. If we don't have to raise prices, we'll eventually have a bigger share of the market for our products (or service). This will not only enable the company to stay in the black, but also assure us of keeping our jobs."

Reasoning and Principle Involved

When adopting an austerity program, it pays for management to explain to employees why it is necessary and what management is proposing to do. Talks to employees should include steps that may be taken and how they would help to reduce costs. The primary objective of a talk, however, is to get people thinking in the right direction and cooperating in the overall effort. The implementation of cost-cutting measures will then be more readily accepted.

PROBLEM NUMBER 3

What to say to the supervisor whose people have poor quality and productivity records.

The Situation

The department that you manage has not been doing well. Product quality has dropped off and the department has failed to meet its production quota for the last two months. You decide to talk to the supervisor of the department about these problems.

What You Should Say and Some Responses

"Andy, I'm sure you're aware that our department's performance has been a disappointment to management the last two months. Not only have rejects have been high, but the department didn't make its quota. What's the problem?"

Andy looks grim. "I'm not completely sure, but it looks like a combination of things. I'm trying to work it out."

"What do you mean?"

"Well, one of my people made two serious mistakes last month. Joe is usually very reliable—maybe he's got problems at home. And another guy, Pete, I think is an alcoholic. He just doesn't put out like he used to. Both of them have been absent quite a bit."

"Is that what you mean by a combination of things?"

"Yes. But I'm working on it."

"What are you going to do? Do you have something specific in mind?"

"Sure do. I'm going to make it clear to them that we won't put up with lousy production, shoddy workmanship, and poor attendance. I'm going to let those guys know that if they don't get on the ball, they'll be fired."

"I'm not sure the hard line is the answer with Joe and Pete, Andy. I'd suggest you talk to both of them, separately of course, and see if you can learn more about their problems. Then, call me and we'll talk it over. We should be able to come up with some answers."

Andy does as you suggest. He shows up at your office the next day. "I talked to both Joe and Pete yesterday afternoon. As I thought, Joe's been having a rough time at home. His wife is very sick, and there's no one to take care of the kids during the day. When he can't get a baby sitter, he has to stay home.

"And Pete is an alcoholic, or very close to it. But, of course, he won't admit it."

"Well, Andy, why don't you see if you can arrange a shift trade, at least temporarily, for Joe. See if you can get him on the 4 to 12 shift. That would solve his baby-sitting problem. He'd be home during the day, and a neighbor or someone else would be able to help out in the evening. That would put his mind to rest both on the kids and the job. If that doesn't work out, we'll think of another way to help him out.

"As for Pete, I'll talk to the Personnel Dept. about offering him some help. If he's truly an alcoholic, neither you nor I should get involved. We're simply not qualified to handle such problems. I think that if both Joe and Pete go along with these suggestions, our department will begin to make a better showing and continue to do so."

Reasoning and Principle Involved

The most effective and successful supervisors in business and industry today are the ones who are most human and compassionate. Unfortunately, sometimes there is a conflict between acting like a human being and carrying out the responsibility of a supervisor. A guideline for such situations is to do everything you possibly can to help people help themselves.

PROBLEM NUMBER 4

What to say to the supervisor whose people have poor attendance records.

The Situation

Tom Pace, your office supervisor, is trying something different to combat absenteeism. Upon returning to work after an absence, his people must personally explain the cause of their absence to him. Despite this approach, attendance has worsened instead of getting better. You decide you must do something about this problem. You call Tom to your office to discuss it.

What You Should Say and Some Responses

"Tom, I see we continue to have a serious attendance problem in our department. If we can get at the reason, maybe we can find a way to turn things around. From your experience, what do you think is the main cause of the excessive absence in particular?"

Tom shakes his head. "All I know is what the absentees have been telling me. Bad colds, the flu, a virus, stomach problems, the usual. Frankly, I don't believe most of it. They're just goofing off and taking advantage of the company. I would bet on it."

"Tom, I've checked the records and most of the absences are for one or two days at a time, most of them on Fridays or Mondays. So I agree with you that it looks like they are mostly avoidable. But the question is, why should our department be getting so much more than its share?"

Tom takes a deep breath but says nothing.

"You know, Tom, excessive absence along with lateness is usually symptomatic of some deep, hidden problem, often difficult to uncover. If it's OK with you, I'd like to do a little checking on my own to see if I can come up with an answer."

"Are you kidding? At this point, I really need some help to solve this problem."

After paving the way for an investigation on your part, you have some informal discussions with other supervisors and group leaders who know Tom. You also interview a few of the more conscientious and productive employees after assuring them your purpose is to improve conditions, not establish a case against Tom for any wrongdoing. Then, you meet with him again to report your findings.

"Tom, I know you'd like to have the answer to this attendance problem just as much as I do. So I'm going to give it to you straight, just as I received it from the people I talked to. Of course, I'm not going to mention any names."

"That's fine with me."

"First, a few people said you were too set in your ways and behind the times with what motivates and unmotivates people. This hard approach turns people off, and in some cases, makes them resentful. Second, most supervisors today suggest that their people do things— you, on the other hand, issue orders. Also, astute supervisors *listen* to subordinates to learn how they think and feel. You don't do enough of that according to the people I talked to. They say that most of your communication is one-way.

"Another thing that was mentioned was that many supervisors try to determine their people's job preferences in order to make the work more interesting. You seem to be insensitive to your people's problems and needs.

"Tom, I believe that if you think about these things, you'll agree that they make sense."

"Well, you're probably right," Tom weakly answers.

"Why don't you give these suggestions a try, Tom, to see if it'll made a difference."

"OK, I'll do that."

Reasoning and Principle Involved

Studies have shown that the hard line approach to managing people just doesn't work in today's society. Poor attendance, lateness, work disruption and bad workmanship are the symptoms of insensitive management.

PROBLEM NUMBER 5

What to say to an employee whose productivity hasn't improved after several warnings from you.

The Situation

In checking the time sheets on projects completed and jobs currently in process, you notice that Tom Johnson's productivity continues to be poor. Johnson is one of your painters in the maintenance department. You have spoken to him twice before about his failure to meet the department's production standards, yet he seldom does so. You also gave him a written warning two weeks ago and put a copy in his personnel record. This letter stated that he would be disciplined if his output didn't improve. You see that you must now act on that.

What You Should Say and Some Responses

"Tom, I've checked the time sheets, and I saw that you're still painting the tanks in Building C. If you look at the standard for that job, you'll see that it should have taken you no more than three days and you're now on the fifth day. Why is it taking you so long?"

"I don't know. I've been working as fast as I can," says Tom. "Maybe those standard figures are wrong."

You shake your had and say, "No, we've had these standards for many years. Other painters had no problem with meeting them. You know, we've talked about you not doing enough work before. I'm sorry, Tom, but I'm going to have to suspend you for two days."

Tom appears stunned. "That's not fair. I don't deserve it."

"It's anything but. And if you don't start doing much better, I'm going to recommend that you be fired. I've sent your suspension notice to the Personnel Dept. Don't come back to work until Thursday."

An Alternate Approach

"Tom, I see that the painting job you're doing is going to take you at least five days to finish. Why is it taking so long?"

"That's a tough job, and it's stinking hot in Building C. I've had to take a lot of breaks and also work much slower than I usually do. Besides, I haven't felt well the last few days."

"I didn't notice that it was overly hot there when I made my round, and those tanks weren't in any worse condition than when we painted them four or five years ago. I was aware of that when I gave you the job.

"No, Tom, you simply haven't tried to do more work. We've talked about your poor performance before, and you've been given a written warning. I have no choice now but to suspend you for two days, starting now. Also, I want to remind you that if you don't improve your output, the next disciplinary step is dismissal."

Reasoning and Principle Involved

Management has specific objectives in mind when it establishes production or work standards. The standards enable supervisors to plan and schedule jobs efficiently. Also, without the standards, some employees might shirk their duties. The standards are based on what should be expected of an average employee working under normal conditions. As such, they are fair and reasonable.

Tom Johnson was told more than once that his performance was unsatisfactory, and he was given opportunities to improve. His failure to do so indicates that he hasn't tried to be more efficient and probably doesn't care. For this reason, the suspension is justified. If he continues to perform below the standards after the suspension, you should recommend that he be terminated.

PROBLEM NUMBER 6

What to say to a manager whose department's costs must be cut.

The Situation

Word has come down from upper management that the company must greatly reduce expenses. Costs must be cut as much as possible.

There will be no new hiring, and existing staff and line people should be cut to the bone. Since you are to implement these orders immediately, you arrange to talk to your Development Department manager, Betty Elton, that afternoon.

What You Should Say and Some Responses

"As you may have heard, Betty, the competition in our industry has recently gone all out to get a larger share of the market, and to some extent, they've succeeded. Our company had to cut prices to hold the customers we have, and this wiped out our profits.

"Management decided to trim production costs as much as possible and to lay off some of the hourly people. In addition, we've been asked to work out a plan for making do with reduced staff for the near future at least. We will have to cut some of your people."

"Oh, no!" Betty responds. "This doesn't make sense. I was just about to put through a request for two more people. The company shouldn't cut Development at a time like this. Besides, take a look at the workload I have."

"I know this is hard to take, Betty. I don't enjoy doing this any more than you do. But the company is in a tough spot. We all have to cooperate with this program."

"Cooperation is one thing," Betty replies. "Solving design and development problems is another. My workload is bigger than ever. I'm working my people overtime now."

"All right, Betty, let's talk about that workload, or better yet, let's look at it on a job-by-job basis."

"What do you mean?"

"Let's see if and where you can afford to drop some jobs and where dropping jobs isn't feasible. Our objective should be to cut costs wherever we can without hurting the operation. As much as we want to cut costs, we know that false economies don't pay off. If it's not feasible to cut your staff, management will probably understand."

Betty breathes a long-suffering sigh. "OK, where do we start?"

"Let's start with your list of projects and work assignments. I'd like to compare them with those you had two years ago, if you can dig those out."

Betty looks bewildered but quickly recovers. "No problem. They are in this same file. Here they are."

You and Betty then make a generalized job-by-job comparison for a couple of representative months, current workload against the workload two years ago. You break the projects down by hours and weeks taken to handle each job.

"Betty, it looks like you had pretty much the same workload two years ago that you have now, looking at it overall."

"That's right," Betty says. "And as you can see, we had a lot of overtime then just as we have a lot of overtime now."

"Now let's look at your list of personnel, then and now."

You and Betty do that. "Look here," you say. "Your department has four more people today than it had two years ago, even though the workload is just about the same. What do you think of that?"

Betty doesn't know what to think, or what to say either.

"Don't let it get you down, Betty. This is not at all an unusual situation. When business is good, we tend to put on more staff people, even if the amount of work remains the same. The workload always seems to mesh in to the available labor, with overtime included."

Betty remains glum and silent.

"I can imagine, Betty, that you're wondering how you can cut the amount of work your department does to the point where you can get along with less people. But you'll be surprised how much tightening you can do if you put your mind to it.

"From my experience, the best way to start is to make a detailed list of all the assignments and jobs your people perform. Then ask the question of each: is this job absolutely essential? I'll work with you on that. Also, I'll try to induce as many departments as I can to reduce the number of development requests they give you and also eliminate reports they can live without. Since this cost-cutting program is company-wide, the amount of work your department will be requested to do may be reduced significantly.

"Of course, there is other cutting that you will have to do. You can, for example, check for duplication and overlap on jobs, eliminating unneeded steps or combining others where feasible. Another thing to do is to review all functions to determine what might be done faster or more efficiently elsewhere. At the same time, you should determine if some work could be done faster by someone other than the person presently assigned to it."

At this point or sooner, Betty should perk up and show more interest in what you are saying. Don't be surprised if she starts taking notes. Also, be sure you show that you are confident in what you are saying and doing. Seeing that you are determined to reach your objective should point out the seriousness of the situation to Betty.

"Training is another time and work saver, Betty. By training your people to handle jobs other than their own, you'll not be hurt by absences or layoffs. You can also avoid working overtime in some situations."

Betty asks you a question. "How can I sell my people on this cost-cutting program?"

"Tell them why management is doing it, and how important it is to keep costs in line. Show them how it will be to their advantage to help reduce costs. Ask them, 'How can I help you with your work? Where are you having problems?' You may be surprised at what you can find out if you ask."

"Well, what do you think, Betty? How many people do you think you can spare? Four?"

"No way!" Betty replies. "Let me see what I can do. Maybe two."

Reasoning and Principle Involved

Every employee must participate in controlling costs if a company is to keep up with the competition, prosper and grow. Managers can't do the job alone. But they can get help and cooperation in the effort by selling subordinates on why and how the job can be done.

PROBLEM NUMBER 7

What to say to a supervisor when the department's operating costs are on the rise.

The Situation

In studying the performance and productivity charts you have been keeping, you notice that Department C is not doing as well as A and B. Although costs of Department C have not increased suddenly, there has been a gradual rise over the past four months that you can't explain. Determined to correct this trend, you visit the supervisor of the department to discuss the problem.

What You Should Say and Some Responses

"How are things going, John?"

"Oh, just about normal as far as I can see. But it seems to get more and more difficult to meet our production schedule each month."

"What do you mean?"

"Well, as I remember six months ago, I never needed to work people overtime. In the last few months, that seems to be the norm. Yet, I believe our quotas haven't changed much in over a year."

"You're right about that, John. But what about your people? Have you had any transfers in or out of the department? Excessive absenteeism? Accidents that resulted in lost time on the job?"

"No, I still have the same number I had a year ago. We haven't made any job changes in a couple of years. Maybe some of the people are getting bored or just lazy."

"How about materials? We haven't changed any suppliers for your department, but that doesn't mean the material quality hasn't changed. Have you had any off-spec product, rejects or a lot of waste?"

"No, nothing like that. In fact, things have been sort of humdrum around here. We haven't made any process changes, installed any new equipment, or tried any new procedures in the past year that I know of."

"John, I think you may have hit upon something. Both A and B departments are quite different from what they were a year ago. The company brought out a new product in Department A. That required new machines and retraining of some of the people. And we made a major process change in Department B where we also promoted one of the people to supervisor. In addition, the work areas in both departments have recently been painted.

"Your department could probably benefit if you would stir things up a bit. I'm suggesting, for example, that you train some of your people to handle other jobs. Then you can switch a few and rotate others. Look for some new procedures too, so you can get away from the old routines. Also, dress up the place a bit by pushing housekeeping and cleaning the machines and equipment.

"Why don't you try these things, and then let's see what happens."

Reasoning and Principle Involved

Workers can become bored with the same day-to-day routine. They get listless and restless, and it may show in their productivity. Sometimes change for the sake of change itself can make a difference.

If a Union/Management agreement prohibits some of the changes you'd like to make, discuss the problem with the Union leaders; they may have some suggestions, and may be willing to go along with you. Although the world hates change, it is the only thing that has brought progress.

PROBLEM NUMBER 8

What to say to a foreman whose people are bored because their work is highly repetitious.

The Situation

Your department consists of several groups of people, each performing a different operation in the manufacture of a multi-component product. While some of the operations are handled by machines, others are almost completely manual in nature. But since your management is progressive, all of the operations are carried out in the most scientific and efficient way possible. However, one group of workers is significantly less productive than all the others. You decide to talk to the foreman of that group, Jack Willis, to discuss the problem and suggest a remedy.

What You Should Say and Some Responses

"How are things going, Jack?"

"I was expecting you," Jack replies. "That last productivity report made my department look bad. I suppose you'll be looking for someone to replace me pretty soon."

"Not necessarily," you say. "I always felt you were cut out to be a good foreman, Jack, and I still do. But we've got to find out what's wrong and do something about it."

Jack nods to show his agreement. "I've been trying to come up with some ideas to get more production out and also keep the quality up, but I can't seem to get my crew interested. It seems they just don't give a damn."

"This thing about your people not being interested—does that apply to all of them?"

"Yeah, at least that's the way it seems to me."

"Do you have any idea why?"

"That's what I've been trying to figure out. About the only comment I get when I try to push them or get them more enthused is that the work is too boring. They do the same thing hour after hour as if they were robots instead of humans. The work is very repetitious, but it has to be done."

"Of course it has to be done," you say. "The problem is, how is it done?"

"Well, in the most efficient way possible. I've gone over all the assembly operations, and everything is done according to the book. There's not a wasted motion anywhere. Maybe we're too efficient."

"I hear you. Keep talking."

"I'm not sure if a person can be too efficient. We all like to be efficient in what we do. But what good is efficiency if people don't care about their work and what they're doing for a living? Nobody wants to be bored to death."

"You're right, Jack, on all counts. The problem is how efficiency is defined. There's more to it than simply eliminating wasted motions. Maybe you can't get true efficiency and better productivity unless you change some people's attitudes on those matters.

"Not too long ago, a new management philosophy was introduced that dealt with the problem that many jobs are very boring. It's called job enrichment, and it takes into consideration that people on the job are human beings, not robots or machines. They need to get satisfaction from their work and to have a feeling that they're contributing.

"Some large companies have been promoting it with good results. Jack, I'd like you to study this idea and then get back to me on what you feel we could do with it in the department. There's no reason why we can't work out a few good human strategies to get your people more involved and thereby more interested in their work."

Reasoning and Principle Involved

Attitude surveys have shown that many of today's workers, particularly young people, want more than just a job. They want to get satisfaction and a sense of achievement from their work. Educators and psychologists say that jobs must be enriched and enlarged if these desires of workers are to be achieved. Fortunately, there are several ways this can be done. The good part is that both the workers and management benefit from adopting them.

PROBLEM NUMBER 9

What to say to a supervisor when suggesting that he level with his people.

The Situation

Hector Wilson accepted the job of supervisor three months ago. He stepped into a tough situation in that he had taken over with very little training. Also, the people in his crew are mainly veterans who wanted one of their members to be supervisor rather than Hector. Productivity of the crew has dropped off. You sense that Hector is having trouble contending with their poor performance and doesn't know what to do.

What You Should Say and Some Responses

As you enter Hector's department, you find him hard at work at his desk. "Good morning, Hector. Can you spare a few minutes so we can talk?"

"Sure can," Hector replies.

"Let's go into the conference room where we won't be bothered."

Hector nods agreement and the two of you go to the back of the room where you can talk in absolute privacy.

"I've noticed that the output of your department has dropped off. Tell me about this, and why it is happening. Maybe if we talk about it, we can see where we could do something."

Hector hesitates. "It's hard for me to know where to begin."

"That's not really important. Start anywhere at all, just so long as we can discuss it." When Hector is slow to respond, you say, "Are your people giving you trouble?"

"Are you kidding? I know what their jobs are, and I'm pretty sure about how they should be doing them. But getting them to go along with me is an entirely different matter."

"Why?"

"I don't know. I can't figure it out. I'm simply not getting any cooperation."

"Why?" you persist.

Hector rubs his chin and blinks his eyes while thinking. "Well, I guess it starts with my becoming supervisor in the first place. Everyone around here knows that there were others who wanted the job. Bob Smith for one, and Jack Steele for another."

"Have they been making it rough for you?"

Hector nods no. "No more than the rest. If it were just them alone, I believe I could handle it. But each one has his friends. I think most of the guys in the group would have liked to see Smith get the job. He's the fair-haired boy around here. The men resent me and don't try too hard to hide it.

"They make me feel like an outsider. I get the impression they would like to see me go, figuring that if I'm fired, Smith will get the job. Some of them are even giving me the silent treatment. I don't mind that so much as their lack of cooperation."

"Hector, I've run into this kind of thing before. I mean the kind of situation where there's misunderstanding, where people are resentful and where there's little if any communication. For a variety of reasons most if not all of these things are unjustified.

"It's simply a case where many of your people are prejudiced against you. And when it comes to running a department productively and efficiently, prejudice is poison.

"As for what we can do about it, I think our only hope is for you to get the air cleared. You'll have to get together with your people and let them know what the score is. Tell them that you want to do the job you're being paid to do, and that you need their cooperation to do it.

"Say that you're trying to be fair and impartial, but that you are going to insist that standards of work and behavior be met. Let them know as a group and individually, that if they have any suggestions or gripes you'll be more than willing to listen to them, but that under no conditions will you tolerate shirking of responsibilities.

"Hector, I feel sure that if you get this message positively and forcefully across, you'll get the cooperation you need."

Reasoning and Principle Involved

Although leveling with employees usually consists of being honest with them about their performance, discussing their good and bad points, and saying what they should do to improve—it can also be used to state a manager's needs.

One of the best ways to level effectively with people is to make them responsible for their own behavior. Hold them strictly accountable for results. Describe behavior in terms of "more-or-less" rather than "either-or." The more-or-less approach stresses quantity which is measurable, rather than quality, which is judgmental.

Chapter 3

COMMUNICATION

In the following situations, note how the manager assures that subordinates understand assignments, and how rumors and bad news should be handled. Notice, also, the advice given on writing proposals, suggestions, and conducting meetings to make these means of communicating useful and cost-effective.

PROBLEM NUMBER 1

What to say to a supervisor who fails to fully explain when he makes assignments.

The Situation

Ralph Jones is a young, new supervisor who reports to you. His department's performance has been slipping ever since he accepted the job. While you had hoped that time and experience would turn things around, this has not happened. You suspect he may have problems communicating with his people. You decide to talk to him and try to help him.

What You Should Say and Some Responses

When you visit Ralph, you find him busy at his desk. Even though it is just after the lunch period, he looks up tiredly as if he had spent a whole day on the job.

"How goes it, Ralph?"

He shrugs. "I'm doing the best I can."

"Having problems?"

"Yeah, I guess so."

"I thought you might be having a problem or two. Try not to be overly concerned, Ralph. Every new supervisor has problems. It'll take you a while to get into the swing of things. Can you use a little help?"

"Sure can."

"Good. That's what I'm here for. Do you feel like telling me about it?"

"I'd like to, but that's the problem."

"I don't get you."

"What I'm trying to say is that if I could put my finger on the problem, maybe I could come up with an answer—but things just don't seem to be working out as they should. Our production figures continue to drop, and this month they're worse than ever. I simply don't know why."

"Are your people cooperating and not goofing off?"

Ralph frowns. "I feel that they are. Most of them are conscientious and seem to be trying to do a good job. But boy, they make a lot of mistakes and do too many things wrong. As a result, there are too many rejects and too much work that has to be redone."

"I see. Well, the sooner we can get to the bottom of this, the sooner we can do something about it. Tell me something Ralph—you said your people are making too many mistakes. What kind of mistakes?"

Ralph scratches his head. "I don't know. Different kinds, as if they're not sure of themselves."

"What about the work itself? Is your department getting any jobs that are tough to handle?"

"No, but most of the jobs are specials, and some of them are pretty complicated. But they're not any worse than what we got before I became supervisor."

After this response, proceed to ask Ralph questions concerning the various jobs that his department performs. You will probably find him completely knowledgeable and ready to talk about all the work that is done.

"Tell me, Ralph, how do you assign these jobs?"

"Well, it's rather simple. When the jobs and orders come to me from the planners and schedulers, I just hand them out to the people who are experienced with those jobs, as far as I can determine."

"And that's all there's to it?" you ask.

"Yes, what else is there to do?"

"Let me put it this way, Ralph. I can't guarantee that this is the answer to the problem, but I have a hunch that it is. Being handed a job is one thing, completely understanding it, is another. In my experience, the more a person knows about a job the better he will do it. He should know not only what he's doing, but also why he's doing it, what happens when he's through with his work, how the product or item will be used and by whom.

"Thinking about a job only in terms of what a person does without relating it to the end use of the product or overall goal of the company, forces people to work like machines, and not think. When people on the job stop thinking, they make mistakes. Do you understand what I'm saying?"

"I sure do," Ralph replies. "I should be giving my people as much information about the jobs as I can."

"Right," you say. "Something tells me it may make a big difference."

Reasoning and Principle Involved

It's been proved time and time again that people take more interest in their work and get more satisfaction from it if they know how what they do contributes to the finished product, increases its salability or pleases its user.

All workers also like to feel that what they do is important. Supervisors are the best persons to tell them that.

PROBLEM NUMBER 2

What to say to a supervisor who has trouble communicating with subordinates.

The Situation

Clyde Hanson, a former group leader, was made a supervisor about four months ago when Bill Butler left the company. He recently had some problems with two of his people. Their output has been declining steadily, and by now is well below standard. In addition, his department's overall performance has been slipping.

What You Should Say and Some Responses

"How goes it, Clyde?"

"Not bad, I guess."

"I've noticed that our output of model F has dropped off the last two months. This suggests to me that you might have a problem or two."

"Two is more like it: one is Benton, the other is Clark."

"Aren't those the two fellows who used to give Bill Butler a hard time?"

"Yeah, they are. But someway or other, Butler was able to control them and keep them in line, something I've been unable to do."

"How do you mean?"

"Well, Benton and Clark have never been more than average when it comes to getting the work out. They're the kind of guys you have to constantly watch. Their performance drops below standard every now and then, but apparently Butler knew how to crack the whip and make them toe the line again. In the four months I've been supervisor, their output has been declining steadily, and today it is way below standard. I guess I'm not too good as a whip cracker."

"Have you had any luck in learning what the problem is?"

"No, I just can't figure it out."

"Do you ever get the feeling those two guys have something against you?"

"No, they've never said or done anything personal."

You nod thoughtfully. "You mentioned cracking the whip. Did you take any action on getting those guys to put out more?"

"I thought I did. I talked with each one at least twice and tried to lay down the law. I even told them the consequences if they didn't do more and much better work. They've both been with the company a long time, but I suppose in time I could build up a case against them and get them fired. But I'd probably wind up looking like an ass."

"You may have a point there, Clyde. Firing is sometimes unavoidable in extreme cases, but I always felt it should be an absolute last resort. Tell me, though, what kind of reaction did you get when you talked to them?"

"Nothing bad. Neither one denied he wasn't doing a real good job. They both promised to do better in the future."

"And then didn't follow through on their promises?"

"That's right. What do you make of it?"

"Well, I've got another question. Specifically Clyde, in trying to make your point with those guys, what aspects of their performance did you concentrate on?"

"Nothing in particular. I just let them know they weren't doing an acceptable job."

"That's what I figured, and it might just be the reason we're not getting anywhere with those guys. In my experience, criticizing shoddy and sloppy performance isn't enough. You have to be specific. You have to spell out in clear and concise words exactly what quantity and quality you expect on every job you assign your people.

"And you have to continually follow up and check to make sure your people are maintaining the levels you specified. That's especially true with guys like Benton and Clark—they need special attention. You have to set up goals for them and keep those goals in mind at all times."

Clyde shakes his head in agreement. "That makes sense. It's sure worth a try."

"I'd say so," you reply. "Let me know how you make out."

Reasoning and Principle Involved

Successful supervisors have found that they must be firm, forceful and very specific when making assignments or giving instructions to certain individuals. This is necessary for several reasons, two of which are quite important:

1. Some workers look to their supervisor for detailed guidance. They don't like to think for themselves.
2. There should be no misunderstandings or questions of your intentions if you communicate clearly and fully. Under such situations, nobody should be able to offer an excuse of not knowing what was expected of him or her.

PROBLEM NUMBER 3

What to say to an employee who delights in originating and spreading rumors.

The Situation

Mary Smith, a clerk in your department, is a compulsive talker. Her job requires her to deliver reports, mail, and memos to various offices, a task that takes her two to three times longer than it should because she has a conversation with at least one person at each office. Your problem with Mary, however, is that she originates and spreads rumors; you can find no other source of the gossip and rumors that periodically circulate through the company about your department.

What You Should Say and Some Responses

"Mary, I've noticed that you are slow on some of your deliveries to the offices. One manager mentioned to me that he is accustomed to handling his mail at 10 A.M. each day, and twice last week he did not receive it till much later. Are you having a problem with sorting it or getting it distributed?"

"Oh, I'm sorry. I didn't think the mail delivery was so important," Mary replies. "I'll try to start out earlier."

"That's not the answer to the problem, Mary. You waste too much time talking to people at each stop you make. That's not good for two reasons: you waste the time of the people you talk to, and you don't get your other work such as filing done on time."

Mary meekly nods agreement with what you're saying, but doesn't make any comment.

"I assume most of your conversations are on department activities, Mary, but I really don't know what you talk about. What do you discuss with the people you talk to?"

"Oh, lots of things, like the amount of mail, and the new people who come into the department, and the amount of work people have to do, and . . ." But from her manner of speaking, you know she is not telling you everything.

"I see. The reason I asked you that question is that many people simply don't try to separate rumor from fact; both are something to talk about."

A guilty expression shows on Mary's face, but she quickly recovers.

"You know, Mary, no one should repeat or start a rumor. There are too many bad things that can happen when rumors are spread in a department. Some people get upset, and others get hurt. I'd like you to come to me if you hear a rumor instead of talking about it with anybody. If I don't have the facts, I'll get them for you as quickly as I can, whether they have any truth to them or whether they are just rumors."

Reasoning and Principle Involved

Note that it would not be proper to confront Mary about originating or spreading rumors. You have no proof of this.

The best way to dispel rumors is to give people the facts. If there is no truth to a rumor or no information concerning it, that should be said. Above all, workers should be asked to never repeat a rumor. Supervisors must show their people that they intend to do everything possible to keep them fully informed.

PROBLEM NUMBER 4

What to say to a promising young employee who says he has accepted another job.

The Situation

One of your supervisors has just informed you that Matt Carney, a good worker, has resigned, saying he wanted to take advantage of a better opportunity elsewhere. Since Matt had given you no indication that he was dissatisfied and planned to leave, you question his supervisor, Smitty, about it. But Smitty doesn't have an answer other than to say that Matt had frequently brought up the subject of his future with him. Smitty added that he didn't give him an answer, because he didn't want to build up false hopes or make promises that couldn't be kept. You decide to talk to Matt yourself.

What You Should Say and Some Responses

"Matt, I respect your decision to quit, and since you've made up your mind, I won't try to get you to change it. But I'm in a little bit of a spot. My boss gets upset any time a good person decides to leave the company. He thinks it indicates poor management or a working condition that ought to be changed. He wants me to find out your real reason for leaving if I can. Can you help me out?"

Matt shifts uneasily in his seat. You can tell he is reluctant to speak. "I don't like to bring other people into this," he says finally.

"I understand that. But this needn't be something to be concerned about. No one is going to blame anybody or find fault with anyone. All management wants to do is improve its relations with employees."

"Well . . ." Matt looks away, undecided on what to say.

"Maybe I can help you. Smitty tells me you asked him about your job status a few times, whether you would be transferred, what your chances were for advancement, and so on. Is that what caused you to start looking around for something else?"

"Yeah, I guess it did. Smitty is a nice guy to work for, but I felt he was stalling me. He promised to talk to me about it one of these days, to let me know where I stood as soon as he could, but he never did. I felt I was not getting anywhere here and that I could probably do better some place else."

You nod your head. "I don't blame you for feeling that way. Thanks for leveling with me. Strictly for your own information, we were going to shift you from one group to another to give you some experience before promoting you.

"Smitty felt he couldn't tell you anything about your future until something definite was decided. He didn't want to make any promises he couldn't keep."

Matt let his breath out with a sigh. "If only I'd known that . . ."

You smile. "Matt, it's still not too late to change your mind. But like I promised, I'm not twisting your arm."

Reasoning and Principle Involved

While it is true that building an employee's false hopes is as dangerous as stalling the person, mentioning the company's long range plans for the person without making any definite commitments would probably help the person's attitude.

The point to be made with supervisors however, is that when there is a job to be done, delaying tactics can be fatal.

PROBLEM NUMBER 5

What to say to a subordinate whose pride won't let him admit he doesn't understand a project you asked him to handle.

The Situation

Your department activities involve the use of many machines, conveyers and auxiliary equipment. Downtime of this productive equipment has become a problem, especially since some of the machines must be coordinated with others. Recently you prepared a downtime control system which you gave to a subordinate, Dave Barnes, to implement. Although he said he understood what you wanted him to do, he has been slow in taking action.

What You Should Say and Some Responses

"Good morning, Dave. How are you doing on that downtime control system?"

"Uh, er, I'm trying to get it set up," Dave replies.

"I hope you're not making it a big project. In my opinion, it's relatively simple and should have been set up by now."

"OK, I'll try to get it going just as soon as I can," Dave replies, but he doesn't sound too sure of himself.

"All right, Dave, give me a call when you're ready. I'd like to review what you've done."

Late in the morning, you receive a phone call from Dave. "I seem to have run into a bit of a problem in trying to get that downtime control system underway," he reports.

"I see," you reply. "Why don't we get together the first thing after lunch to straighten it out?"

Dave agrees and you go to his office when you return from lunch.

"OK, Dave, what seems to be the problem?"

Dave moistens his lips and begins. "The other day when you explained this system to me, I thought I understood it, but I realize now I was mistaken. There are a couple of things I can't figure out. This alpha-numeric labeling isn't clear to me, and I don't see how you make the timing adjustments on the conveyors."

It takes you about five minutes to answer Dave's questions and clear up other problems. Sensing that he is no longer confused, you ask, "What do you think? Do you understand it now?"

Dave nods that he does and says so. He starts to gather up the papers and gets up from his desk.

"Tell me something, Dave. How much time did you spend trying to figure this out on your own?"

Slightly taken aback by your question, Dave answers slowly, "More time than I should have, I guess. I felt that since you had already explained the system to me once, I should be able to figure it out by myself."

"Could it also be that you were a little too proud to admit that you didn't quite understand all of it, that part of it was difficult for you to figure out?

"Being unable to solve a problem is no crime. But it's a mistake to delay and become flustered without help to avoid admitting you don't know the answer. I'd rather have you come to me for help when you need it than waste valuable time in an effort to prove how independent you can be."

Reasoning and Principle Involved

Pride is often a reason for making mistakes, and false pride tends to trip people up. While it may be difficult for a person to swallow his or her pride, consideration should be given to what might happen if it isn't done.

On the other hand, problems involving comprehension and understanding can often be avoided in other ways. Managers who hand out assignments which could be misconstrued or misunderstood should protect themselves by asking questions of the subordinate concerning the assignment. Requesting that the subordinate repeat his or her understanding of the assignment in his or her own words is also helpful.

PROBLEM NUMBER 6

What to say to a foreman who lost a good employee because of his failure to communicate effectively with her.

The Situation

Linda Eden, an employee in her late twenties, has been with the company about eight months. A very productive person who is also bright and cooperative, she is one of the most promising people the company has. A week ago she was given a small merit increase in pay. But today she announced she was quitting. You go to her foreman, Ron Black, to learn why she is leaving.

What You Should Say and Some Responses

"Ron, I just heard the bad news. How come Linda Eden is leaving? I thought you had big things planned for her?"

"Yes, I did," Ron replies.

"Has her husband been transferred to another city?"

"Not as far as I know."

"Then what made her resign? Did you talk to her about it? Try to get her to stay?"

"Yes," Ron slowly replies. "She wasn't interested in staying. She told me she feels she can do better elsewhere, that her new job pays more than she's getting here."

"Didn't she know about the plans the company had for her? Did she have any good reason to believe she wasn't in a dead-end job?"

"Well, I think one of the reasons she came to work for us was because I assured her she would have a good future with the company."

"And how long ago was that?"

"About eight months ago," Ron replies.

"In all this time did anything happen to confirm the original assurance you gave her regarding her future?"

Ron thinks a bit, frowning. "No, I guess not. But I figured the merit raise was a way of letting her know we were pleased with her work. And in her evaluation interview I let her know we were very satisfied."

"Telling someone you like his or her work, and convincing the person of a good future with the company don't necessarily relate to each other. Also, the merit raise apparently didn't persuade her. My guess is that she expected a promotion of some kind. That would have increased her responsibility and status. A small merit raise looks like slim pickings if you expect much more.

"Ron, in my opinion, the most important problem managers and supervisors have to contend with in dealing with employees is communications. Insufficient communication produces the greatest amount of confusion, bitterness and misunderstanding. More projects and programs are fouled up or fail completely as a result of its inadequacy in too many offices and plants.

"More people make bad decisions and judgments because of management's failure to communicate effectively. Had you communicated effectively with Linda, she would never have quit. Your failure to let her in on your plans and explain that they had to be deferred until our expansion program started only reinforced the doubts she already had. You didn't say anything, so she expected the worst and acted accordingly.

"I hope you've learned something from this. Management must go all out to keep good employees. One of the best ways to assure this is to maintain good communications with them."

Reasoning and Principle Involved

Management must be sure that the employee who has great potential or is doing an excellent job is not neglected. This is especially necessary with young or new employees who may be less willing to look for another job if they are assured of a good future.

One responsibility of the supervisor is to show concern about the person's future. The greater the person's abilities, the greater the obligation to see that this person knows of the company's plans for him or her.

PROBLEM NUMBER 7

What to say to a group leader who exaggerates when communicating with subordinates.

The Situation

Your company recently adopted an information and data control procedure involving the computer. As soon as it was brought into your department, you explained the new system to your group leaders and answered all the questions they had about it. The system is now working well in all areas but one. Joe Wilson's people have apparently not accepted it judging by their mistakes and record-keeping omissions. You go to Joe to talk about the problem.

What You Should Say and Some Responses

"Good morning," Joe greets you with a smile. "What can I do for you?"

"Good morning, Joe. I hope you have an answer to an important question I'm going to ask you. I just heard from the data processing people that the production report is messed up again. The problem is centered around your people's input. What's wrong and why is that happening?"

The smile on Joe's face quickly leaves. "I was afraid you were here to ask about that. Frankly, I can't understand what's wrong. My people are just not following orders, and I can't figure out why."

"Maybe we can work it out by going over the entire procedure again. Remember when I brought all the group leaders together to talk about what was involved? After I finished, I suggested that you and the other leaders explain it to your crews the same way. Management felt that the introduction to the system would be most effectively communicated to the employees by their most direct and immediate supervisor."

"Sure do," Joe replies.

"How did your explanation and discussion with your crew work out?"

"Good. I got all my people together and gave them the whole story. I thought everything went smoothly."

You nod thoughtfully. "I wonder what went wrong." You pause and think a bit, and then say, "Joe, would you mind if I talked to a few of your people to get their reaction to this system?"

"Not at all," Joe replies. "I'd sure like to know what's wrong."

After you've talked to a few of Joe's crew, you get back to him to report what you learned.

"Joe, I talked to some of your people about the new system yesterday afternoon. While two people admitted they weren't cooperating as much as they should, others said they had simply lost interest and preferred the old way of making records. One person said that you tried to trick him by saying that everyone would get special training on the computer, and only two people did.

"Another said you mentioned that all the crew would probably get raises as a result of the new system. He said he didn't see any signs of this happening. Were these people telling me the truth, Joe?"

Joe sheepishly lowers his eyes. "Now that you're telling me about it, I suppose so. I guess I was so anxious for the crew to accept the new system and make it work, I might have exaggerated a bit in trying to sell it. I didn't think they'd take everything I said so literally."

"But they did, Joe. It's human nature for people to believe and make the most of every word their boss says. By saying what you did, you falsely built their hopes and expectations.

"The company needs your people's help and input to make this system work, so I'm going to call them all together with you present Joe, and explain what happened. I'm going to tell them that you hadn't properly understood the situation and apologize for your deception which was unintentional. I believe they'll accept this, and we'll soon see a change in their attitude and behavior."

Reasoning and Principle Involved

If there's one thing that's essential for a computer system to be successful, it's the cooperation and support of every person who plays a part in its operation. Since clear and honest communication is required to get cooperation and support, management must ensure that no facet of it is neglected.

The only way to win people over to a new procedure or system is to motivate them. It has been proved time and again that trickery and manipulation don't work.

PROBLEM NUMBER 8

What to say to a leader whose meetings aren't accomplishing much.

The Situation

Your subordinate, Ed Deal, is a conscientious person who tries hard to carry out his responsibilities. He understands the importance of good communications for efficiency in the department. With that objective in mind, he conducts a meeting with his people every Friday afternoon, bringing them up-to-date on department matters and inviting their suggestions and comments. However, he feels the meetings are not popular or turning out well, and has said so to you.

What You Should Say and Some Responses

"Tell me about your meetings, Ed."

"Getting the attendees to participate is like pulling teeth. I get the impression, too, that some of them are bored. We don't seem to get much accomplished."

"Suppose I sit in on one of your meetings. I won't contribute or make any comments, I'll just see how the meeting goes. How do you feel about that?"

"That's OK with me. The next meeting is tomorrow, starting at two."

You attend the meeting, trying to make yourself as inconspicuous as possible by sitting in the back of the room. It doesn't take long for you to see that the meeting is quite dull. During the meeting, Ed says a few words about work in progress in the department. When he asks for comments or questions, there are none. He then talks about new work and future projects for the department. After about 10 to 15 minutes of this, he again asks if there are any questions. Nobody speaks. You slip out of the room a few minutes before the meeting appears to be coming to an end.

"So what's the answer?" Ed asks you later. "Do I fail the course on communications?"

"I wouldn't say that," you reply, "but I have a few ideas about what might be the problem. For one thing, experience has proven that the most effective meetings are those that are called with a special purpose in mind. Examples are to announce or explain a major or significant change, to fill people in on a new procedure, or to discuss a problem that has come up.

"Simply calling a meeting to communicate rarely works if the subject matter isn't new and important, and of special interest to the meeting attendees. Even if the reason for a meeting is important, you'll have trouble if you follow the same routine all the time. The idea is to change the procedure or format from time to time. Try something new once in awhile.

"For instance, you might give one of your promising people a chance to run a meeting. This adds variety and interest, perks up the participants, and is good training for the individual selected. Just make sure the person you pick is articulate and outgoing, and be sure to brief him or her beforehand.

"Recognize too, that a meeting is only one form of communicating with people, and it's not always the best one. The main reason for meetings is to give people the opportunity to exchange ideas and opinions. One idea or remark sometimes triggers another and you may get different viewpoints. But under other circumstances, the best way to communicate may be by telephone, a letter, or a memo, or a person-to-person talk. It depends on the situation.

"Sometimes the best way to talk to your people is to have a stand-up, impromptu meeting. When people have to think and talk on their feet, it saves a lot of time and effort."

Reasoning and Principle Involved

Successful leaders are seldom guilty of calling unnecessary meetings. If they hold a meeting, they have a good reason for it to justify taking busy people from their work. These leaders also make sure to conduct their meetings efficiently. Meetings are good for identifying and recognizing problems. They usually are not good for trying to solve them.

PROBLEM NUMBER 9

What to say to an individual who dominates your meetings.

The Situation

As the leader of a group of research and development people, you continually try to promote creativity and innovation. You also want to keep your people informed and up-to-date on current problems. You have found that periodic meetings are one of the best ways to accomplish both of these objectives. However, Tom Pearson, an extroverted individual in your group, has become a problem because he talks too much. When Tom takes over in your meetings, other people experience difficulty in joining in or simply withdraw. Ignoring him in a meeting has not worked. You decide to talk to him before your next meeting.

What You Should Say and Some Responses

"Tom, I want you to know I appreciate your contributions and suggestions at our development meetings. Not only are they usually very good, but they are also right to the point. I don't have many people who are as enthusiastic about their work and the company as you are."

"Thank you," Tom replies with a smile. "I *do* like my work and I enjoy the challenge of problems."

"However, I frequently have trouble in getting others in the meetings to speak up and say what they think. Have you noticed that?"

"No, I haven't."

"I thought maybe you could help me with that problem. I know that you are far ahead of most of them in thinking and reasoning. Also, you are not afraid to say what you think in the presence of others. As you may have heard, some engineers and scientists are introverted and not good at expressing themselves orally."

"Yeah, I know what you're are saying. I've never had any problem that way. But how could I help you with that problem?"

"There's at least one thing that you can do. If you would withhold your suggestions and comments in meetings until all of the others have had a chance to speak, I think we'd get more out of our meetings, and we wouldn't have so many reticent people just sitting there."

Tom looks thoughtful but also skeptical. He starts to speak but then decides not to.

"Don't worry, Tom, about my thinking that you might not have anything to say, because I know you usually do. It's just that some of our people seem content to keep quiet, especially when you have the floor. I would have a better chance to draw these people out if you kept quiet, at least until you sense that nobody has anything more to say.

"What do you say we try this at our next meeting, Tom?"

Reasoning and Principle Involved

Controlling a person who talks too much in a meeting may require direct action by the leader, but instead of bluntly telling the person to "shut up," that message can be put across in other ways. Appealing to the person in private should be tried first. Another approach with a severe case is to challenge the person to justify a statement or an idea, particularly if it is farfetched. After one or two embarrassing situations, the talker may think twice before speaking.

However, the person who talks too much in meetings may not be as serious a problem as it may seem. It should be recognized that a loquacious person can keep a discussion active and moving. If other people are reluctant to speak up, this person may be the catalyst to draw them out. Thus, it may not be wise to suppress such a person completely.

PROBLEM NUMBER 10

What to say to a worker who has poor listening habits.

The Situation

Betty Simpson, one of your department people, is an excellent worker from a productivity viewpoint, but she makes too many mistakes. As a result, the quality of her work often suffers. Although you thought that haste was her problem because she sometimes seemed impatient when you gave her assignments, now you suspect that she simply wasn't listening. You approach her to talk about the problem.

What You Should Say and Some Responses

"Good morning, Betty. How are you today?"

"OK, I guess, but I don't like this hot weather."

"Betty, I noticed that you made quite a bit of waste on your machine yesterday. What happened? Did the heat bother you?"

"No, I wasn't too uncomfortable yesterday. I guess I misunderstood your instructions on that order for Smith & Jones Co. Just before I finished the job, I rechecked the spec sheet and found that I'd cut the pieces wrong, so I had to do the job over."

"I remember telling you to watch out for that odd-size cut-out. Didn't you hear me?"

"I'm not sure that I did, but I'll make sure to listen more carefully in the future."

"You know, Betty, the same thing happened a week ago on the Beatrice job when you made three dozen of those gizmos. I had specifically asked you to make only two dozen. You are either very forgetful or you are not listening. I don't think you could forget something that quickly, so you must not be listening.

"There are several reasons why people have poor listening habits. Some people fail to listen because they're too busy talking. Others think that listening consists simply of not talking.

"People may not listen for a variety of reasons. For example, they may be waiting for their turn to speak, or they may be thinking of what to say next, or they may not be paying attention. Whatever the reason, these things prevent them from truly listening.

"Some people don't really want to hear. Their minds are already made up. Others tend to be judgmental. They react to what they hear depending on how it affects them personally. They may be more concerned with whether they like or don't like what a person says than in understanding the person.

"Then there are people who are preoccupied with themselves. The more wrapped up these people are in their own feelings, needs, and problems, the poorer a job they do in listening to others."

You pause a bit to see if Betty has anything to say, but she remains quiet. You go on.

"Once people begin to recognize some of the causes of their failure to listen properly and take steps to eliminate them, they will soon be on their way to becoming better listeners.

"Betty, I'd like you to think about what I've said, and sincerely try to listen better. You'll find that you'll feel more confident about what you're doing, knowing that you'll be making fewer mistakes."

Reasoning and Principle Involved

Good listening habits can be acquired with practice. Therefore it pays for leaders to help their people be better listeners by periodically talking about the art of listening with them. When employees have learned how to listen, a leader's job of giving instructions and explaining work situations will be easier. More important, communications between all parties will improve resulting in fewer mistakes and misunderstandings.

Chapter 4

RULES AND REGULATIONS

In the following situations, note how every company must have **rules and regulations** concerning the running of the company and the behavior of its employees. These must be communicated and enforced if management is to maintain control. Notice also, how the manager handles the problems which arise because of these rules and regulations.

PROBLEM NUMBER 1

What to say to a supervisor whose worker violated the no smoking rule.

The Situation

Although a no smoking sign is posted on the wall in the stockroom of your company, this morning one of the employees was found smoking there. When the smoking led to a fire in the area, other employees put it out before it caused much damage. You begin your investigation of the incident by talking to Walt Rogers, supervisor of the guilty employee.

What You Should Say and Some Responses

"I heard we had a serious situation in the stockroom this morning, Walt. Do you know how that fire got started?"

Walt looks down. "I think I do," but he is slow to continue.

"OK, what happened down there?"

"I was walking through the stockroom when I saw Ed Smith puffing away on a cigarette. I asked him if he couldn't read the no smoking

49

sign, and told him to put out the butt. I was in a hurry so I didn't wait to see if he did.

"Apparently he flipped the butt into a trash barrel. It probably smoldered for awhile, then caught on. Luckily, a couple of fellows from the shop smelled smoke and investigated. They put the fire out. Only a few nearby cartons were charred and no real damage was done."

"Walt, what is a supervisor's first and foremost responsibility over all other responsibilities?"

Walt replies in a quiet voice. "To do everything necessary to protect the safety and health of his people."

"And what is a supervisor's second most important responsibility?"

"To protect the company's assets to the best of his ability."

"Do you realize that this plant might have experienced a big loss through a major fire? I hope you don't think it couldn't happen. Would you like to hear the details of how some plants were burned to the ground because of some employee's carelessness or some supervisor's neglect of his responsibility? I have a file on such incidents."

Walt lowers his eyes and doesn't respond. After you see he is not going to answer, you continue.

"How long have your people been smoking in unauthorized areas?"

"I can't say for sure," Walt replies. "I know we enforce the no smoking rule very strictly in the vulnerable areas. But in other places like the stockroom, I guess we haven't been tough enough."

"From what you've said, I take it that other employees have been smoking in the stockroom."

"Yes," Walt replies. "It's happened before."

"What do you intend to do about Ed Smith?"

"I was discussing that with Frank (another supervisor) when you called. He thinks we should set this up as an example, and give Ed a week's suspension."

"I'm not so sure that's the complete answer. Despite the seriousness of the situation, Ed is not entirely to blame. If you had seen to it that discipline was strongly enforced, chances are Ed wouldn't have been smoking that cigarette to begin with.

"When you walked into the stockroom and saw him smoking, bawling him out for it and ordering him to put the cigarette out was tantamount to no discipline at all, particularly since this was common procedure. Effective discipline does not rule out words, but it implies that action is required in situations where words aren't enough.

"I recommend that you give Ed a clear official warning, telling him that smoking is absolutely prohibited wherever no smoking signs are posted, and that the next time he's caught, he will be suspended or even lose his job, depending on the situation. Once you get this message across to him and all of your people, you must then enforce it."

Reasoning and Principle Involved

Of all the fears of management, a fire in the office or plant is one that's most dreaded. For this reason, companies have safety experts or fire specialists designate certain areas as vulnerable and others as non-vulnerable; no smoking signs are posted in the vulnerable areas.

It behooves management to see that no smoking rules are enforced. Not to do so courts disaster for both employees and the company.

PROBLEM NUMBER 2

What to say to the employee who has a poor attitude toward the rules of the company and how operations are conducted.

The Situation

You are in charge of a group of women who sew garments and costumes. Claude Thomas, one of your employees, operates a supply truck to bring fabrics, thread and other material to them. He has been criticized for moving his truck too fast through the workplace aisles. Today Claude told the women that he would make a delivery only when at least two people called to say they were out of material, and he had done that once this morning. Clearly, Claude needs to be talked to about his attitude and his responsibilities.

What You Should Say and Some Responses

When you enter the sewing room to look for Claude, you find him smoking and drinking coffee in the canteen area. "Got a few minutes to talk?" you ask him.

"I'll take some," Claude answers. You motion to him to follow you as you walk to a nearby meeting room where your conversation won't be overheard by others.

"Say, Claude, a couple of the women told me you weren't giving them good service this morning. What's the problem?"

"Oh, there's nothing much to it. They're thinking only about themselves. They'll run me to death if I let them. I can't see where letting a woman wait a bit for material is so bad."

"I can," you say emphatically. "When the women run out of material they have nothing to do. As a result, the department falls behind in filling its orders. We can't operate this company and make a decent profit if some of the employees are idle part of the time.

"Regardless of that, Claude, your job is to keep the women supplied with materials *at all times,* not just when you feel like doing it."

Claude isn't bothered by your remarks and shows it. "Well, I've been doing my job. I can't help it if the women don't like the way I do my work. I usually try to get the fabric to a sewing machine operator quickly when I hear she's out."

"Yes, I've noticed that, and I've talked to you about it, too. We can't allow stock trucks to be moved faster than that of ordinary walking in these congested tight aisles. There's too much risk of an accident. Yet I've heard that you sometimes move your truck at a near run. Why do you persist in doing this?"

"That's a crazy rule to have. You just said you had to get the production out, and here you're criticizing me for trying to do it. I can't see where making my rounds in a hurry should bother anyone. I'm careful and always watch where I'm going."

You reply quickly, "That rule was put in effect to prevent accidents. Since I'm responsible for the safety of all people in this department, I'm going to enforce it. You can consider this a warning that the next time I see you moving that truck too fast, I'm going to suspend you.

"Also, I want you to start making more trips with materials to the sewers. There's no reason why you can't keep them supplied so they never have to call for it."

Claude shows his dissatisfaction with your words by saying, "You can't ask me to make more trips. I won't have time to take my personal and smoke breaks that I'm entitled to. I'm going to the Union representative about this."

"That's your right, but I suggest you reread your job description before you do."

Reasoning and Principle Involved

Union—management agreements invariably give management the right to run the business or operation and discipline employees for just cause. There has to be discipline, obedience to authority, and respect for the rights of others in any successful organization. Without these, order and efficiency would be impossible. Supervisors and foremen fit into the picture in that they determine an employee's need for discipline and mete out penalties for infractions.

PROBLEM NUMBER 3

What to say to a foreman about being consistent in enforcing rules and regulations.

The Situation

This morning your foreman, George Jackson, suspended one of his people five days for insubordination. The employee, Buck Rowe, had parked his car in a restricted area of the plant, and had refused to move it to the employee's parking lot when asked to do so by George. This afternoon Buck came to your office with his Union representative, claiming the penalty was completely out of line. The representative stated that if a rule is set up to apply to one employee, it must apply to all employees. You see that you must get the full story from George.

What You Should Say and Some Responses

"George, I just had a meeting with Buck Rowe and his Union representative. They claim that your suspension of Buck is unfair. I told them I would discuss the incident with you and get back to them. Does Buck have a justifiable complaint?"

"In my opinion he doesn't. It's well known to all employees why parking out by the shipping platforms is forbidden. For one thing, permitting employees to park in an area within close access to the plant and its products would be bad security practice."

"I agree," you reply. "Also, it wouldn't be practical from an operations standpoint. With trucks frequently loading and unloading at the platforms, automobiles might interfere with their movements. That's why the company went to the trouble and expense of providing an employee parking lot."

George then proceeds to tell you that Buck says there's nothing in the contract nor in any written rule that says he has to park in the employee lot. He claims that it's right to park where he wants.

You ask, "But why did he park at the shipping dock in the first place?"

"Buck told me that he had tripped at home and hurt his leg. He felt that walking the greater distance to the parking lot would aggravate the condition. I asked him to move his car anyway, first early this morning and then again at lunch time. He still hasn't done it. As I see it, the guy is guilty of both insubordination and noncooperation."

"I told the representative that it's management's prerogative to establish rules designed to maintain the efficient and profitable operation of the plant. But the rep said he wasn't arguing that right at all. He was only saying that if the rules applied to one employee, they should apply to everyone. Exceptions shouldn't be made."

George's face clouds when he hears those words. You continue the account of your meeting with Buck and the representative.

"I asked him what he meant by that, and he replied that some employees have been allowed to park there from time to time, and nothing was said about it. He said that Bob Wiley parked there all day a week ago."

"That's true," George replies. "But Wiley received special permission. He was given an OK to borrow a portable sander from the maintenance shop for a flooring job he was doing at home. Since he was going to pick up the sander at quitting time, I approved his request to park there. He didn't just park there on his own in defiance of the rules and in defiance of his foreman's request that he move his car. There was no insubordination involved."

"I was unaware of that incident," you say. "But I agree that Wiley had the decency to request permission, whereas Buck took it on his own to do as he pleased, whether you liked it or not. That is insubordination, whether he intended it to be or not. However, when a ruling affects plant security and operating procedures, it shouldn't be waived for the convenience of one employee in favor of another. Even though Wiley got your permission, it shouldn't have been granted.

"Of course, that doesn't justify Buck's attitude and behavior," you add quickly. "But I feel it's essential that management insist on equal treatment for all employees, and to demonstrate it with its actions. For this reason, I'm going to change Buck's suspension notice to read one day instead of five.

"Relax George, I'm not going to give you a long lecture. But I am annoyed. Every time management has to back down on its dealings with employees, some degree of respect is lost in the process. I'm sure you now know the reason for being impartial. And as much as you may be tempted at times to enforce rules prejudicially in favor of people you like and against people you dislike, prejudice never has and never will pay off."

Reasoning and Principle Involved

If the rules and regulations of an organization are to be meaningful and effective, they must be impartially enforced. That's not always easy when dealing with a notorious and uncooperative employee on the one hand, and a conscientious and considerate one on the other. When this happens, it's natural to lose sight of the need to be impartial and give the good employee a bit more equality than the bad one. But in a democratic environment, that is a dangerous mistake for a foreman to make.

PROBLEM NUMBER 4

What to say to a supervisor who follows rules to the letter.

The Situation

Joe Kelly is a competent and conscientious leader and technically well qualified for the job of supervisor in your department. But he is weak in human relations and lacking in imagination. Today you learned that one of your most capable workers, Bob Wilson, had a run-in with Joe, the outcome of which was Bob quitting his job. Bob's reason for leaving was that Joe refused to allow him to temporarily work hours other than the customary eight to five workday because of problems that Bob was experiencing at home. Since you don't want to see the company lose employees like Bob, you discuss the incident with Joe.

What You Should Say and Some Responses

"Joe, what's this I hear about Bob Wilson quitting?"

Joe's face becomes very serious. "That was his decision, not mine. I told Wilson that the company rule calls for an eight to five workday, and if I altered the rule for him, others might want the same thing. That would screw up our schedule."

"You've got a point, but don't you think that rules have to be broken at times, when circumstances require it?"

Joe doesn't waver. "I don't believe in giving people special treatment. Company rules are made for a purpose. If you break a rule for one guy, pretty soon someone is going to ask you to break a rule for him. Bob Wilson is a good employee, but he's no better than anyone else."

"I'm not going to argue with you Joe, but it's been my experience that, rules or not, a supervisor has to use good judgment."

Joe shrugged. "My judgment is that you go by the book. That is the way I operate, and it has worked well for me."

"I'm not so sure of that. Rulebook management can cause a lot of resentment and antagonism. Some employees will not take the initiative when they should. Others will hesitate to be aggressive when doing so would help the company.

"When you think about it, Joe, in one sense all rules are useless. The good employee doesn't need them, and the bad employee doesn't comply with them conscientiously. I think Bob Wilson is too good an employee to lose. I plan to call him at home and offer him a job in another department.

"Joe, I'd like to see you bend a bit more in your relations with your people. You'll find they'll think more of you if you let a rule go by the board now and then. You'll probably get more cooperation, too. In my eyes, you'll also be a better supervisor."

Reasoning and Principle Involved

Strict and unbending compliance with all rules, regardless of circumstances, can undermine an entire organization. Not only may productivity suffer, but it may be difficult to establish a rapport between management and employees. Equally as bad, many of today's workers will refuse to work in such an environment.

PROBLEM NUMBER 5

What to say to the worker who won't stretch a rule.

The Situation

You assigned one of your workers, Roger, a job that was very urgent. A customer's order was behind schedule and a truck was waiting to take it as soon as it was completed. At the time you gave Roger the job, you told him to stay on it until it was finished. But when you check on the order later, you learn he did not follow your instructions.

What You Should Say and Some Responses

"Roger, our shipping supervisor told me that urgent order didn't leave till after 1:00 P.M. He said he had to wait for you to return from lunch to complete it. Why did you leave the job when you knew the order was behind schedule?"

"Nobody told me to stay," Roger replies.

"Common sense should have told you."

"But the plant rules say we go to lunch at 12, and that's what I did."

"That may be so, and I'm not one to understate the importance of rules and regulations, but sometimes you have to allow for a situation. You knew a truck was waiting for that order. Also, it wouldn't hurt you to take your lunch break later."

You pause for some words from Roger, but he says nothing.

"Roger, our employees are told to never leave a machine running unattended. But suppose a fire broke out and you had to quickly leave a machine. Would you take the time to turn everything off before you left because you didn't want to break the rule?"

Roger looks exasperated. "Of course not. But that's a different situation."

"What's different about it? If rigidly applied, almost any rule can be harmful. If you have to stretch or even break a rule to meet a worthwhile objective, sometimes it's the only sensible thing to do."

Roger slowly nods agreement, but you are not sure you made your point.

"OK, Roger, you can go back to work. But remember, rules are made to help an operation or procedure, not to hinder it. Your good judgment and intelligence, if you're acting in the best interest of the job and the company, should come first. If you're ever in doubt whether a rule should or shouldn't be stretched, all you have to do is ask. Do you understand?"

Reasoning and Principle Involved

There are always some people on the job you can never reach concerning matters like rules and regulations. Your only alternative is to allow for their weaknesses in dealing with rules. Merely talking about a rule will not cause trouble.

PROBLEM NUMBER 6

What to say to the worker who strictly follows specifications, making it difficult for the company to carry out its objectives.

The Situation

This morning you gave Guy Henderson, your maintenance man, a pump repair job. The bearing had failed and needed to be replaced. You told Guy that the Production Department wanted to have the pump back as soon as possible. Since this job usually takes 1 to 1½ hours, you follow up 2 hours later to see if the pump is back in use.

What You Should Say and Some Responses

"Did you get that pump repaired and running, Guy?"

"No, it's still not done," Guy replies.

"For gosh sakes, why not? I gave you that job before nine. You should have finished it by now."

"It wasn't a matter of time," Guy says. "It was parts. The job writeup calls for a Smith bearing. We don't have one in the house. I checked the storeroom, the bins in the shop, and two other departments. Now I'm trying to figure out what company in town I should call to get one."

"What's this you're saying? Guy, you've been around here long enough to know that if you're all out of Smith bearings, you can substitute Black bearings and get the same results. We're overstocked on Black bearings. In fact, that's probably the reason no more Smith ones were ordered. We want to get the inventory on Blacks down first."

Guy's jaw was set. "The job writeup says to use Smith bearings."

"But," you start to say, when Guy goes on.

"I go by the book. If you go by the book, you don't make a mistake."

"You learned that in the Army, I suppose."

"That's right," Guy says defiantly.

"Guy, for Pete's sake, this isn't the Army. It's a manufacturing plant." You take a deep breath and continue, "Let me have your copy of the job writeup. We'll make it official."

Guy hands you the writeup. You take a pen and add a sentence where the specs call for the Smith bearing: "or a Black bearing if a Smith is unavailable." Then you initial the addition.

"OK?" you ask Guy.

"Yeah, sure."

"Fine, now please get that pump handled like I asked you to, using a Black bearing in place of the Smith."

Guy nods in agreement as you turn to leave. Then, you turn back to him.

"One thing more, Guy. The Production Department really needs that pump. Please don't go to lunch until it's finished, installed, and ready to operate."

Reasoning and Principle Involved

Wherever and whenever possible, managers must try to anticipate when a specification, manual or rules could thwart their objectives. And then make provisions in advance to keep it from happening.

PROBLEM NUMBER 7

What to say to a foreman about permitting horseplay in the workplace.

The Situation

You just received a phone call that an employee in the machine shop was injured. The injured person, you were told, had a big gash, half an inch from his eye, and was now being attended to in the company nurse's office. You immediately head for the machine shop area to talk to his foreman, Vince.

What You Should Say and Some Responses

"What happened, Vince?"

He doesn't look you in the face. "I'm almost afraid to tell you. Two of the fellows were on a rest break, Ross and another guy. They were tossing a ball of twine around, and the other guy threw it too high. Ross slipped and fell against a machine. A sharp edge cut his face near his left eye."

"Horseplay!" you say.

"Yeah, I guess so."

"Another inch . . ." you don't finish the sentence. Vince is looking guilty and probably feeling miserable.

"Where were you, Vince?"

"I was checking out a machine nearby. I noticed them throwing the twine around, but they weren't getting too rambunctious. My thinking was that a little fun and relaxation once in awhile doesn't hurt. I guess I was wrong."

"I thought your people were better trained than to horseplay on the job. When grown men start fooling around like a bunch of teenagers, the likelihood of an accident shoots up a thousand percent."

You pause a bit to let your words sink in.

"I'm not an advocate of harsh authoritarian management, but there's one exception. You can't get too tough when safety is involved. When a safety rule is broken, you've got to be very rigid about it.

"Other rules may be broken at times when there are special circumstances. But a safety rule can never be broken, not even bent. Nothing can ever excuse horseplay. Innocent or not, it's always a danger as we have seen here today. Ross was lucky. He got off easy. The next victim of horseplay might not be so fortunate."

Vince has been listening carefully, and now replies earnestly, "Yes, I guess I had to learn the hard way, but there'll be no more horseplay in my area without my taking strong disciplinary action. I'll see to that."

"OK, Vince, I believe you."

Reasoning and Principle Involved

There's nothing wrong with a bit of well-timed fun and relaxation on the job, but horseplay is no proper form for fun and relaxation to take. Once a manager starts compromising his or her standards, the standards are automatically weakened. That applies to any kind of management including safety management.

Chapter 5

DISCIPLINE

In the following situations, note how the manager puts across the importance of disciplining subordinates fairly, equally and immediately. Notice, also, how positive discipline is administered.

PROBLEM NUMBER 1

What to say to a supervisor about administering discipline fairly.

The Situation

It's common knowledge around the company that your supervisor, Bob Simpson, has been feuding with one of his workers, Tod Ronson; their personalities are very different and continually clash. Bob is 50, hard working, conscientious and "square." Although he is steady and reliable, he doesn't seem to like people and they respond in kind. Tod, 27, is a mod dresser, wears sideburns and a mustache which Bob especially dislikes. Brash, handsome, and single, he is liked by the girls in the office. Tod's performance on the job is average, his attendance good and he is seldom if ever late. This morning you were handed a copy of a suspension notice that Bob gave Tod for fighting in the plant. The notice, however, requires your approval before it can become effective. Shortly afterward, Tod came to you to discuss it. Now you see that you must have a talk with Bob.

What You Should Say and Some Responses

"Say, Bob, I have the suspension notice you gave Tod Ronson, and . . ." Before you can say anything more, Bob interrupts you.

"Good, I've been waiting for that guy to step out of line so I could zero in on him. I intend to build up a case so we can get rid of him. As far as I'm concerned, we don't need people like Tod on the payroll." Bob is excited about what he has done.

"Fighting is certainly a serious matter, and we won't tolerate it, but . . ." Bob breaks in again.

"Yeah, he and "Buck" Jones really went at it, but Tod started it. I happened to pass by when the fight started, and Tod was clearly the aggressor. He was the one who was throwing all the punches. The fight was about some of the work which was messed up. Both guys said it was the other's fault. But Tod's attack was unwarranted and vicious. That's why I made the suspension for two weeks."

"Bob, everyone in the department knows that you and Tod don't get along well. I'm aware that Tod has a way of getting under your skin, and I'm certainly not condoning it. Nor am I condoning your style and approach which has a way of inviting this kind of response from young people. Whatever the case, in fairness to Tod and in deference to fair play in general, I have to carefully check out this incident before approving the discipline."

Bob appears deflated when he hears your words, and wisely decides to keep quiet. You go on.

"Tod came to my office a short while ago to talk to me about what happened. You know what my policy is here—I've often mentioned it to the department people: if an employee, whatever his or her level, believes he's not getting a fair deal or is unable to communicate with his supervisor, my door is open and I'm always ready to listen."

Bob starts to say something, but thinks better of it.

"The story I got from Tod is that all the punches he was accused of throwing don't even qualify as a fight. He admits to getting very angry with Jones and maybe shoving him, but it was hardly a fight. What's more, he says he has witnesses to prove it.

"He was quite calm and sincere in coming to me. He also said he wasn't complaining about the severity of the discipline, had your accusations been true and not greatly exaggerated. What bothered him most was the mark on his record. His attitude impressed me, and somehow, I'm inclined to believe him.

"For those reasons, Bob, I'm not going to approve this suspension." You pause, waiting to see if Bob has anything to say. He remains quiet.

"I hope you learned a lesson from this. If there isn't anything more you have to say, I suggest you immediately go to Tod and tell him you've reconsidered and the suspension is off. I think everyone will feel relieved once you do this."

Reasoning and Principle Involved

Supervisors should expect that they will occasionally find themselves directing employees who are difficult to get along with. Some employees may appear to be misfits or have personalities that are hard to accept. However, such people should not be judged in light of the supervisor's preferences.

Bias and prejudice should never be factors in how people are treated by their supervisors. Also, supervisors should never attempt to discipline when there is a possibility that emotion rather than reason is controlling their thinking. They will be less likely to make the mistake of being unfair to both the employee and the company.

PROBLEM NUMBER 2

What to say to an employee who has not responded to discipline.

The Situation

One of your craftsmen, Bill Otis, is very skilled and efficient in maintenance work. He has frequently repaired machines in much less time than that required by other craftsmen. Bill's behavior, however, is not good in that he has little respect for authority, is frequently late, and has a poor attendance record. He has been warned both orally and in written form about this, and has received several suspensions. Yesterday he was absent without notice. You call him into your office today to discuss the situation.

What You Should Say and Some Responses

"Bill, two of our Braber machines broke down yesterday and we lost a lot of production. Where were you? Were you sick?"

Bill looks surprised. "I had some personal business to take care of. I mentioned that to you the day before. Don't you remember?"

"No, I don't, and with all the repair work we have backlogged, I certainly wouldn't have given you the day off, especially since you already have such a poor attendance record.

"I don't understand your behavior, Bill. Despite all the warnings and suspensions you've had, you don't seem the least bit worried about your job. I have all the justification and documentation needed for firing you."

Bill is not alarmed with your words. With a slight smile on his face, he says, "I don't think I'm doing so badly. I'm taking home a lot more pay than the other mechanics because I'm good at my job and I get the work out. There aren't many people around with my skills."

"Maybe so," you reply, "but there's a limit to what management will put up with on an employee's violation of rules and regulations. Also, I sense that the rest of the guys in the shop resent it.

"When you didn't show up yesterday, I talked to the Personnel Manager about you. His recommendation was that you be fired. But I want to give you a final chance to save your job. There will be no more suspensions, but one more infraction on your part will result in your termination. I am putting this in a letter to you with a copy to the Personnel Manager so there will be no misunderstanding on anyone's part."

Reasoning and Principle Involved

No matter how skilled and well qualified an employee may be, letting him or her get away with violation of rules and regulations is unfair to everyone else. Running an organization or department must be a team effort if the organization is to be successful. No other arrangement is acceptable.

PROBLEM NUMBER 3

What to say to a foreman about disciplining employees uniformly and equally.

The Situation

When an employee struck another one yesterday in Sam Klein's department, Sam, your foreman, investigated the incident and then wrote a warning notice to be given to the guilty employee. You must approve such notices. When you read it, you saw that you needed to talk to Sam. Fighting on the job is a serious offense which ordinarily calls for a five-day suspension.

What You Should Say and Some Responses

"Sam, I don't understand this notice you're asking me to sign. Are you simply giving Conn a warning for fighting on the job?"

Sam gulps and weakly replies, "Well, ordinarily I would have given him a suspension. But Conn is one of the best men I have. He was probably provoked into hitting Foster. Besides, he's got an outstanding record, and I need him badly on the job this week."

"You should know better than that. Don't you remember the two men that got into a fist fight in the warehouse a month ago? What discipline were they given?"

"They got five-day suspensions," Sam quietly replies.

"If Foster had struck Conn instead of the other way around, what would he have gotten?"

"Five days."

"For gosh sakes, Sam! You've been with the company long enough to know that you can't sock one man with a suspension for fighting and let the next guy get away with it, no matter how much you'd like to.

"You can't discipline today without considering what the consequences will be tomorrow. If you let this incident go by, next time you catch two men fighting and try to suspend them, they'd raise the roof about unfair and discriminatory treatment. And what's more, they'd be right. What goes for one employee has to go for another if you don't want the Union and everyone else on your back."

Reasoning and Principle Involved

The purpose of discipline is to correct, not punish. If discipline doesn't succeed in reforming an individual, it fails in its objective. With this in mind, the thing management should try to do is tailor discipline to the individual or specific situation.

PROBLEM NUMBER 4

What to say to an employee who drinks on the job.

The Situation

One of your accountants told you this afternoon that the office storeroom was out of the voucher forms he uses. You cannot understand this because you knew a shipment of office supplies came in just

a few days ago. Since you've had problems with the storeroom atten-
dant about drinking, you go there to talk to him and to see for yourself.

What You Should Say and Some Responses

"How are you doing today, Cal?"

"Pretty good, I guess. What can I do for you?"

"How about seeing how many voucher pads, Form 87B, you've got
in stock?"

"Oh, that's the form we're out of. I looked for it a half hour ago."

"Humor me," you say. "Check the item again."

Cal complies and returns moments later. "Like I said, no more left."

"May I take a look at your receiving folder?"

Cal hands over the folder, and as he does so, you smell liquor on
his breath. "You've been drinking again," you say.

Cal begins to deny your charge, but you continue.

"I can smell it on your breath, and I have a good sense of smell."

"Well, OK, I just had a couple of short ones. I've got a cold and the
booze helps me get rid of it. A couple of drinks doesn't hurt anyone. It
doesn't affect my work."

While Cal is talking, you have been looking through the receiving
slips. You find the one on the voucher pads and note that it had been
recorded two days ago.

"Here it is Cal," you say. "You probably misplaced them in stock
because of drinking too much. You know, I've talked to you before
about drinking on the job and the effect that alcohol has on your work.
Two warning letters about your drinking are also in your personnel
file. The company cannot continue to overlook this. You already
made some serious mistakes and your attendance is also beginning to
suffer."

"The only time I drink is when I'm having lunch. That's not drinking on the job," Cal replies.

"It's just the same as that when you come back from lunch with
too many drinks under your belt. I'm sorry, Cal, but I'm going to
recommend that you be replaced."

"I'll never touch another drop. One last chance; that's all I ask."

"That's what you said last time."

"This time I mean it. I swear."

"Tell you what I'll do, Cal. I'll give you one last chance, if you see
the company doctor for treatment. He's experienced with this problem
and will be able to help you."

"OK, I'll go," Cal replies.

"That's a good decision," you say. "I'll make an appointment for you."

Reasoning and Principle Involved

Management should try to help employees who have drinking problems, especially if they have been with the company a long time. Many of the larger companies have established programs for dealing with alcoholics and drug users. But there's a limit to what can be done, particularly if the drinking employee or drug user refuses to be helped.

PROBLEM NUMBER 5

What to say to an employee about not obeying an emergency order.

The Situation

It was 11:30 A.M. when you received a call from the Production Department that a conveyor broke down in the assembly room, completely shutting down the production line. As supervisor of the Maintenance Department, you promised to put someone on the job immediately. After going to the area and seeing that a bearing had failed, you quickly go to Dave Stone, your most experienced mechanic, who was repairing a pump in the maintenance shop.

What You Should Say and Some Responses

"Dave, I want you to drop what you're doing and hurry over to the assembly room. The main conveyor broke down, and ten people are idle. I just looked at it, and a bearing has to be replaced. It shouldn't take you more than a half hour or so to repair it."

Dave nods he understands and says, "OK, I'll get on it."

You decide to get a snack from the canteen for your lunch and head back to your office. On your way, you pass Rick Wallace, a new employee who had just finished a job. You tell him about the breakdown, say it's a rush job, and tell him to help Dave until it's done.

Forty-five minutes later, you receive an angry call from the Production Department saying that nobody has gone to the assembly room to repair the conveyor. You apologize and quickly go in search of Dave and Rick. You find them in the employee cafeteria having lunch.

"I gave you two an emergency order more than 30 minutes ago. What happened?"

Dave speaks up. "Oh, that job is number one on our list. We were planning to get to it right after lunch."

"You were told to get over there right away. That doesn't mean after lunch."

Dave pleads ignorance. "I figured after lunch was good enough."

"It's not good enough for me. When I say right away, I mean right away. Dave, I'm going to suspend you for this. You've been here long enough to understand the problem and the cost involved when a conveyor breaks down.

"Rick, I'm going to give you a written warning. I realize that a new employee can't be expected to know the full significance of a conveyor breakdown. Also, I can't fault you too much for going along with Dave's decision and failing to follow my instructions."

Reasoning and Principle Involved

Because of its demanding and authoritative tone, managers and supervisors should seldom use a direct order. They should limit its use to times of emergency to indicate the urgency of the situation or when working with people who don't respond to any other type of order. Employees can expect to be disciplined if they ignore a direct order, and management would be amiss if it was not imposed. But, here again, discipline is used to teach, not to punish.

PROBLEM NUMBER 6

What to say to a supervisor about the importance of administering discipline immediately when it is needed.

The Situation

While walking through the workplace, you noticed an employee running a machine with the safety guard removed. You told the employee to replace the guard and then went to tell his supervisor, Bill Jones, about the safety violation. Since Bill was out of the department at the time, you left a note on his desk asking him to look into the employee's previous safety performance to evaluate other infractions, if any, and to take whatever disciplinary action he felt necessary on the current violation. Four days have past and you have not heard from Bill. You phone him to come to your office to discuss the matter.

What You Should Say and Some Responses

When Bill enters your office, you greet him and motion him to sit down. Before he does so, he hands you a copy of a suspension notice. You glance at it but don't comment. Instead you wait for Bill to speak.

"I know," he says meekly. "I really goofed. This notice should have gone out four days ago, on the same day I got your memo."

"Why didn't it?" you ask.

"I had so many projects going and things to do that it just slipped my mind."

"That sounds like you have a poor reminder or tickler system. For gosh sakes, Bill, how long did it take you to write up this notice?"

"About five minutes," he answers sheepishly.

"That just about speaks for itself, doesn't it? Bill, what's the most important thing you must do when you discipline someone?"

"Be impartial and fair."

"OK. What's also very important?"

"Do it immediately. Don't let any time pass between the violation and when you do something about it."

"Right!" you say. "I thought you learned that years ago, and by now, it would be something you would do automatically. You can't tell me you were so overloaded with high priority jobs that you couldn't find the time to fit in a crucial five-minute one."

"No," Bill replies. "I kept putting it off, and after a while, I forgot about it."

"All right, Bill, I'm not going to harp on this. And I have to admit that this often happens in business. Although most managers and supervisors are well trained in business basics, they often fail to adhere to them as they should. In my opinion, one of the most important basics is to take action when action is called for, not before and not after."

Reasoning and Principle Involved

When an employee commits an infraction or violates an important safety rule and is caught doing it, he or she becomes an object of public interest and concern. Word gets around quickly through the workplace and everyone is curious to find out what will happen to the employee and what discipline the person will receive, if any. If management forgets to take action, or postpones doing it, the impact of the discipline is reduced. The chief purpose of discipline isn't to punish—it's to teach. When discipline is handed out immediately following a violation, the teaching impact is strong and effective.

PROBLEM NUMBER 7

What to say to an employee who is not responding to oral and written reminders that her behavior is not acceptable.

The Situation

You have been having problems with Laura Brown, a programmer in your department. Over the last six months, Laura's attendance has been poor, she has been late frequently, and her productivity has dropped considerably. In addition, she has a lax attitude and doesn't seem to care. You have discussed these matters with her to no avail. Oral and written reminders had no affect on her behavior. After being absent again yesterday, you decide to take a critical step with her today.

What You Should Say and Some Responses

"Laura, we missed you yesterday. Were you sick?"

"Yes, I wasn't feeling well, and when I overslept, I figured it was too late to call and say I wouldn't be in."

"You know, of course, that you have a poor attendance record. We've talked about this before. You have received both oral and written reminders that the company cannot continue to employ you under such conditions. I feel that we have reached the point where you must decide whether or not you want to continue working for the company.

Laura looks off in the distance and doesn't say anything.

"I don't want you to come to work tomorrow. Instead, take the day to decide whether or not you want to continue to be employed here. You will be paid for the day, but you must understand that the next violation of company policy such as being late or absent will result in your termination."

Reasoning and Principle Involved

The use of positive discipline is a relatively new way of dealing with problem workers. Reasoning instead of punishment to correct and prevent behavioral problems has proven to be very effective. Positive discipline differs from punitive discipline in two ways:

1. Early discipline steps consist of oral and written reminders instead of warnings.
2. A decision-making "paid suspension" of one day is the final disciplinary step.

Chapter 6

MOTIVATION

In the following situations, note that successful managers know that the most significant factor in achieving profit objectives is people rather than materials or machines. Notice, also, that lower level managers sometimes have difficulty identifying a motivational problem in a subordinate's performance.

PROBLEM NUMBER 1

What to say to a worker to increase that person's enthusiasm for the job.

The Situation

As supervisor of the Assembly Department, you are a bit concerned with how your new employee, Linda Pope, is going to fit into your department. Although you recognize that she is inexperienced, you are not sure she will enjoy the work and get satisfaction from it. You decide to do as much as you can to get her interested and enthusiastic about her job. An opportunity to do this arises during her second day on the job when she comes to you while you are talking with another worker.

What You Should Say and Some Responses

"I hate to bother you, but do you have a minute?"
Linda has a partially assembled machine component in her hands.
"Any time, Linda," you say. "Excuse me, Sarah. What do you have there, Linda?"

She shows you a piece of work she has been assembling. "You said to check with you after getting this far."

You look at the work with undisguised admiration. "Oh, this is real good. You're doing just fine, Linda. Now let's talk about the next step. Here's what you do. . . ."

As you guide her and explain the work, you do it gently and slowly, watching her for comprehension. You also show you are keenly interested in her progress. After explaining the next step, you tell her why it is being done now and mention what will follow. Lastly, you ask Linda to repeat in her own words what you and she had decided was to be done. This ensures that she understands the procedure thoroughly.

As Linda turns to leave, say, "Keep up the good work, Linda. I couldn't be more pleased with the job you are doing." Then, make sure you do not turn your attention to Sarah until she is on her way to her workplace, just in case she has a final question or comment.

Reasoning and Principle Involved

Personnel experts say that workers are effectively and properly motivated when they are convinced they are performing useful and challenging work, and when they share a feeling of enthusiasm and optimism about what they are accomplishing. One of the best ways to get people enthusiastic and satisfy their need to feel appreciated is to give them your full attention and show an interest when they communicate with you. People especially appreciate this when they know you are busy.

PROBLEM NUMBER 2

What to say to a supervisor who is overly friendly with one of his workers.

The Situation

Management recently formed a new department in your company. In selecting a supervisor for the department, the contest had been between two men who were very close friends, Henry Clark and Joe Green. Clark was eventually chosen. You had explained the reason for his selection to both men because of their close association and friendship, and the fact they would be working together. You had also told Green that the next opportunity for advancement that came along would be his. In the last few months, however, the new department has not been doing well either from a quantity or quality point of view. Production is down and rejects are up. You visit Clark to discuss the problem, bringing with you the department performance records.

What You Should Say and Some Responses

"Henry, I'm sure you're aware of the figures in this report. I thought you might be able to use some help in getting to the reason or reasons why they're so bad. Maybe if we discussed the situation we could learn what the problem is."

"I sure wish I knew," Henry replies gloomily. "It's been bothering me for weeks. Most of the guys in the department are pretty good men, at least I always thought they were. But the way they're acting now, you'd think they'd never heard of the standards we're supposed to meet.

"I thought these guys were my friends, but now I'm not so sure. Maybe they're mad that I got the supervisor's job instead of Joe, and Joe would have done a better job. I'm beginning to think they may be right."

"Bull," you say. "If management thought Joe was more qualified than you to handle the job, he would have gotten it, and both of you know it. Are you having any trouble with him?"

"With Joe? Are you kidding? He's the only guy in the department who cooperates with me."

"Do you really think the rest of the guys are intentionally making it rough for you?"

"I hate to say it, but sometimes it certainly seems that way."

'Have you talked to any of them about it?"

"Yes, I had talks with a couple of them. If they have any gripes or complaints, they're keeping them to themselves."

"You didn't learn anything at all?"

"Nothing specific. When I asked if they had any complaints, they had none. They answered most of my questions with yes or no answers, saying as little as possible. I thought I detected some resentment or hostility, but I couldn't put my finger on it. The way things have been going, I'm not sure of anything anymore."

"Don't let it get you down," you say. "It may take a while, but we'll eventually find out what's wrong."

Now you pause a bit to see if Henry has anything else to say. If he doesn't, open the conversation again.

"Henry, I've been wondering about your relationship with Joe, and how you two are getting along."

"We've always been good friends. We're still good friends."

"I know, but let's face it. You've been equal and at the same level in job status all these years. Suddenly, you're not because you're the boss. Something has to be different now."

"Like I said. . . ."

You break in. "I know what you said, but think about this a minute. Do you really believe there's been no change at all, that your becoming supervisor makes absolutely no difference in your actions and attitudes towards each other?"

Henry thinks a bit, then says, "I'm not sure I know what you are getting at."

"Suppose I put it this way—would you say Joe Green is doing the same job he's always done?"

"He does more and works harder, if anything."

"What about the work he does, the assignments he's given? Same as before?"

Henry scratches his head. "I would say so. No, on second thought, it's more diversified. He gets interesting and new jobs, sometimes jobs we haven't done before."

"Which requires special training?" you ask.

Henry frowns. "I suppose so. But he has the most potential and is also the hardest working guy in the department."

"That may be true, Henry, but he's also a special buddy, and everyone knows it. In the eyes of all the guys in the department, he's the fair-haired boy, the guy who can do no wrong. He gets all the breaks and opportunities."

After pausing a bit, you go on.

"If that's what's bugging the guys, it could knock out any morale that existed. What do you think, Henry? Does what I say make sense?"

Henry shifts his weight about. "Could be," he slowly admits.

"There's a good way to confirm this, Henry. I'll get Joe transferred to another department after explaining the situation to him. Since he's on his way up, he wouldn't be with you for long, in any case. You'll miss him, but it will be best all around."

Reasoning and Principle Involved

When old friends who formerly worked side by side on the job are suddenly put into a supervisor/subordinate relationship, anything can happen. There is a strong likelihood that the new arrangement may result in problems for both of the individuals involved, either immediately or sometime in the future.

PROBLEM NUMBER 3

What to say to an employee who complains that the work is boring.

The Situation

Andy Perkins is one of the company's veteran employees. Hired nine years ago, his performance on the assembly line has been better than average. In recent months, however, Andy's productivity and workmanship has steadily slipped and now it is well below average. This is evident from both his piece-work earnings and the amount of off-spec material he turns out. Since you are not sure what the problem is, you must talk to him about it.

What You Should Say and Some Responses

"Andy, you've been with the company more than nine years."

"Don't I know it!" he replies.

You smile, "Do I detect a bit of regret?"

"Nah, I guess not. I don't think I've got any complaints. The company's been good to me."

You nod your head in agreement. "I suppose you could say that, at least from a financial viewpoint. You've had a few merit increases and some cost-of-living increases over the years. But are you happy here, Andy? Do you like working for the company?"

Andy takes a deep breath. "Well, I dunno. What's happy?"

"Do you enjoy your work? Or do you hate having to come to work every day?"

Andy looks at you warily. "Why are you asking all these questions? Am I in trouble with the front office?"

"Not exactly. At least not right now. But let's face it, Andy. We both know you've been slipping. Up until six months ago, you were doing OK. But from about that time, you've been going downhill. I'm going to level with you, Andy. If you were just another guy with a year or two of service, it might be a different story. You'd have two or three warnings about your work by now, and if it didn't improve, you'd be fired."

Andy looks forlorn and discouraged.

"But you're a nine-year veteran," you continue. "That makes a big difference to my boss and to me. You've spent a good part of your life with the company, and you've made some valuable contributions. We don't want to simply write that off if we can help it."

Andy, listening intently, doesn't reply.

"Here's what I'm getting to. According to my thinking, a person doesn't change from above-standard to below-standard without a good reason. From what you've told me now and then, you have no troubles at home and your health has been OK. These are common reasons which explain why people change in doing their work or why they have a different attitude.

"Since they apparently don't apply to you, we'd like to know what the problem is. If something's wrong, we'd like to know about it. Maybe we can correct it, or maybe we can help in some other way. You and I agree that your performance is down. What I want to know is why."

Andy moistens his lips and gets up his courage to talk. "I don't know. It's not that I'm deliberately doing a poor job."

You wait for him to continue.

"It's hard to find words to explain it. Maybe the work has gotten too easy, or maybe I'm getting older. I don't know which. I guess the simple truth is I'm bored. Sometimes I find myself falling asleep on the job. Do you know what I mean?"

You nod. "Yeah, I think I do. What you're objecting to, if I may use that word, is having to do the same tasks day after day and week after week without variation.

"Repetition is the key word. Some people can take it, even welcome not having to think. But others, like you, Andy, find repetition painful and boring. It seems to take all the zip out of them, and also gives them a grim outlook when they realize that it can go on and on. If you're bored to death, you can't do a good job. I'd feel the same way.

"Andy, I'm going to try to make your and your fellow workers' jobs more interesting. Maybe we can rotate some of the jobs and get some variety into others. I've heard that participating in problem-solving and decision-making also helps. I'm willing to share some of those functions with you fellows, so I'm going to talk to my boss about this and see what we can come up with."

Reasoning and Principle Involved

Boredom with one's work is common today, particularly on jobs which are mostly repetitive in nature. Management can take several possible approaches to the problem: disciplinary action, rewards for better performance, appeal to pride, and enrichment of the job. Each course has its advantages and weaknesses, but job enrichment and participation in other activities have proved to be best for solving or at least alleviating the problem.

PROBLEM NUMBER 4

What to say to an employee who fails to accept responsibility in an emergency.

The Situation

Late Friday afternoon, your department received a call from the company's sales department that an order must be shipped very early Monday morning. An important customer needed the material; their employees would be idle if it did not arrive soon. You notified one of your workers of the situation and asked him to work on Saturday to get out the order. He agreed to have the order on the shipping dock by 7:00 A.M. When you arrive at 8:00 A.M. Monday, you learn that the order has not been shipped. You immediately contact your worker for an explanation.

What You Should Say and Some Responses

"Bob, what happened to the Superior order? I just talked to the shipping department and they haven't seen it. Were you sick Saturday?"

"No, I felt fine. I ran out of the No. 3 fasteners and could not finish the job. I tried to call you several times to find out what you wanted me to do. When I couldn't reach you, I went home."

You shake your head. "I don't believe this! It's unreal! Bob, you've worked on jobs like this before. You know that No. 1 or No. 5 fasteners can be substituted for the No. 3's."

"Yeah, but the No. 1's are more expensive and the No. 5's are cheaper. I didn't know which ones you wanted me to use. You've always said that it's better to be safe than sorry."

You take a deep breath and try to remain calm. "But that does not mean you shouldn't think and use good judgment in an emergency. The few cents more or less that the fasteners cost don't mean a thing in a situation like this. We might lose that customer because we didn't get the order out on time."

Bob looks down, "Gosh, I'm sorry. I just figured I didn't have enough authority to make a decision like that."

"You've got to use your head in an emergency. The least you could have done was get the units you completed packed up and ready to go."

"I never thought about that," Bob says apologetically.

"Well, get that done immediately, and then use the No. 1 fasteners to complete the rest of the order. That's the least we can do for the customer if we still have his business."

Reasoning and Principle Involved

When employees have been conditioned to do their jobs without solving problems or making decisions, they literally are turned into robots. Thus, when they are called upon to deviate from their accustomed routine, they're lost because they've never been given the opportunity to develop the habit of thinking for themselves.

Overspecialization is one of the most effective ways to dull employees' abilities and desires to think for themselves. Employees may need more opportunities to solve a few problems and make a few decisions on a day-to-day basis.

PROBLEM NUMBER 5

What to say to a supervisor whose excuses have gotten him in trouble.

The Situation

Ken Caldwell was a hard working employee before being made a supervisor. He has a higher than average IQ and constantly tries to improve himself. It was common knowledge in the company, however, that when he got the job, there was a lot of grumbling from another employee who felt that the job should have been his because he had more seniority and also a following of sorts. Recent company reports show that Ken's department ranks low in meeting production quotas. In addition, waste has been increasing in the department and product quality is down. When this month's report shows further declines, you head for his department to talk to him.

What You Should Say and Some Responses

As you approach Ken at his desk, he glances up at you unhappily. "I've been expecting you," he says.

"I'm not here to criticize you, Ken. I'd like to help if I can."

"Thanks. I certainly can use some."

"OK. To start, I don't see any point in hashing over the figures on this month's report. You and I have both seen them and know what they mean. The only constructive approach we can take is to try to find out why they are so bad. One of the other managers told me he thought you might not be getting the cooperation you need from your people."

"That's really an understatement."

"Why? What's going on?"

"Tim Hanson is causing me trouble. But it's not him alone. He's got quite a few backers."

"Meaning what?" you ask.

"Meaning there's a plan under way to push me out of this job so that Tim can take over."

"How do you know this, Ken? Do you have any proof? What happened to cause you to feel this way?"

"That's the problem. I can't come up with anything specific or concrete. Whenever I try to do that, I get a lot of double talk from the guys. They're either evasive or talk in circles. If a job gets messed up, a mistake made, or the work isn't finished on time, they find 18 reasons to explain why it couldn't be helped and wasn't their fault."

"Instead of results, you get alibis, is that it?"

"Right! That's what's happening."

"Ken, have you tried to find the cause of these problems? For example, the report shows a low machine utilization. Have you analyzed this to determine if the problem is due to the machines or the operators?"

"No, I haven't," Ken replies. "I've had too many other things on my mind."

"How about absenteeism? Did you check to see if these people are sick, as they claim? Did any of them bring in doctor confirmation slips?"

"I've been intending to ask them to do that," Ken replies, "but I've been swamped with paperwork."

"Rejects and waste? What are the main causes for those? Are your people careless or indifferent? Have they had enough training? Is poor quality raw material the problem?"

"I can't tell about any of those things until I get the right cooperation from those guys."

You pause and think a bit. Then you look directly into his eyes.

"Ken, I'm going to level with you."

"OK." He appears apprehensive.

"Your problem, in my opinion, is plain and simple—too many alibis."

Ken looks relieved. "I think you've got it. Those guys . . ."

You interrupt. "Not just 'those guys.' You're just as guilty as they are. You've got enough training and know-how to see that when a mistake is made or something goes wrong, the only way to correct it is by investigation and follow up.

"Yet everything I've asked you about, you couldn't answer. Instead you offered all kinds of excuses why it hasn't been done. This is the same thing that your people are doing. Alibiing. The sooner you quit it, and stop your people from doing it, the sooner you'll get your department straightened out. I suggest you start immediately by checking out some of those things I mentioned."

Reasoning and Principle Involved

People who really want to do something find a way. Others find an excuse. Supervisors must accept full responsibility for what goes on in their department. They should stop to think before they tell their superior they could have done something if they'd had the time. Such words are just an excuse for lack of motivation or interest.

PROBLEM NUMBER 6

What to say to a supervisor who labels one of his workers as lazy.

The Situation

The operating costs of one of your departments are much higher than they should be. You decide to discuss the problem with that department's supervisor, Harold Trout. But before you do, you review the personnel file of Harold's people and see indications that their performance is generally below average. One person, Tom Ralston, is particularly poor in this respect. You wonder if motivating Ralston to better performance might help the department.

What You Should Say and Some Responses

"How goes it, Harold?"

"Well, I've got problems and headaches. But isn't that what supervisors should expect?"

"Ain't it the truth?" you say.

"What's on your mind?"

"One of your problems. His name is Tom Ralston."

"Oh, you mean 'Lazy Tom.' Yeah, he's certainly one of my problems."

You act a bit surprised. "'Lazy Tom!' Is that what people call him?"

"That's what *I* call him. I'm sure that someone must have told Tom that hard work never killed anybody, but he doesn't want to take any chances of becoming a victim. I don't think I've ever seen such a lazy guy. I can't prove it, but I swear he sometimes goes to sleep standing up."

Caught up in the subject, Harold continues before you can say anything.

"I've been meaning to talk to you about him. He's had a few warnings from me, and I've discussed his poor performance with him several times. But it hasn't helped. He promises me he'll do better, and sometimes he does for a day or so. But then he begins goldbricking again. I've even called him lazy to his face. Frankly, I've had it with him. I think it would be good for the department if we fired him; it probably would be good for him too."

"Harold, I just reviewed his personnel record. His pre-employment tests were above average and the personnel man who interviewed him rated him very intelligent. The records show that his first four months on the job he did exceptionally well. But ever since that time, he's gone downhill.

"Why is his output now far below standard? Why has this eager young fellow with apparent potential and demonstrated ability had a change of heart and begun to act like an unhappy, tired old man?"

Harold acts uncomfortable and ill at ease. "I don't know," he replies in a quiet voice.

"I think your characterization of Tom as lazy isn't accurate. His problem goes deeper than that. You know, a lot of amusing remarks have been made on the subject of laziness. Also, considerable research has been conducted on why people appear and act lazy.

"In my experience, Harold, few people are really lazy. Psychologists have confirmed this. When an employee appears lazy on the job, it's usually because the employee doesn't have rapport with or isn't understood by his or her supervisor.

"I know you are hard-working and conscientious. But it takes more than good intentions to manage people well and to motivate them. It may be that Tom wants more interesting work and a chance to get ahead. You may be able to confirm this by some probing to find out what makes him tick.

"I'm inclined to believe that you've failed to get through to him, to communicate with him, and to motivate him properly. There may still be time to reach him and get him going in the right direction. I can't say for sure, but I think it's worth a try."

Reasoning and Principle Involved

Since it's against man's nature to be lazy, managers should look for more plausible reasons to explain inefficiency and low productivity in an employee. Lack of motivation is one of the major reasons for poor performance. There are very few people on the job who don't have a motivational trigger of their own that can be set off by proper action and follow up of their supervisor. The supervisor is the key to efficiency and productivity in most organizations.

PROBLEM NUMBER 7

What to say to an employee who leaves the job early without notice.

The Situation

Your company has adopted a work standard program under which employees are assigned specific tasks for each working day. These tasks are considered the daily work quota, but additional compensation is given to employees who exceed their quota. All this is covered in an agreement with the Union. One of your people, "Slug" Jackson, feels that the standards are too tough and has said so, even though he is capable of meeting and beating his quota more often than not. Although the normal working day in your department is 8:00 A.M. to 4:00 P.M., yesterday Jackson clocked out at 2:45 P.M. without saying a word to you, his supervisor. You approach him today for an explanation.

What You Should Say and Some Responses

"What happened yesterday, Slug? I saw that you clocked out early. Did you get sick?"

"Nah," Slug replies. "I felt fine. Since I'd made my quota for the day and didn't feel like starting a new job, I figured I might as well go home."

"You were out of line, Slug. Your daily quota has nothing to do with the length of the work day."

"Show me in the agreement where it says you have to do more than your quota."

"You show me where it says an employee can take off when he feels like it."

"Well, it makes sense to me. You do a day's work for a day's pay, right? The way I see it, there's no reason a guy can't take off if he makes his quota for the day."

"The way you see it is wrong, and I'm going to suspend you for one day. Also, I'm going to give you a warning letter which clearly spells out management's position on this, and also says that a repeat performance on your part will result in more severe discipline."

"No way!" Slug replies. "I'm going to the Union with this."

"That's your right," you reply.

Reasoning and Principle Involved

Work standards and compensation never dictate the length of the work day, but an unmotivated employee might want to test management on the issue. While some employees welcome an opportunity to earn extra income, others, not so productive, may complain that the standards are too tough.

Chapter 7

DEVELOPING PEOPLE

In the following situations, note how important it is that managers be skilled in leading and developing subordinates. Without that skill, there may be a lot of wasted effort, costs may increase and productivity may decline. Notice, also, that managers must be sympathetic and empathetic but not softhearted and permissive.

PROBLEM NUMBER 1

What to say to the new supervisor who continues to be "one of the boys."

The Situation

With the early retirement of one of your supervisors, you've had to find a new one. In contrast to his predecessor who was a rough and tough character, the man you selected, Terry White, is a quiet, easy-going individual. But ever since he took the job, the department has not done well. When the department's performance declined for the third consecutive month, you go to Terry to try to help him.

What You Should Say and Some Responses

You find Terry hard at work at his desk. He looks up anxiously at your arrival. "I thought you'd be coming to see me."

You smile and take a seat. "I guess the way things are going, you probably did. What seems to be the problem, Terry? Why is the department's output going down and the scrap and waste going up?"

Obviously unhappy, Terry replies, "I don't know. I just cannot figure it out."

"Maybe if we talk about what you're doing and not doing, we can get some clues. Let's start with how you're handling your people. One of the other supervisors thinks you're too free and easy with them. Could he be right?"

"Well, that's possible, I suppose. Certainly my style is a lot different than Joe Toth's. I don't get after some of the workers the way he did. I've always felt that if a person is properly motivated, you shouldn't have to hound him all the time."

"There's a lot of truth to that," you say.

"That's what I thought. But it doesn't seem to work out that way in my case."

"Tell me, Terry. How do you get along with your people? Do they willingly accept your assignments? Do they cooperate with you?"

Terry takes some time before he answers. When he does, he hesitates and speaks slowly. "I'm not sure about that. I like to think that they're good friends and my buddies, that they'd do anything for me. We get along fine when we go to ball games, and I'm on their bowling team. I think they like it when I have lunch with them, which I try to do as much as I can. Yet, somehow the work doesn't seem to get out the way it did when Joe was supervisor. Maybe I'm not supposed to be a supervisor."

"Terry, from what you've told me, I believe we can get your operation back up where it should be. This may surprise you, but you've got to break away from the hourly people and stop being "one of the boys," so to speak. You have to set yourself apart from the group and function as a representative of management.

"The course you've followed up to now never works out. There are times when you have to be tough and firm. I'm not saying that you have to go as far as Joe did, but remember, he got results.

"There are times, too, when you have to discipline someone. And, invariably, you'll find there are some people who automatically take advantage of a too friendly supervisor.

"Although a good supervisor and his people may work together well as a team, in a sense, they're natural rivals. Supervisors have a management responsibility and profits are their objectives. Very few workers and hourly employees have this attitude. They tend to overlook and forget why the company is in business, and it's the supervisor's job to keep them going in the right direction. This is difficult to do when both parties are good friends or buddies. The supervisor who decides he wants to be very popular with his people is headed for trouble."

An Alternate Approach and Some Responses

You find Terry hard at work at his desk. "Got a few minutes?" you ask.

"Sure do," Terry replies.

"Have you seen this report on the plant operations?" you ask as you put it down on his desk.

"Yes I have, but I wish I hadn't. My department doesn't look very good."

"Right," you say. "No one knows this operation better than you, Terry. What's the problem?"

Terry rubs his chin thoughtfully. "I wish to hell I knew."

"That figures," you say. "I guess if you could pinpoint the problem, you would have done something about it. OK, let's talk about it. Are your people slowing down or refusing to cooperate?"

Terry shakes his head no. "They're good workers. I've got a good group of people working for me."

"Then why the poor attendance, excessive waste, and failure to make the schedule?"

"I don't know. As I said, I worked with most of them before I became supervisor, and they're my friends. I can't see where they're doing anything differently now than before."

You see that you're not getting anywhere so you say, "Mind if I talk to a few of your people?"

Terry doesn't mind at all and says, "Anything you can do to help me would be appreciated. I can't figure it out."

You proceed to talk individually to various people in the department. Everyone seems to like Terry, and all his people have a good word for him. Nowhere do you find any bitterness, resentment or hostility.

At this point, you decide to take a different approach. You start checking the records, log books, schedules and work assignments. What you find is revealing. In more than one instance, you learn that the wrong person was put on a project. You also see where employee infractions were either overlooked or ignored. In addition, you find an important customer order behind schedule, yet no overtime work assigned to it. You're ready to talk to Terry again.

"Say, Terry, I've been looking at some of your department jobs and I found that the Superior Company order didn't go out on its scheduled shipping date. Couldn't you have worked some overtime to avoid the order being shipped late?"

"That's the night our baseball team played the Johnson Company team from across town. Quite a few of the guys wanted to watch the game and no one wanted to work."

"Don't you think the job should come before baseball?"

Terry doesn't have an answer for that.

"I've been wondering, too, about how you decide who should do certain jobs in the department."

"That's easy. I generally ask the guys which jobs they want to do. After all, I've known these guys a long time. They're my buddies. I have to give them a break."

"I see," you say.

Further conversation with Terry accounts for the general attitude of laxity in the department. You learn that when infractions are committed, Terry tends to overlook them. He simply cannot bring himself to discipline an old friend. It becomes clear to you that Terry is more concerned about how his old friends think of him than about his obligations as a supervisor.

"Thanks for your time, Terry. I'll get back to you later."

"How does it look?" Terry asks anxiously.

"It doesn't look good," you say as you leave.

Reasoning and Principle Involved

When a person is promoted from a worker to a supervisor, he or she goes through a major transition. To perform effectively, the person must no longer continue to maintain old social relationships. Focus must now be on the job, its responsibilities and its objectives. To achieve these objectives, the person must take a position apart from the rest of the group, be friendly but not fraternal, sympathetic to the needs of his or her people but not lax or permissive. Not everyone can adjust easily to this kind of change.

PROBLEM NUMBER 2

What to say to the department head who doesn't know how to say no.

The Situation

Linda White has been head of a production department for six months. The department's output has been poor ever since she took over. While the first two or three months can be explained by transition and workers adjusting to new supervision, the downhill slide appears to be continuing. If you can learn what the problem is, you may be able to save Linda's job and also correct a bad situation. Your plan calls for first talking to Linda.

What You Should Say and Some Responses

Linda looks up from her desk and smiles as you approach. She appears tired, probably because she has been putting in long hours on the job.

"Good morning, Linda. How are you today?"

"Just fine," Linda replies. "What can I do for you?"

"I thought we ought to talk a bit about your department's production. It hasn't been very good you know, and seems to be getting worse. If we can determine what's wrong, we should be able to take steps to turn things around."

Linda nods. "I hope you can help. I can sure use it."

You smile and look around the workplace.

"Where is everybody?" you ask. "I thought you had more people than this."

"I do. One of the girls is on vacation, another is out sick, or so she claims, and a third I loaned to Dick in "B" department. He's more short of people than we are and has a rush order to get out today. When he explained his situation, I sent Mary Porter over to him for the day."

"That's certainly generous of you. But aren't you behind schedule on important jobs yourself?"

"Sure, but Dick is worse off, and his order is top priority. I couldn't turn him down."

"I see. Well, let's get into your problems. How many people do you have now compared to six months ago?"

"There's been no change. I've had 12 all along."

"I guess that figures. Business has been pretty steady over the past six months. But you don't know any reason why your production volume has dropped so much?"

"No. It's been driving me nuts. Everybody's working most of the time. Of course, we've all been under pressure with all the overtime we're working, but that shouldn't be enough to make the figures so bad."

"Is the morale still good with your people?"

"I think it's gone down. With all the stress and strain, it's hard for people to keep their cool. But it isn't that bad. I've got a good group of people here, and most of them are cooperative."

"What about the workload, Linda? Has it increased in the last few months?"

"That's a good question. Let's look at the work schedules." She takes a file from her desk and looks at the monthly reports. She finds three projects and a couple of studies currently being done on a regular basis that weren't in effect six months ago.

"That's interesting," you say. "You're doing more work with the same number of people. If that does nothing more, it causes more overtime which adds to the department's operating costs."

As you are speaking, Linda's phone rings and she answers it.

"I don't know," she says. "We're pretty busy." She listens for a bit again. "Well, I suppose so, if you really need the information. I'll get it done as soon as I can. Oh, that's OK, Tom. I'm glad to oblige."

"What was that all about?" you ask after Linda hangs up.

"Tom Olson wants us to make a study and work up some figures on an idea he has. He thinks that it might save the company some money."

"Why couldn't he do it himself?"

"I suppose he could. But he thinks it would be faster and more convenient if we do it for him, since we have the information available. He's probably right."

You think a bit and then say, "Linda, how often do you do this type of work as a favor?"

"Every once in awhile. It's nothing, really. I don't keep a record of it."

"What about loaning your people to other departments?"

"Only when they're on the spot and badly need help. I'm certain that Dick, for example, would do the same thing for me if I asked. I don't keep track of such things."

"OK. But how often, in the last six months, have you asked?"

Linda doesn't answer at once. "Very infrequently. In fact, I can't remember one time when . . . ."

"Linda, I think I have an answer to your department's poor showing, or at least a partial one. I believe you're taking teamwork too seriously. You don't know how to say no when someone asks for help or wants you to do them a favor.

"The way I see the situation is that if you increase the amount of projects and studies you do on an off-the-record basis, you're not going to be able to keep up with your own work for which you're held responsible. Sometimes you simply have to turn down requests for help because you have priorities that are more important to you.

"I want you to seriously think about this. I think you'll reach the conclusion that you're going to have to say no more often. I'm going to be watching the amount of overtime your department works in the next couple of months and the department's production figures. I don't think I have to tell you the conclusion I'll reach if those figures don't go in the right direction."

Reasoning and Principle Involved

No supervisor who is an asset to his or her company needs to be told the importance of cooperation and teamwork. But even these virtues, however desirable, can be carried to extremes. If such work or effort may have an adverse effect on the output or productivity of the supervisor's own department, it must be avoided. The supervisor simply has to know when to say no.

PROBLEM NUMBER 3

What to say to the employee who doesn't know the difference between worry and concern.

The Situation

Early in the morning you were notified by your superior that an order for the Acme Company should be shipped that afternoon. You immediately notified your expediter, Hank Clark, to make sure the order was handled. Around noon, you call Hank to ask if any problems had arisen with the order. He assured you that the order would go out on schedule. Shortly after that, your superior calls to say that the Acme Company order had not yet been put in the mail to your company. You then go to Hank.

What You Should Say and Some Responses

"So you're 100 percent sure the Acme Company order will be shipped on time, and you won't have any problems with it?"

Hank's face shows he's very embarrassed. "Sir, the fact of the matter is . . ."

"I know exactly what it is. I just got a call that we haven't yet received the order. Now I've got a pretty good idea how you spent most of the morning. It was searching for that order, wasn't it?"

"Yes, I was." Hank cannot look you in the face.

"How many people did you talk to in an effort to find it?"

"At least seven or eight."

You shake your head. "Did it ever occur to you to phone Acme to find out when they sent it and to whom?"

"Yes, I thought about doing that, but decided against it. I figured that would suggest to them that something happened here which would make matters worse. I figured if I could put my hands on the order . . ."

"OK, that makes sense. But why didn't you let me know you couldn't find the order?"

Hank takes a deep breath and hesitates.

"You thought I might consider you inept or a poor expediter. You were worried that it might somehow lower my opinion of you. Isn't that it?"

"Yes, I guess so," Hank replies.

"So you ran around all morning and worked up a sweat over an order that didn't even exist."

Hank doesn't say anything.

"Hank, there's a big difference between being worried and being concerned. A worried person sees a problem; a concerned person solves the problem. Early in my career with the company, I learned that it was foolish to worry about anything. I'm sure that your job would be much less stressful if you would do the same."

Reasoning and Principle Involved

Efficient and astute managers concentrate more on concern than on worry when a problem arises or trouble occurs. This means that they take the most sensible and practical action they can in response to the difficulty. They leave the worrying to others.

PROBLEM NUMBER 4

What to say to the supervisor who is too softhearted and permissive.

The Situation

The Personnel Department has just informed you that one of your employees has been booked by the local police for assault, disorderly conduct, and drunken driving. You have the problem of deciding how the company should react to this. After you learn a few details of the incident, you go to the office of his supervisor, Mark Benson, to discuss the problem.

What You Should Say and Some Responses

"Mark, from what I understand, Wayne Pike is in serious trouble."

Mark nods and says, "Yeah, it looks like he's really in the soup this time."

"I guess 'this time' tells the story from what I've heard. One of the fellows told me this morning that Wayne has a reputation for hitting the bottle too hard and carousing too much. I'd like to talk to you about what the company should do about him."

"I suppose you'd like to look at his record."

"Yes, that would help."

Mark goes to a file, unlocks it, pulls out a folder, and hands it to you. As you leaf through the various papers inside, what you see shocks you. The records show that Wayne had two previous arrests, and had received warnings about drinking on the job. He also had been suspended for fighting. In addition, he had a very poor attendance record.

You shake your head and look at Mark who appears uncommonly glum.

"Mark, this guy is a big liability to the company and to himself as well. I don't understand why he wasn't fired, given psychological treatment or rehabilitated, or something a long time ago. His atrocious behavior goes back for years."

Mark isn't surprised at your words. "That's what I thought you'd say. I can't tell you the number of times I've talked to the guy. I can't tell you how many times he said he'd stop drinking. Each time, I believed him, but . . ."

"Then he should have been fired!"

"That's easier said than done. He's got a wife and four kids, and he's badly in debt. How can you fire a guy like that? If he loses this job, he'd be really in serious trouble. He could even be kicked out of his apartment.

"Wayne has been on my mind for months. All the facts say he ought to be fired. But when a guy's down and out and desperate, how can you lay one on him?"

"That's one way of looking at it," you say, "but sometimes a good kick in the rear is just what's needed to drive some sense into an unruly person."

"I'm not sure I get you."

"OK, then consider this. So long as Wayne continues to drink and carouse around, he's going to be in continual trouble. Apparently he's a weak-minded person and can't figure that out for himself. He may need something or someone to jolt him to reality.

"Then consider the company. Your and my responsibility is to do our best to keep our department running as efficiently and productively as possible. Wayne is clearly counterproductive and a dead weight for both himself and the company.

"Lastly, this is the second time Wayne's been booked for drunken driving. How many times do you think he's driven while intoxicated without being caught? Up to now, it's luck alone that has kept him from injuring or killing someone, wouldn't you say?"

"Yeah, you're right." Mark looks thoughtful. "The sooner we can stop him from drinking and driving, the better for everyone."

You nod agreement. "Mark, sometimes you have to take the hard line, even though it may seem tough. If you seriously think about it, you'll realize that it's something you should have done long ago."

Reasoning and Principle Involved

Although companies have certain responsibilities to all employees, particularly long-term ones, management cannot be permissive concerning their behavior as it relates to efficiency and productivity. Management's right to discipline an employee can never be questioned. Just because you have been permissive in the past doesn't mean you have to continue to be that way.

PROBLEM NUMBER 5

What to say to a supervisor who is insensitive to employee's problems and needs.

The Situation

Bill Stein is one of your supervisors in the Production Department. He replaced a well-liked supervisor who, six months ago, decided to leave the company. Although Bill is a serious-minded, hard-working, conscientious fellow, production has fallen off in his area the last few months and his people are also making more and more mistakes. Rumors are that Bill is not very popular with his people because he is rude, cold and has no regard for their feelings. One of his people quit without notice a few days ago. You decide that it's time to have a heart-to-heart talk with him.

What You Should Say and Some Responses

"Bill, I've noticed you've been having difficulty in meeting the production schedule the last few weeks. I think we ought to talk about it. Maybe I can help. I understand you have a reputation for being a tough taskmaster. Could that be the reason?"

Bill shrugs. "The way I see the job, that's the only way to get the work out. I set high standards and try to see that they are adhered to. I also set high standards for myself. I don't see anything wrong with that."

"Do you have any idea why Peterson quit without notice? He wouldn't tell me."

The supervisor looks away. "Maybe, but I'm not sure." Bill seems ill at ease and not wanting to talk.

"What do you mean, you're not sure?"

Bill hesitates. "About a week ago, he made a bad mistake, causing us to shut the process down, and I gave him hell for it. He got upset at the time, but I'm the one who should have been peeved. His mistake put us way behind schedule, not to mention the cost of wasted materials. We never seemed to get along well after that."

"Would you mind if I talk to a few of your people? I'd like to find out if they know why the department is having trouble meeting the production schedule."

"Not at all. If I'm not handling this job right, I'd like to know what I'm doing wrong so I can correct it."

One by one, you talk to Bill Stein's people. Some you find are reluctant to speak freely, while others willingly talk. They all have much the same to say. Now you go back to Bill to tell him what you have learned, level with him, and see how he takes it.

"Bill, I thought you'd like to know what I learned from talking with your people. Of course, I won't reveal any names, but here are a few of the comments I got. One individual said you didn't care if you hurt a person's feelings. Another said you're always finding fault with people instead of helping them and guiding them. A man said that he was shopping around for a new job, and a woman admitted she was thinking of requesting a transfer out of your department."

Bill listens thoughtfully and soberly, but doesn't say anything.

"One of the operators told me that your tough standards didn't bother him because your predecessor's standards were just as tough. But, he said, your predecessor never made him feel stupid and incompetent as you do.

"All I can conclude from these comments from your people, Bill, is that however well-intentioned and conscientious you are, your efforts are being wasted because you're unwittingly triggering resentment in your people."

Bill slowly shakes his head from side to side, and then says quietly, "It all seems so clear and simple, now that you've told me, and there's no question that everything is true. But why couldn't I see it for myself?"

"I don't know. Perhaps it's because we're so caught up with our jobs and getting the work out, that we overlook human nature and the feelings of people who are doing the work. We never stop to consider how others might react to our behavior.

"Whatever, Bill, I think you have learned something very important today. If you now apply it, you should soon have a smooth running and efficient department."

Reasoning and Principle Involved

Insensitivity has been the downfall of many supervisors and managers. Supervisors, in particular, sometimes become so wrapped up in their own bailiwick, they forget that other people have pressing problems and needs. This causes them to appear ruthless, demanding and unforgiving. It also brings on resentment, it results in people making mistakes, and lowers productivity.

PROBLEM NUMBER 6

What to say to the supervisor who doesn't let subordinates think for themselves.

The Situation

About five months ago, one of your most competent supervisors was promoted to another position. In anticipation of the move, management had trained Keith Bond, a young engineer with management potential, to become the new supervisor. Although the training period was rather short, Keith had learned quickly and gave all indications of being a dedicated and diligent supervisor. However, he has had trouble on the job, particularly with getting projects completed on time. In addition, conflicts and arguments among his people have been occurring in the last month. Sensing that matters are getting worse, you visit him at his office.

What You Should Say and Some Responses

Keith looks up apprehensively when he sees you approach. "Hi, what's new today?" he asks.

You waste no time on preliminaries. "I'm concerned with your department's operations. Your people have been late in completing a few important projects, and I've heard that they've been having some arguments. Do you know what the trouble is?"

"No, I don't. Harold Thompson didn't have the problems with them that I'm having. I can't seem to get them to put out for me the way they did for him. I get the feeling sometimes that they resent me, but I can't figure out why."

"I know you're still new on the job, so I wanted to give you a chance to work out your own problems. But things don't seem to be getting any better. Is it possible you might be favoring one or more persons in handing out easy and tough assignments?"

"No. I make sure not to do that. I distribute the work as fairly as possible."

"How about working them too hard, demanding too much of them?"

"No way. My problem is trying to get them to do a fair days work."

"Have you had any arguments or disagreements with anyone?"

Keith shakes his head slowly. "Not that I'm aware of. Once in awhile I get after them to cut down their idle time, but I haven't singled out anyone in particular." He hesitates but doesn't say anymore.

"Yes, what were you going to say, Keith?"

"I'm not sure, but many of the people are cool, almost unfriendly at times. I've tried to tighten up on the operations. My objective has been to streamline procedures to make them run as efficiently as possible. I spell out exactly what has to be done and how to do it so there won't be any confusion. But instead of making things better, it seems to be making them worse."

"Well, that's interesting," you say. "What else?"

"I try to follow up closely, most of the time, to make sure I'm available if my people have any questions. There's nothing wrong with that, is there?"

"Yes and no, Keith. Sometimes it depends on the disposition and attitude of the person doing the work. Many people like the challenge of a job. They like to solve some of the problems that come up by themselves. When you are right there on the spot if something goes wrong, the job becomes a bore.

"From what you've told me, it's likely that some of your people may feel you're treating them like a grammar school teacher. Others may think you have no faith in their ability to do anything right on their own. From a management viewpoint, I would say that you are oversupervising.

"I suggest you think about this, and determine how you can change your style of managing without neglecting your responsibilities. I believe it'll make a big difference in your department's performance."

Reasoning and Principle Involved

One of the most important responsibilities of management is the proper development of self-confidence in employees. The surest way to destroy an employee's self-confidence is to give the person the impression that the supervisor doesn't trust or have faith in his or her ability. A supervisor's job is to train people to do a good job while leaving enough unsaid when giving instructions for them to think for themselves and make their own decisions.

PROBLEM NUMBER 7

What to say to the employee who suddenly is unable to cope with the job.

The Situation

Norman Toll had been an outstanding mechanic for almost five years. About three months ago he missed being promoted to supervisor only because another man had a bit more experience. Shortly after that, Norman started acting surly, belligerent and uncooperative. In addition, his workmanship has steadily declined. Your oral and written warnings have had no affect on him. You gave him a one-day suspension for fighting a week ago, and told him if he didn't straighten out, he would lose his job. Today he became abusive and started swearing at you when you asked him to do a job he didn't like. You tell him to follow you to the conference room.

What You Should Say and Some Responses

"Norman, I'd like an explanation for what just happened. I try to be fair in handing out assignments. I make sure with the dirty jobs in particular that they are equally distributed among the men. And I don't like being sworn at."

"You've been riding my back for weeks, and I'm getting sick and tired of it. It seems that nothing I do is right in your opinion."

"Do you want your job, Norman?"

"Yes, I do."

"Last week when I gave you a suspension, I took a good look at your record. Until about three months ago, it was one you could be proud of. Ever since you came to our department, you had done an excellent job and management thought highly of you. Then, all at once, you made a complete turnabout. I'd like to know why."

Norman looks away. "I don't know."

"That's a remarkable answer. Five years as a respected individual, and now looked down upon. And you don't know why. How about leveling with me, Norman? There *has* to be a reason, and you darn well know it. Is it that promotion you missed out on?"

"No."

"Has your health gone bad? Are you seriously in debt?"

"No."

You try to be patient and wait for Norman to talk. He remains silent.

"Look, Norman, we've got to get this thing settled. You need this job. The department needs good men."

Norman's lips quiver and he struggles to control himself. Suddenly, he spills over. "It's my wife. She's been in the hospital four months. I don't know when she'll be getting out. I've got three kids, the oldest is 11. My married sister has been helping out, but the situation keeps getting worse. I . . ." His voice starts to break, and he stops talking for a few seconds. "I don't know what to do. My nerves are shot, and I lose control easily. If I lost my job . . ."

"You're not going to lose it," you say softly and with compassion. "Hell, Norman, all you had to do was tell me." You glance at your watch and see it's almost quitting time.

"Go home now and do what you have to do. We'll talk again tomorrow and see if we can come up with a way to help. In the meantime, try not to worry. Things will eventually work out. They usually do."

Norman rises slowly and starts to leave. "Thank you," he says in a voice that is just barely audible.

Reasoning and Principle Involved

Empathy and understanding are valuable assets to all leaders in business and industry. But being human and compassionate when an employee is in trouble is not easy for many managers. Without these virtues, a manager might very easily overlook or dismiss an employee who could be a great help to the company.

Chapter 8

INTERVIEWING AND
JOB SUITABILITY

In the following situations, note how the manager makes the point with subordinates that interviewing must be conducted with care and be thorough if there is to be any assurance that both the employee and the company benefit. Notice also that managers have the responsibility of making sure employees are suited for the positions and jobs they request or apply for.

PROBLEM NUMBER 1

What to say to an employee when he or she is not suited to a job opening.

The Situation

One of your supervisors, Ralph Wilson, has decided to move to another city. Your boss has asked you to find someone who would make a good supervisor. Before you have time to do so, Bob Smith, a fellow who has been with the company for many years, approaches you and asks if you have time to talk to him for a few minutes. You know Bob quite well and you don't think he would make a good supervisor.

What You Should Say and Some Responses

"What can I do for you today, Bob?"
"I heard that Ralph Wilson is leaving and the company needs a new supervisor."
"That's right, Bob. Ralph just made it official."

"If I'm figuring right, I'm next in line for the job."

"From a seniority standpoint, yes, but that's only one factor. There's a lot more than seniority that management must consider."

"I know that, but I've got a good record. I have a lot of experience and I miss very few days of work. The way I see it, that makes me a good candidate."

"I don't disagree with any of that, Bob. I think you're one of the best people in the department. But I don't have to tell you that a supervisor's job is a rough one around here. There's quite a bit of responsibility involved, and there are a lot of problems and headaches that go with the job.

"It's hard for me to see you in that position. You're a pretty easy-going guy. It's not your nature to keep on people's backs and make some of them toe the line when you have to."

What had been a smile on Bob's face disappears. "I could learn to do that, and I certainly could use the extra money."

"Everybody could. The point is that with your seniority, you will be earning nearly as much as a supervisor when the next cost of living increase comes through. And it looks like you're due for another merit increase in a couple of months."

"I don't know what I should do," Bob says slowly. "I hate to pass up an opportunity for a promotion."

"I wouldn't be concerned about that. You're a top-notch operator and you should be proud of it. I'm sure you'd enjoy the job you're doing now more than a supervisory job where you'd have to handle people when that's not your cup of tea.

"Think about it, Bob. I believe you'll agree with me. Getting enjoyment and satisfaction out of your work and the respect that it brings is more important than a small increase in your pay."

Bob slowly replies, "You may be right," but he still looks uncertain.

"What you should do is try to imagine yourself as a supervisor. Remember last year when you were a group leader on the new process line? I got the impression from watching you that you weren't comfortable handing out orders, even if you only had one or two guys working for you. A lot of people are like that. They enjoy working side by side with others. But when it comes to taking charge and telling people what to do and how to do it, they're not at ease."

"Yeah, I remember." Bob scratches his head.

"There's something else to think about, too. Right now you've got a lot of security, and your future with the company is assured, provided you don't do something way out of line. If you tried this supervisor's job and it didn't work out, you'd be jeopardizing the security it took you all these years to build. If I were in your spot, I'd be glad to stay put."

Bob nods, a thoughtful look on his face. "OK, thanks for your advice."

An Alternate Approach and Some Responses

"How are you doing, Bob?"

"Pretty good, I guess, but I'd like to talk to you about becoming a supervisor, now that Ralph Wilson is leaving. I understand you'll need someone. I think I can handle that job, and I'd like to try it."

"I'm sorry, Bob. I think a lot of you as a person and a good operator, but I don't think you're right for this job. I have to decide as I see it."

"How do you know whether or not I can handle the job unless you give me a chance?"

"Of course, nothing's certain about things like that. All I can do is use my best judgment."

"All I want is a chance to show you what I can do," Bob says. "Even if I goof up, what have you got to lose?"

"Plenty. A lot of valuable time for one thing, the time it would take to break you in. Another supervisor would have to work with you for quite a while before you could go it on your own. Also, as you know, it's company policy not to demote anyone except under very unusual circumstances. If you didn't work out, the company would lose one of the best people it has. When you think about it, getting a person set in a key job is a big and costly investment."

"If you don't give me a chance, I'll probably get a supervisor's job somewhere else. I've got enough experience, and I feel I can handle a job with more responsibility."

"I'd sure hate to see that happen, Bob. We'd certainly miss you in the department. If I were in your position, I'd think a long time about quitting and looking for a supervisor's job with another company. That's a big step and a risky one, in my opinion, especially when you've got a lot of security right here."

Reasoning and Principle Involved

Some people are born followers while others are born leaders. If followers are promoted to supervisors or managers, the idea that they're regarded as part of the management team may make them ill-at-ease and uncomfortable. As a consequence, they don't get satisfaction from their work, and may even dread going to work each day. An unhappy supervisor doesn't do his or her best and is not an asset to a company.

If a manager has a choice between a person who is seemingly suited for a key job and a person who might not make it, more often than not, the manager's best bet is to rely on his or her instinct. Having a good record of performance on a nonsupervisory job plus years of service to the company are not justifiable reasons for promoting a person to a management position.

PROBLEM NUMBER 2

What to say to a manager who is doing a poor job of interviewing and hiring.

The Situation

Patrick Foley became manager of the Pattern and Mold Shop about a year ago. Prior to that he had been a supervisor of another department with five people in his unit. Now he has more than 20. You've noticed that the turnover in Pat's department is quite high, higher than in any other department in the company. The high turnover means that Pat is continually interviewing and hiring people, a practice which is detrimental to the company from the productivity viewpoint in addition to incurring high training costs. You begin your investigation of the high turnover problem by talking with Pat.

What You Should Say and Some Responses

"Hi, Pat, how's the job going?"

"OK, I guess, but the backlog of work to be done keeps increasing, and I don't seem to be able to cut it down. I'll have to hire some more people."

"I've noticed your high turnover. The employment records indicate that you hire more people that don't work out than any other department head. I was wondering why."

Pat becomes very serious. "I've wondered about that myself. It seems to be getting harder and harder to find good reliable people these days."

"That's nothing new," you say. "Even though the unemployment figures are high in the area, good, experienced people are always hard to find. But that isn't all that concerns me. When reviewing the records yesterday, I saw that more of your new hires don't last through their probationary periods than those of any other manager. What bothers me even more is the question of how many new hires are getting past their probationary periods and becoming permanent employees who aren't really qualified and won't turn out to be loyal and conscientious workers."

"I guess that's something to worry about," Pat says thoughtfully. "But good people are tough to find. Here's a good example." Pat picks up a newspaper clipping from his desk and shows it to you.

"We placed this ad in the paper a few days ago and got six calls about it. Three of the people who called didn't have suitable experience and had to be rejected right away. One guy is doubtful and two others weren't very impressive, but they're possibilities. They're scheduled in for interviews tomorrow. Even if they aren't just what I need, I'll have to hire one of them."

"Why? Who says you do?"

"Well, it's either that or we get further and further behind in our work. We're really hurting. I need someone in a hurry."

"Maybe so," you say, "but let me tell you what I learned from the Personnel Department before I came to see you. Out of the last five people you hired during the past year, four were hired within one or two days of the ad's publication. Hard as it is to find and screen good people, that's almost unbelievable.

"What it tells me, Pat, is that your hiring practices are poor; you're hiring the best person available at the moment instead of trying for a more suitable applicant. This turns out to be a vicious circle because the unqualified individual doesn't get past the probationary period, and you're again looking for another person to hire.

"Pat, do me a favor. When you interview those people tomorrow, don't hire anyone unless you're sure he's exceptional. Tell them you'll let them know. I'll talk with you in the morning on what we can do.

"What I want to do is go over that backlog and see if we can cut it down. Also, we'll see if working overtime for a short period will handle the problem until better replacements can be found."

Reasoning and Principle Involved

Hiring is one of the most important functions that a manager performs. If it isn't done wisely, every other management function suffers. Costs increase and bottlenecks get worse. It takes competent and cooperative employees to cut down backlogs and get the work up to date.

Although it may take time and patience to find the right people, a manager's time couldn't be spent better than when it's allocated to hiring qualified, superior people.

PROBLEM NUMBER 3

What to say to a manager about assigning a critical and difficult task to a subordinate.

The Situation

An experienced and skilled staff individual, Ed Steffy, recently announced he would soon take early retirement. Your law department will sorely miss him. Some of the projects handled by Steffy were complicated and complex, requiring foresight and special judgment. It will probably take months before his replacement develops the knowhow required to handle certain assignments. You decide to talk to your department manager about who should be assigned to do Steffy's work until a person can be hired.

What You Should Say and Some Responses

"Do you have a few minutes, Steve?"

"Sure do," Steve replies.

"You know, we have to find a replacement for Ed Steffy and that may take some time. The Personnel Department will be interviewing people starting next week, but a new person may not be brought in for several weeks. Meanwhile, we will have to distribute the work that Ed has been doing among other members of the department. What concerns me most about this, is the Contract Status Report that Ed works up for the Vice Presidents every two weeks. That's a complex report, one that's difficult to write."

"I know what you're saying," Steve replies. "I've been thinking about it and figured that Ben Adams might be best suited for the job. He's had some experience with contracts, is thorough and conscientious."

"But . . . ." you begin to comment.

"Yes, I know. There's an unknown here. Ben's never worked on anything that difficult or complicated before. I *think* he could probably do it, but I'm not sure."

"How did you plan to handle this?" you ask.

"I was going to ask Ben if he's interested in taking over the report, and if he is, giving him a shot at it."

"Is anyone other than Ben qualified for the job?"

"I believe Alice Miller and Frank Williams are probably just as qualified, but Ben is more familiar with the contract language. Of course, I'm not sure about any of them until I see what they can do."

"I believe you just gave me the answer," you say.

Steve looks closely at you. "I'm not sure what you mean."

"Why don't you see what Ben can do before committing yourself? Ed will still be here for another four weeks. When is the next Contract Status Report due?"

"By the end of next week."

"OK," you say. "Explain to Ben that Ed is being assigned a special project to summarize where several accounts stand and would be hard pressed to get out the report. Assign Ben to help out on it. That way, you'll have a good chance to work with Ben on the report, see how well he does, and see if he understands what's needed. You can do all this without committing yourself in any way."

Steve nods his head, and a smile begins to appear. "That way, if Ben doesn't work out, I can pick someone else without disappointing him or letting him down."

"Right," you say with a smile.

Reasoning and Principle Involved

One of the worst things a manager can do is to build up a subordinate's hopes, give the person an opportunity, and then have him or her fail to deliver or perform acceptably. A manager is better off delegating on a trial basis which will always give the manager an out if the delegation doesn't prove out.

PROBLEM NUMBER 4

What to say to a supervisor who didn't handle an unsatisfactory employee properly.

The Situation

During a recent business upturn, the company hired some temporary people, one being the brother of an employee. This temporary employee proved to be a poor one in both attitude and productivity. But for the sake of the brother, and anticipating a downturn in business, the temporary employee was kept on the payroll past the probationary period. Then when production slowed, he was laid off. Now, six months later, business has begun to pick up again. The company has rehired the same temporary employees except for the previous unsatisfactory one. Within a week, the brother questioned the company on this. When told why the company did not rehire the person, the brother claimed discrimination because the person is a member of a minority group. You go to the supervisor involved, Avery Toth, to discuss the situation.

What You Should Say and Some Responses

"Avery, the Personnel Department just informed me that Juan Espera is claiming that the company is discriminating against his brother by not rehiring him along with all the other temporary people recently put on. What do you know about this?"

"Oh, you mean Filipe Espera. He was the 'temp' that didn't work out about a year ago. He just couldn't get the hang of the job, and he also goofed off a lot. He's not at all like his brother Juan, who's a pretty good worker."

"Apparently he was on the payroll for several months. Why didn't you get rid of him and hire someone else?"

"I figured there were just three or four weeks involved and we could put up with him for that length of time. Also, he's Juan's brother. Unfortunately, business was good and we didn't lay off the temps for another two months."

"Did you know that Juan is now claiming his brother is being discriminated against because we didn't rehire him?"

"No, I didn't," Avery gloomily replies.

You shake your head in dismay. "Avery, when it comes to performance, there's only one course that management should follow. If an employee won't or can't do the job, the first thing to do is to learn why and correct the problem, if possible. If this doesn't work, the person has to be fired.

"Telling a poor employee that he or she doesn't qualify is one of the most unpleasant and disagreeable jobs for a supervisor to do. But it's one you can't put off or get around. In my opinion, tolerating substandard performance is the primary sin of management, and as you can see, it can lead to all kinds of trouble."

Avery has nothing to say.

"Do you think keeping Filipe on the payroll despite his incompetence helped either him or his brother? I hope you don't."

"What are we going to do?" Avery asks meekly.

"What can we do?" you say. "Send Juan to see me. I'll try to convince him there is no discrimination involved, just that management handled the matter very poorly."

Reasoning and Principle Involved

When management finds that an employee can't do his or her job, immediate action must be taken. The situation cannot be permitted to continue. Either the problem must be corrected or the employee must be removed from the job.

PROBLEM NUMBER 5

What to say to a manager who is reluctant to try a female on what is traditionally "a man's job."

The Situation

Your company expanded its operations and more orders are being received. Another truck driver is needed. When the job was posted, two employees applied for it. One was Jack Miller, a warehouse employee, and the other was Rosa Pirelli, a shipping clerk. Both have good records with the company, but Rosa has three years' seniority. Your manager, Wilt Ellis, has decided that Jack should be given the job, and sent you the Job Transfer form for your approval. You ask Wilt to come to your office to discuss the matter.

What You Should Say and Some Responses

"Good morning, Wilt. How are you today?"

"Real good," he replies as he takes a chair close to your desk.

"I would like to talk about the new truck driver's job. I see you picked Jack Miller for the job. Why him instead of Rosa Pirelli?"

"That's easy," Wilt says. "Driving a truck, even if you get help loading it, is heavy work. It's no job for a woman."

"I'm not so sure of that. It may be no job for *some* women, but that doesn't mean it's no job for *all* women. Some of the girls in the office might not be qualified to fill that job, but Rosa is a strong, well-muscled woman. Moreover, I've seen her carry some heavy boxes from the shipping office to the loading dock."

Wilt looks skeptical. "I still have my doubts."

You smile. "That's understandable. We can't be sure about how any given employee will perform on any job until we see how they handle it and evaluate the results.

"But there's something else we should consider, Wilt. Things have changed in labor relations and job placements from what they were years ago. Rosa knows that you plan to give the job to Jack and is angry about it. She thinks you are discriminating against her. I wouldn't be at all surprised if she turned in a grievance if Jack was awarded the job. You know she has seniority over Jack. If the case ever went to arbitration, the company might lose it.

"Wilt, I'm not asking you to make a final and irrevocable decision, but I have a hunch she could handle the job without any difficulty. Besides, that's what probationary periods are for. You'll have 30 days to make up your mind. If it turns out during that time that the job is too tough for her, I'm sure that Jack will quickly take it. All things considered, I think Rosa deserves a chance to show us what she can do."

Wilt looks thoughtful. "OK, I guess that's the least we can do for her."

Reasoning and Principle Involved

Times have changed in the marketplace. There are not many jobs today that some women can't do just as well as men. Management must therefore consider all the facts and circumstances when placing employees on jobs which were traditionally "men's jobs."

PROBLEM NUMBER 6

What to say to an employee who objects to filling out a personnel questionnaire.

The Situation

The Personnel Department of your company recently gave you some forms requesting that you have your people fill them out and return them to the department. A memo with the forms stated that the department was conducting a company-wide survey to determine the organization's population from the standpoint of ethnic, religious, and other minority representation. The forms asked employees to indicate the information requested for race, religion, national origin, color, age and other data. Shortly after you handed out the forms, an employee comes to your office with the form in his hand and a defiant look on his face.

What You Should Say and Some Responses

"Do you have a question about the form?" you ask.

"Not a question, but a protest. This form violates the Civil Rights Act."

"No violation is intended," you say calmly.

"Maybe not. But the law specifically prohibits an employer from asking about race, religion, age and the other things on this questionnaire."

"Well, you're both right and wrong," you say with a smile. "You are absolutely correct in saying that such inquiries are illegal if they are made before employment or during the screening process. But they're legal if asked for nondiscriminating purposes, especially in compliance with the Civil Rights Act of 1964.

"You've made a good point, however. I think the Personnel Department should have handled this a better way. They should have prefaced the questionnaire with a sentence or two explaining its purpose and use."

Reasoning and Principle Involved

With more and more government interest in protecting the rights of workers, employers need more information about their employees to make sure the company's balance of minority and non-minority employees is proper. Some employers also need the information to conduct programs designed to help minority groups.

Chapter 9

PERSONAL QUALITIES

In the following situations, note how the manager deals with and promotes the principles of good human relations when guiding and working with subordinates. Notice also that managers who are lax and permissive create problems rather than solving them.

PROBLEM NUMBER 1

What do you say to an employee who refuses to dress appropriately for the job.

The Situation

Al Silvers has done an excellent job for the company as a sales-service engineer the past year. A clean-cut fellow, 20 years old, he was eager, enthusiastic and neat in appearance when he was hired. Recently, however, he began going through a transformation. Some of his fellow engineers said it was the new crowd he was running with. Others said he was unhappy with his pay and your refusal to give him the large raise he requested. Whatever the cause, he started letting his hair grow and began wearing mod clothes on the job. When both the hair and the dress approached extremes, you decided to talk to him about his appearance.

What You Should Say and Some Responses

"Say, Al, it looks to me like you could use a haircut."
"No way, man, that's the way I wear it. I can't see anything wrong with it. In fact, I'm going to continue to let it grow."

"I also don't think those tight jeans and loud shirts are appropriate dress for the job you're on. What's happened, Al? The Al Silver of today and the one we hired more than a year ago are not the same person."

"Bull," Al replies. "That's just a figment of your imagination. Besides, this is a free country. I can dress as I please."

"Al, I don't particularly care what you wear to the plant. You could come in boxer shorts for that matter. But it's the nature of your job that creates a problem. You knew that when you were hired and started your training, you would eventually be sent to customer plants for engineering service work.

"You can't show up at a customer's plant looking like a weirdo or a hippie. It's bad for the company's image."

"I can't see how I dress, has anything to do with it. I do good work, and that's all the customer needs to be concerned with."

"I'm sorry, Al, but I disagree with you on that. If you had shown up for your employment interview in the costume you're presently wearing, and with that hair style, you wouldn't have gotten past the receptionist's desk. I believe many of our customers feel the same way."

"Well, it hasn't happened yet, so why the big hassle?"

"I'm going to make sure it can't happen. You have just two days to get some clothes so you can come to work dressed the way you used to. And get that hair taken care of, too. If you don't comply, you can plan on looking for a new job next week."

Reasoning and Principle Involved

Although dress and appearance codes have been substantially liberalized recently, most companies are still concerned with the impression their employees make on customers. A company's image influences the kind and amount of business it does.

PROBLEM NUMBER 2

What to say to a manager who treats subordinates like machines.

The Situation

A new data processing system involving the computer was recently introduced into one of your departments. The system was expected to increase the productivity of the workers and also reduce the number of errors they made. You've been following the operation every day or so by talking with the workers and checking their output. Productivity has not increased and there are more mistakes being made now than before the system went into effect. You decide to visit the manager of the department, Toby Prior, to discuss the problem.

What You Should Say and Some Responses

Toby is hard at work at his desk when you approach, and he looks worried. "It can't be all that bad," you say as he looks up.

While that brings a smile to his face, it is only temporary. "I'm afraid it is. This new data processing procedure is giving me fits."

"Do you think there's something wrong with the system? Maybe the software?"

"I don't know. Probably not. Everything works fine on paper, but it sure isn't working in the department."

"Why not?"

Toby takes his time in answering. "I guess it's because everybody hates the system."

"Why? Is it complicated?"

"No. In fact, it's simpler than the old way."

"Then what's wrong? What's the problem?"

"What's supposed to happen isn't happening for a number of reasons. People forget to add to the database to keep it current. Also, they put information in the wrong place. This leads to duplications in some cases and apparently no inventory in others."

"Have you asked your people about these things?"

"Time and time again. They don't have any answers. They complain the system's hard to understand, that the old way was better; that they forget to do certain things, and on and on."

"Would you say these problems and difficulties applied to everyone?"

"No," Toby says quickly. "Most of them aren't doing well, except for Becky Stopher or Jim Cornwell. They may be exceptions, but, as far as I can tell, they aren't having any trouble with it."

"That's interesting, because I talked with Jim the other day. He told me a few things about the system that might explain why your people are having problems. For one thing, he says a couple of the steps are duplicated unnecessarily, and a couple of them have the order reversed from the way we've been doing them. He said that 'nobody consulted us and we're the ones who have to work with the system.' He feels that management just sprung the system on them."

Toby's face is grim, but he doesn't say anything.

"Jim said also that some people think the only reason for the new system is to check up on them. Also, a few people feel threatened by the system; they feel they might lose their jobs because of it.

"What do you think about this, Toby?"

"Well, it makes sense. I guess I've been so busy thinking about the mechanics, the computer and the details of getting the work out, I neglected to consider the people aspects of the job."

"Yes, I think that's the answer."

Toby doesn't look too happy. "So where do we go from here? Now that I've got most of the people bitter and resentful, how do I turn them around?"

"By leveling with them. By explaining the real purpose of the new system. Tell them it's designed to make their jobs more secure by making the company more competitive. Ask them how they think the system should be run—you may be surprised with what they say. I believe you'll also find them more cooperative after you've talked to them."

Reasoning and Principle Involved

When management decides to make a change involving the employees, the new system or procedure should be discussed with the employees before anything is done. Change cannot be forced down peoples' throats. Their feelings and interests must be considered, and they must be sold. Astute managers see to it that this is done.

PROBLEM NUMBER 3

What to say to a supervisor who is too easy going.

The Situation

Ruth Wallace is one of the hardest working supervisors in the company. Intelligent, fair-minded and well-liked, you had every reason to believe she would make good at the job when she was promoted to it six months ago. But her department's performance keeps heading down with no sign of an upturn. Since one of your company's objectives is to have more women in supervisory and management positions, you'd hate to see Ruth fail. With the intention of learning what her problems are and helping her with them, you ask her to come to your office.

What You Should Say and Some Responses

"How goes it, Ruth?"

"Do you really have to ask? I know you've seen the monthly performance report and I'm guessing that's what you want to talk about. If my department sinks any lower, I'm afraid you'll shut it down, although I'll probably go first."

"Wrong assumption, Ruth. Management has a high opinion of you. I feel you probably have a problem or two. If I can help, I'd be glad to."

"I can use all the help I can get, but I really don't know what's wrong."

"Are your people cooperating as much as they could?"

"I suppose so. They do the assignments they're given and follow the instructions that go with them. But rejects are on the increase and there are too many errors."

"Anyone giving you a hard time?"

Ruth hesitates before answering. "No, I guess not. At least no open and obvious insubordination."

"What about Chuck Hollis? I hear he's a rough and ready character."

"Yes, he gets a little crude sometimes, and he doesn't do anymore than he has to. But he's smart enough to know where to draw the line with his remarks and his petty behavior."

"Do you think you're having problems because you're a woman running a department consisting mostly of men? Hollis, for example, has the reputation of being very macho. He may resent having to take orders from a female."

"You're probably right. But how can you be sure about something like that? If I ever brought up the subject, he'd deny it, and put on a big act about such an accusation having no foundation."

You think a bit and then say, "Ruth, would you mind if I talked to some of your people privately about the department's problems?"

"Mind? Not a bit. In fact, I'd appreciate it."

You proceed to interview three or four of Ruth's people, both male and female, always assuring them that you weren't doing it to get anyone in trouble or place the blame for anything that may have happened. All these people offer their opinions and comments on how Ruth is doing as supervisor, and generally they are in agreement on what her problems are. The next day you again talk with Ruth.

"Ruth, your people were very helpful in giving me their opinions on the department's problems. And since many of their comments were similar in nature, I have to feel that they are probably right. In essence, they think you are trying too hard to be a good guy, if you know what I mean."

"I think I do, but spell it out anyway."

"OK, they feel you are too easy on people, that you're afraid to offend them or turn them against you. So they lose respect for you, and some of them take advantage of you. Two people mentioned Hollis in particular as getting away with murder.

"When I asked them to compare the way things are now with the way they were before you took over the department, they said that things were a lot easier now but more work got done before. As for what they meant by easier, they said you didn't get on their backs if they took extra time doing a job. One person said you were too lax and permissive. The trouble with that is when you're a supervisor, decent treatment and permissive treatment aren't the same thing.

"In my opinion, Ruth, we're dealing with an accountability problem here. You're accountable to me, and I'm accountable to top management. The people you supervise must see and accept the fact that they're accountable to you as a representative of management. This means they're obligated to perform to the standards established for the work they do.

"One of the most difficult things for a supervisor to do is to toughen up when there is a need to do so. I'm not advocating being tough just for the sake of it, but being tough to the point where you refuse to accept substandard performance. If you take this position starting today, I feel sure your problems will soon disappear. And I can think of no better place to start than with Chuck Hollis."

Reasoning and Principle Involved

Managers and supervisors must continually audit and evaluate employees to make sure they are carrying out their responsibilities and meeting the company's standards of performance. In addition, leaders must be careful about being permissive. When they are too easy going, they lose the respect of their subordinates.

PROBLEM NUMBER 4

What to say to a foreman who uses fear in an attempt to gain cooperation and good performance.

The Situation

When Randy Welch, your veteran foreman, decided to take a three-month leave of absence, you selected his group leader, Rick Ellis, to take his place. The first week Randy was gone, however, productivity in the department dropped almost 10 percent. The next week, it dropped another five percent, and the same thing happened last week. You decide to talk to Rick about the problem.

What You Should Say and Some Responses

"Rick, I realize that you haven't had a lot of time to get your feet wet on this job, so I've hesitated about talking to you about how you're doing. But things don't seem to be getting any better. I'd like to help you if I can."

"Thank you," Rick replies. "I appreciate that."

"So what seems to be the problem? Why is production down and continuing to decline?"

"I really don't know. I guess maybe the gang misses Randy. He's a terrific foreman. I wish I had half as much on the ball."

"That's something to shoot for. I don't know anyone who does not think well of Randy. But he's about 55 years old and has a lot of experience. You're only in your 30's. You've got plenty of time to develop. Do you have any other ideas?"

"I suppose some of the gang simply don't like my style."

"Why do you say that? You've been around for a while as a group leader. Did you ever have problems before?"

"Not that I know about. But I was never in charge before."

"Has your style changed since you took over?"

"I suppose it has, in a way."

"What way? How would you describe your style?"

Rick thinks about that a bit. "Well, I guess it's the way I handle people, how I hand out assignments and show my authority, that kind of stuff."

"OK, let's say you give someone a job to do. How do you go about it?"

Rick seems uncomfortable. Then he answers slowly, "Well, now that I'm the foreman, I think it's important that those guys know for sure who's the boss. I believe that if you don't show your power and authority right from the start, you weaken your position. You wind up with people stepping all over you."

"OK, but how do you show your authority? What things do you do?"

"One thing is I try to put enough fear into those guys so they will do their work without stalling or arguing about it. When I give someone a job, I let him know he'd better do the job right, or else."

"Or else what?"

"Or else he'll be suspended or fired, depending on the seriousness of the situation."

"You haven't done anything like that yet."

"If I have to set an example with someone, I will. And I think everyone knows it." Rick pulls out a notebook from his rear pocket. "I keep a detailed record of mistakes and foulups; everything goes down in this book."

"What about excellent and outstanding performance?" you ask. "Does that go down, too?"

Rick hesitates. "Well, no, but I suppose it should, shouldn't it?"

"Definitely! But there's something else that's very important which you should be aware of. When it comes to influencing people and gaining their cooperation and loyalty, honest persuasion and reasoning is the only way to go. Fear has never worked and never will.

"With a few exceptions, successful foremen do not carry out their responsibilities by telling the world, 'I am the boss. You do as I say.' They also do not pressure or coerce people into doing what they want done. Some foremen do this without realizing it, perhaps because they are more drivers than leaders.

"A driver doesn't seek respect or cooperation but relies mostly on authority to get his or her way. Rick, you'll get much better perform- ance from your people if you act as a leader, not a driver."

Reasoning and Principle Involved

Managers cannot get more work or better performance out of employees by threatening them. Similarly, punishment has little, if any, effect on productivity. Introducing fear into people's minds usually results in low morale, dissatisfaction and high absenteeism, matters that have a negative affect on performance and productivity.

PROBLEM NUMBER 5

What to say to a young supervisor about how to handle a much older subordinate.

The Situation

When your supervisor, Joe Bailey, retired, his successor was Bat Jenkins, a much younger man. Bat is an ambitious and conscientious individual with outstanding potential. He is also a mod character, at least in his style and the way he dresses. Even though considered good at handling people, Bat has had problems with Sam Pierce, a veteran employee who has been one of the steadiest and most dependable workers in the department. But Sam, a man of 60 with fixed ideas about life and work, has recently been irritable and noncooperative. When you heard that Bat would like to have Sam fired, you decided to talk to Bat.

What You Should Say and Some Responses

"How goes it, Bat?"

"Oh, pretty good, I guess. We're getting the ticket out, and most of the gang have been cooperative, but I've got one big problem."

"What's that?"

"Sam Pierce. He's become a real headache. If I want a job done one way, he'll try to do it another way. He's clever enough not to swear at me or refuse outright to do a job, but he doesn't have to. His eyes and his attitude speak for him. I guess the word to describe him is disrespectful. If I continue to let him get away with it, I believe it may undermine supervisory respect throughout the department."

"Tell me, Bat, what makes him act the way he does?"

"Heck, I'm no psychologist. I can't figure him out."

"I thought we might try to be objective about this. You know, if Sam were a troublemaker or turned out poor quality work, I wouldn't think twice, long-service employee or not. I'd either try to get rid of him or do whatever was necessary to get him off your back as soon as possible. But for as long as I can remember, he's been a better than average worker. You simply can't ignore that. Suddenly, he makes a complete turnabout and changes his attitude and outlook. I want to know why."

"I wish I knew. I'd try to do something about it."

"Does he disobey orders?"

"Yes he does. Let me give you an example. This morning I noticed him assembling a finished system and saw that the job was taking a long time because he didn't have any clamps to hold the various components and parts in place. So I got him some clamps and explained to him how they worked and the savings involved. Then I did a few assemblies for him to demonstrate the procedure. Before I left him, I made him put together two of the systems himself. He got it right away."

"What happened?"

"Nothing happened. I checked back an hour or so later. He had set aside the clamps and was doing the job the same way as before, as if I had never showed him the faster way. There were others guys around and they saw it too. They must have had a big laugh at my expense. I simply can't put up with that kind of nonsense."

You think a bit and then say, "I try not to be too positive about the way people feel and think because when emotions and attitudes are involved, logic and reasoning may not apply. All I can do from what you've said is make an educated guess at what is going on. It seems to me that this situation is a classic one.

"We have a conventional and unimaginative employee in his 60's who rather suddenly finds himself in a situation where he is required to take orders and instructions from an energetic and ambitious young supervisor less than half his age. Even for a flexible person, that's a tough row to hoe.

"The more I think about this situation, it would surprise me if Sam, after being supervised for years by someone approximately his own age and with his own background, could respond willingly and without resentment to a bold young fellow like you, however talented you may be. It would depend on the way you handled him, and a man like Sam certainly would require special handling.

"What it comes down to is your need to understand Sam's problem and the conflicting pressures that he's exposed to. It's essential that you be very tactful in dealing with him. In other words, make suggestions rather than give orders, and ask his advice on how to handle some tough problems.

"Also, Bat, you've got to recognize the many advantages to the company of having older workers like Sam on the payroll, and let him know you are aware of those advantages. Treat him with respect and he will return the favor. I suggest you start on that track immediately. I'll be very surprised if he doesn't become much more cooperative within a short period of time."

Reasoning and Principle Involved

Young supervisors sometimes encounter hostility from workers who are older than themselves. Although the most common reason why an older person may be hostile to a younger supervisor is fear, jealousy may also be a factor. Hostility is usually shown by antagonism or withdrawal. The best way to contend with it is to take the person aside and talk to him or her about it.

PROBLEM NUMBER 6

What to say to the supervisor who needs to be more firm with employees.

The Situation

You've noticed that your department operating costs have been increasing the past four months, ever since Jack Green was promoted to supervisor of the department. Labor costs have risen because of excessive absences, and material costs are high because of too many rejects and too much waste. Rumors are that Jack lets people walk all over him and is too polite. This morning when you walked through the department, you found several people either idle or talking with others. In addition, you saw only about half of the people you knew the department employed. These observations prompted you to stop at Jack's office.

What You Should Say and Some Responses

"Hi, Jack, how are things going?"

"Well, they could be better. What's new with you?"

"I just came through your department and saw only a few people. I thought you had about 15 employees. Where are they?"

"Well, two are out sick, or allegedly sick. The others are either taking breaks, in the john, or at the canteen machines."

"How come you don't crack down on them?"

"What am I supposed to do? Keep on their tails? How do you tell someone he can't go to the john or to get a drink of water? What do you do if an employee calls in sick, send someone to his house to check up on him?"

You shrug. "If the situation calls for it. That's been done, you know."

"Maybe I *should* start cracking down. But I've always felt that the best way to get people to do a good job is through fair and decent treatment. I always thought if you treat people with respect and give them the benefit of the doubt, they'll feel obligated to treat you with respect in return. That's what I try to do, but it doesn't seem to be working."

"Jack, I'm going to level with you. To do a good job of supervising, you have to be flexible in your treatment and approach. There's no other way."

A mystified look appears on Jack's face. "What do you mean?"

"What you said about treating people with respect and expecting the same kind of treatment from them makes a lot of sense. That approach works with most people. But like it or not, every organization has a certain number of people who understand only one type of management—you do the job you're paid to do, or else. If you're too timid or wishy-washy with such people, they'll take advantage of you.

"Then there are other people more or less in the middle. They will do an acceptable job if the department's standards and work practices require it. But if they see a fellow worker getting away with murder or goofing off, they'll goof off.

"While every manager can be a nice guy and be noted for it, from what I've heard and also observed in your department, you've been letting too many people walk all over you. If you're not tough enough to lay down the law and take control, you'd better forget about being a supervisor. You can be a 'nice guy' when a strong hand is called for, which isn't really being a nice guy at all, because it's bad for everyone involved including the people who walk over you. Or you can be tough and firm when you have to. It's up to you, Jack. Which will it be?"

"As I see it, I've really got to toughen up. I'm not sure I can do it, but I can sure as hell try."

You nod. "Good, Jack, it's not all that difficult. I'm sure you can do it."

Reasoning and Principle Involved

The best manager is the one who knows what has to be done, how it has to be done and when it has to be done, and lets nothing stand in the way of getting it done. That means laying down the law if it is needed. While it means persuasion when a selling job is called for, it also means being tough and firm when resistance is encountered.

Chapter 10

SAFETY AND HEALTH

In the following situations, note how the manager makes the point that the company is responsible for the safety and health of employees. Notice also that some people on the job resist safety, requiring that managers constantly promote it and insist that safety rules be followed.

PROBLEM NUMBER 1

What to say to an employee whose record indicates he is accident prone.

The Situation

Vince Andrews is an above-average employee and an experienced machine operator. He's a pleasant individual, good worker and well liked around the plant. However, he has a serious problem. He's forever injuring himself or somebody else. Recognizing this, you've tried to assign him jobs where he's subject to the least amount of risk. This, however, has not helped. This morning again he almost seriously injured a fellow worker. You decide you must talk with him about his problem.

What You Should Say and Some Responses

"Say, Vince, I heard that you came close to having another accident this morning."

Vince nods grimly. "Yeah, I still get the shivers when I think about what might have happened."

"I'm concerned about *why* it happened. Do you have any idea or answer to that?"

Vince shakes his head. "No, I don't. I guess I was in a hurry. That's all I can figure out."

"That's what's bothering me. Management constantly talks safety in the plant. We have posters on the bulletin boards and signs all over the place. We hand out safety booklets and we show safety films. I can't understand how a guy like you with a good production and attendance record can be so careless about routine safety procedures. It doesn't make sense to me."

"Anyone can slip once in a while. It's only human."

You nod. "I can't argue that. But once in a while, where you are concerned, means far more than it does for other people."

"All I can say is that I'm sorry. I'll try to be more careful in the future."

"Vince, I know you're sincere with your intentions, but I cannot let matters rest with that. I have an obligation to you as a person, a human being. I must consider what it could do to you psychologically, not to mention physically, should your luck run out.

"You've been lucky up to now. No serious accident. No loss of life or disabling injury as yet. But who knows when that could happen!"

Vince remains silent.

"After many years of experience, I've learned that there really is such a thing as accident proneness. Even in the safest of working environments, some people have a way of inviting accidents more readily than other people, even if they're otherwise conscientious and well-qualified employees.

"Tough as it may be to define, most people seem to possess a kind of sixth sense or intuition that tips them off when danger is imminent. Individuals who lack this capability are labeled 'accident prone.' The best recommendation I could make for such a person is to keep him or her out of situations where the person may be injured or hurt other people.

"Vince, if you were to have a serious accident, I'd always have it on my conscience that maybe I was partly to blame for not insisting that you get out of the plant and into a safer environment."

"You mean working at a desk, I guess. An office job."

"Exactly. In my opinion, the accident prone employee should be transferred out of the plant as a favor to himself, to his supervisor, and to the people around him. I feel you're an exceptional person, one that can help the company, and I'd like you to stay with us. As I recall, you are now taking night courses at the local university. If you're going for a degree in accounting, engineering, or programming, moving into a job with the company in one of those fields could be the best thing that ever happened to you.

"Vince, tell me what your career interests are; let's see if we can work toward a new position for you with the company."

Reasoning and Principle Involved

The accident-repeater, the person who continually has accidents or near misses, is usually well-known to managers. Most managers are concerned about this person and they search diligently for the human factors to explain how and why the person is so accident-prone. One approach to the problem is to transfer the person to a different job, one where the person is unlikely to have an accident or hurt other people. While accidents happen in offices, their likelihood, severity and frequency are less than in the factory or plant.

PROBLEM NUMBER 2

What to say to a supervisor about being responsible for the safety and health of subordinates.

The Situation

You have just walked through the manufacturing area of your plant and are disturbed by the unsafe condition in which you found it. In addition, you observed some of the workmen failing to follow a few basic safety rules. You decide to immediately talk to the supervisor of the area, Bill Jones, about his safety responsibilities.

What You Should Say and Some Responses

"Say, Bill, a few minutes ago I happened to be passing through your department. First one thing disturbed me, then another. I figured I'd better talk to you right away."

Bill appears apprehensive, waiting for you to continue.

"What do you consider is a supervisor's single most important responsibility?"

"Making a profit for the company," Bill replies, but he doesn't seem sure of himself.

"Wrong," you say. "Making a profit happens to be a supervisor's second most important responsibility; it isn't the first. The first responsibility is the safety and health of the people working for him or her. That's more important than profitability and productivity.

"When was the last time you made an inspection and check for safety in your department? I mean a thorough exam of the equipment, tools, and machines to make sure they are in safe operating condition; a check of your department's procedures to make sure all safety rules and regulations are being followed; an inspection of all work and storage areas to make certain no safety hazards exist. When was the last time you did this?"

Bill looks upward, thinking.

You cut his thinking short. "It's been so long ago that you can't even remember? Right?"

Bill weakly replies, "I guess so."

"When I was walking through your department, one of the first things I noticed was the poor condition of the aisles. Some of them were blocked with boxes and cartons of parts or supplies, and they looked like they had been sitting there for some time. In other areas I saw oil on the floor—this is a slipping hazard. Some of the lights were burned out in other areas. A person who isn't alert could bump into something and get hurt. These things all add up to sloppy housekeeping and unsafe conditions.

"The second thing I saw bothered me even more than the first; one of your men, a very young fellow, was working on a machine, making an adjustment or tightening something, I don't know which. But the machine was running, and his hands were close to the drive mechanism. This is contrary to one of the primary safety rules—when a machine is being repaired, the power must be turned off. If he slipped, or was for a moment distracted, it could have cost him a finger or a hand. I didn't talk to him because I was afraid my approaching him could cause him to make a false move.

"And right next to this fellow was a man operating a table saw with the guard removed. I *did* talk to him, and told him to put the guard in place immediately."

Bill nods. "I'll have to talk to them," he says glumly.

"You'll have to do a lot more than that. I want you to make a complete safety check of your department including every person, all the tools and equipment, and every machine.

"Bill, I'm sure I don't have to talk to you about your responsibility concerning safety. If one of your people performs an unsafe act, it's *your* responsibility because you're his or her supervisor. Along the same line, if *you* neglect a safety function or safeguard, it's *my* responsibility because I'm your supervisor. I'd be willing to bet that your department isn't the only one where a safety inspection would probably uncover some hazardous conditions. I intend to talk to the other supervisors about this today.

"As for your department, I want you to get on this problem immediately, Bill, and I want a report on what you find and what you're doing about it by Friday."

Reasoning and Principle Involved

Responsibility for the safety and health of subordinates is one of the most, if not the most, important of all the responsibilities of supervisors. Some workers resist safety, requiring that supervisors constantly promote it and insist that safety rules be followed. Although there are many ways by which accidents can be prevented, supervisors who search out unsafe conditions and unsafe acts of their people and take steps to eliminate both of them usually have the most success in preventing accidents.

PROBLEM NUMBER 3

What to say to an employee whose sickness is greatly affecting department operations.

The Situation

You just received word that your maintenance clerk, Tom Black, was sick again and wouldn't be in to work. Tom has an abdominal condition for which he has been under doctor's treatment for months. At least three times recently Tom had reported that the doctor had changed his medication and that the prognosis looked promising. Yet his attendance was getting worse. This was Tom's sixteenth day of absence within the past two months. While you feel sorry for him, you are concerned about the department as well. His job is critical to the operation because he is responsible for schedules, work assignments, the processing of time cards, and the computation of information required by the payroll department. You realize that you must make a decision about him when he returns.

What You Should Say and Some Responses

"Feeling better today, Tom?" you ask.

"Yes, much better. The doctor is trying another drug and I'm hopeful this will help me."

"I hope so, too. Tom, I want to talk to you about your illness and what effect it is having on our operations in the department. When you are absent, we get into all kinds of problems with our schedules, equipment maintenance and work status records. We even assigned people to tasks they weren't familiar with. Your absences are disrupting the operations and putting undue pressure on people. This is unfair to the crew."

Tom looks very unhappy, as if he is expecting the worst.

"It wouldn't be right if we let you go because you've been an excellent employee and a big help to the company, but we simply can't continue operating the department this way."

"I should be getting well and not have these problems pretty soon, according to the doctor," Tom says, pleadingly.

"Tom, I hope the doctor is right. However, I would like you to take a six month leave of absence. This should give you time to overcome your problems. If, by the end of six months, you can handle your job normally without excessive absence, I'll be glad to welcome you back. I feel this is a fair way to handle the situation, and a solution that's practical from both your and the company's viewpoint."

Reasoning and Principle Involved

Granting or requesting that an employee take a leave of absence in order to handle a health or personal problem is an action that is less harsh than dismissal yet equally effective. It enables the company to operate more efficiently while also providing a compassionate answer to an employee's future with the company.

PROBLEM NUMBER 4

What to say to an employee who refuses to do a job because he considers it dangerous.

The Situation

An unusually heavy rainstorm has flooded a storage area in the basement of your plant. It's been common practice in such situations to have a sump pump put in the area to remove the water. You assign Harry Wilde, a utility worker, to do the job. Ten minutes later, Harry comes to you saying the job is too dangerous, and he refuses to do it. He has learned that an underground high voltage electric line crosses the flooded area.

What You Should Say and Some Responses

"Harry, if I thought there was any danger involved, I never would have given you the job."

"I wouldn't want to find out the hard way that you're wrong."

"Using a sump pump to drain the water is a safe procedure. We have done that several times in the past."

"Just because no one got electrocuted in the past doesn't convince me that it's safe. My life is more important than this lousy job."

"Harry, as I see the situation, there are several things you should consider. I've made it clear to you that the job is a safe one despite your fear of it. As an employee of more than four years, you've been on the job here long enough to realize that other people have done the job I'm asking you to do.

"More important, perhaps, is that, although you have the right to question an assignment if you're concerned about it, there's a specified procedure spelled out in the union–management agreement to follow if you feel the assignment is out of line. You could have consulted your union steward and asked for a safety check. Also, if you felt that you should turn in a grievance, you have the right to do that *after* completing the job.

"The one thing you can't do, something that management cannot permit, is to arbitrarily refuse to do a job you're assigned. Normally in situations of this kind, you do the job and file a grievance later. That's the only way management can function effectively.

"Now, Harry, how about getting that sump pump running? We've got other storm damage work that also needs to be handled."

Reasoning and Principle Involved

Although you did not impose a penalty on this employee for refusing to do a job, union–management agreements invariably give management the right to discipline or discharge employees for just cause. There has to be discipline, obedience to authority and respect for the rights of others in any successful organization. Without them, order and efficiency would be impossible.

PROBLEM NUMBER 5

What to say to an employee who feels he is entitled to extra compensation because of an injury received on the job.

The Situation

Ross Talbot, a carpenter, hurt himself yesterday while operating an electric drill. He claims his doctor told him he'll miss work on his job for 3 to 5 weeks. Ross says he's also going to file a grievance asking for the difference between his regular wages and the money he'll collect from workmen's compensation. After your supervisor, Bob Wilson, told you how the accident happened and the circumstances leading up to it, you phone Ross at his home, asking him to come into the plant to talk to you. You also get the report of the accident from the company nurse.

What You Should Say and Some Responses

"How's the finger, Ross?"

"Pretty bad. I won't be able to work for about a month."

"That bad? I talked to the company nurse this morning, and she said your injury was relatively minor, just the tip of one finger. She also told me you had a more serious finger injury a few months ago. Our department records on that injury show you were back on the job after three days."

"Well, my doctor says I shouldn't handle any tools for at least three weeks, and I don't intend to."

"Tell me, Ross, how did the accident happen?"

"Well, the drill that I was using was unsafe. The chuck was bad causing the auger to loosen and whip around. It caught my finger and cut it badly."

"I talked to your supervisor, Bob Wilson, about the accident, and he told me you were aware the drill was in poor condition when you started using it. He said you complained to him about it. He also said he told you to tag the drill for repair, turn it in to the supply room, and pick up a replacement. Why didn't you do it?"

"That isn't my responsibility. The company is negligent and at fault for furnishing me an unsafe tool."

"Ross, the company has always been strict in applying safety standards, and that's one of them. If a tool or piece of equipment is faulty, employees are asked to report it to their supervisors right away, or to tag it themselves and take it out of service. Had that drill been reported, it would have been tagged immediately. Of course, if nobody reports a problem, we have no way of knowing about it.

"Since you were aware that the drill was faulty, you had no

business using it. There's no question that management has an obligation to provide safe equipment. But that doesn't free you from individual responsibility.

"If you decide to turn in a grievance on this, the company has its
reputation to support. Faulty tools or machinery are never consciously
left in service. If it comes down to it, we can get all the witnesses we
need to back us up, and it would certainly influence an arbitrator.

"In my opinion, you were hurt through your own negligence, and
you're not entitled to extra pay. However, to give you the benefit of the
doubt on the seriousness of your injury, I'm going to ask Bob to put you
on light duty work tomorrow and Friday. Then on Monday, I expect you
to handle your regular job."

Reasoning and Principle Involved

While management has the responsibility to provide safe working
conditions for employees, supervisors must insist on safe work practices in the workplace. Safety is everyone's business. No one is in a
better position to spot safety hazards and to make sure the work is done
in a safe manner than each and every person on the job.

PROBLEM NUMBER 6

What to say to an employee who protests having his eyes
examined.

The Situation

Because of an increase in the number of accidents that are occurring in your company, management asked the Safety Department to
make a study, classifying them by type, location, individuals, equipment involved, and other factors. The study revealed that a number of
the accidents seemed to happen because employees had failed to see
natural or temporary obstacles in their way. One person had tripped
over a hose on the floor, another had bumped his head on a low
overhead conveyor, and a third had fallen down some stairs because,
she said, she had missed the top step. Subsequently, management
decided to require all employees to take eye examinations at company
expense within the next two weeks. By the end of this time, all but one
man, Cal Tingley, had complied. You go to Cal's workplace to talk to
him about it.

What You Should Say and Some Responses

"Cal, I see by the records that you haven't had your eyes examined."

"That's right," Cal replies. "I don't think it's necessary. I'm not having any problems seeing. Besides, I've never been required before to have my eyes examined."

"The number of accidents that employees are having has never been this bad. The company is doing this for your own good, and will pay for the exam. If the exam shows you need glasses or a prescription change, the company will also pay that bill. You should want to do this instead of complaining about it."

"Maybe so," Cal replies. "But this is just another management demand. It's the same thing as imposing another condition of employment. You have to negotiate that with the Union and put it in the contract."

"The company doesn't feel that it's necessary to do that. Eyesight constitutes a critical safety factor in the plant. People work in areas where various hazards exist. An employee with poor vision is a danger to himself and to other employees.

"I know of similar cases in other companies where workers resisted taking physical examinations that management required. A couple of those cases even got as far as arbitration. The deciding factor from the arbitrator's viewpoint was reasonableness on management's part. You know that the people in our plant are having more and more accidents. The study the Safety Department made showed that poor vision could be a determining factor.

"Cal, I hope I've convinced you that you have much to gain and little, if anything, to lose by having your eyes examined. Management feels so strongly about this, that if you don't comply within the next week, you'll be up for suspension."

Reasoning and Principle Involved

One of management's first responsibilities is to safeguard the health and well-being of its employees. Safety can never be taken for granted. No organization attains a good safety record through luck or chance. Behind every fine safety record that a company achieves, there is much planning and a great deal of hard work.

Chapter 11

ASSIGNING AND DELEGATING

In the following situations, note how the manager assigns and delegates in a manner that recognizes the interests and concerns of both the individual and the company. Notice also, the many facets of human relations which are involved, and how the manager tries to assure that all have been considered.

PROBLEM NUMBER 1

What to say to a supervisor who doesn't delegate enough.

The Situation

In going through your files, you notice that today you should receive a report on storeroom operations from your supervisor, Hank Straub. You asked Hank to make a study of the storeroom and gave him two weeks to complete it. Hank has not mentioned it in your recent conversations, nor have you received the report. You ask him to come to your office.

What You Should Say and Some Responses

"Come in, Hank, and have a seat," you say as Hank arrives.

"Hank, I had a note in my files which says that two weeks ago I asked you to make a study of the storeroom operation. I see you don't have anything with you that looks like a report, so how about telling me what you've found and where you stand."

Hank shifts uneasily in his seat. "The fact of the matter is that I've been tied up with other work. I just haven't gotten around to making that study yet."

"Those words have been the downfall of more than one supervisor, and they're not what I like to hear. Anytime a supervisor tells me he or she is too busy to work on a project that could both improve operations and save the company money, I begin to wonder about the supervisor's dedication to the job."

"I know what you have in mind," Hank says, "and I've already discussed the project with one of my most capable staff people, Walt Curtis. The problem is that Walt has a lot of jobs he's working on that can't wait. I know what I'm supposed to do: delegate. But how can you delegate when the one you want to delegate to is already overloaded?"

"Good question. But I thought you knew the answer to it. How many people do you have in your department?"

"Right now, I've got 12. But the trouble is they're not qualified to handle this job or any of the other work I've got to do. Even if they were, they're not equipped to take on the responsibility."

"Hank, do you mean to tell me that in a department of 12 people, there's only one you can delegate to?"

"Well . . . maybe not."

"I should hope not." You pause a bit and then go on. "Here's what I'd like you to do. Starting tomorrow and for a week, I want you to keep a record of how you spend your time. Divide each day into 15 minute periods, and put down in each period what you do and how much time you spend on it. Also, ask Walt Curtis to do the same thing.

"I know that's going to be a nuisance for a while, and will burn up some of the time you're trying to save, but I'm sure it will be very worthwhile. It may turn out to be one of the most useful things you've done as a supervisor. Then, next week, bring your and Walt's records to me and we'll talk about them."

Hank leaves your office with a dour expression on his face. As you requested, he returns a week later with his and Walt's time sheets. As he enters your office, he says, "You'll be glad to hear that I started that study of the storeroom, although I didn't get very far."

"Good," you say, "but let's see what's on your time sheets, first."

You study them with interest, first Hank's, then Walt's. "I can see that neither you nor Walt have been loafing on the job. When you said you were loaded to the gills with work, you weren't exaggerating. But before you feel pleased with yourself, what would you say if I told you most of the jobs you've recorded here could have been delegated?"

"Well, I guess you'd have to show me. You can see that Walt's time sheets are filled in just as heavy as mine, and we both have worked some overtime. Even then we didn't make much of a dent in the backlog."

"OK, let's look at your sheets first. How many of these jobs would you say you could turn over to Walt if he had enough time to learn and handle them?"

"Oh, maybe half of them. Walt learns fast and he's pretty versatile."

"Now let's look at Walt's sheets. I see quite a bit of his time is spent checking out production equipment and seeing that preventive maintenance is performed. He also follows up on oiling and lubrication to see that it is done properly and at the right time.

"Tell me, Hank, when either you or Walt are working on a machine problem, is the operator on hand? Do you take advantage of the opportunity to train him how to trouble-shoot problems on his own?"

"No," Hank replies. "Most of the time . . ."

"Then how do you expect him to become experienced enough to do what you or Walt are doing? I have another question for you. I noticed on your time sheet last Friday you spent 30 minutes to diagnose what the problem was on a machine and another 15 minutes to make the adjustment. After spotting the problem, why couldn't you have instructed the operator to make the adjustment?"

"I guess I could have."

"Hank, if you think about it, I believe that you, and Walt, too, could have turned over to others most of the jobs you did, except the ones that involved a management decision or were confidential. Also, there's no reason one of your crew of 12 couldn't have made a list of the materials and supplies needed for that Thompson project, then gave it to you or Walt for approval. That would have taken only about 15 minutes of your time instead of the two hours you put in on it.

"The same thinking applies to many of the reports you turn out. It might take a bit of time, patience and effort initially to train your people to do such work, but take my word for it, the investment pays off. As your people become familiar with the work you do and experienced, you and Walt will have more time for decision-making, important supervisory functions and creative work, like that storeroom study I asked for."

Reasoning and Principle Involved

Most successful supervisors are skilled in the art of delegation. There is no question that supervisors and managers must practice delegation if they have hopes of moving up in their company. Their skill in delegating could be the deciding factor in whether they can handle greater responsibilities and bigger jobs. Successful managers get things done through others.

PROBLEM NUMBER 2

What to say to an employee you want to train for a higher position with the company.

The Situation

Ellen Thomas has been a senior programmer for about two years. She's an ambitious and exceptional individual and could go far with the company. However, Ellen is getting restless and wants to further her career as soon as possible. Despite receiving two substantial increases in pay in the last 18 months, she now has come to you with a request for another increase. You recognize that she has great potential, and you don't want the company to lose her. So you discuss her situation with the Personnel Manager. Since the company is growing, the manager agrees that Ellen would make a good manager or executive providing she gets the proper training. Together you work out a plan for her advancement. You are now in the position to offer it to her.

What You Should Say and Some Responses

"Good morning, Ellen. How are you today?"

"Just fine. I like this cooler weather we're having."

"I agree with you on that. Last week I hated to leave our air-conditioned offices at the end of the day.

"Ellen, I've talked to the Personnel Department about your position with the company and how you've handled your work. We agree you're doing an outstanding job for the company and are due for promotion. We also feel that you could have a very good future with the company."

Ellen simply says, "Thank you." She is waiting.

"Here's what we would like to do. We would like you to enroll in a systems development program at the university, starting as soon as the courses begin. Of course, the company will pay all your tuition costs. That's step one.

"Step two is that you will be transferred to the systems department of the company immediately as a trainee. That will include a five percent increase in your pay. After nine months of training, your classification would be changed from trainee to Systems Specialist. At that time, you will get another five percent increase.

"I think this plan is a good one for the company, and it does well by you. How do you feel about it?"

Ellen responds quickly. With a big smile, she says, "Great! Thank you very much."

Reasoning and Principle Involved

One of the attributes of astute managers is a sensitivity to the potential of their people. The skill enables them to help individuals discover and attain their full potentials and guide them to levels of accomplishment which they might not otherwise reach. Exceptional employees deserve exceptional treatment.

PROBLEM NUMBER 3

What to say to a foreman who is oversupervising subordinates.

The Situation

George Cornwell had started with the company as a machine operator. Being conscientious, ambitious and a hard worker, it wasn't long before he occasionally served as temporary foreman. When Pete Fisher moved up to manager of another department, George was the natural choice for the job. That was several months ago. Since that time, his department's operating costs have steadily risen. George's response has been to work harder and longer hours than ever before. After a six day week, he often takes paperwork home to go over on Sunday. But this hasn't helped matters. Today you go to his office to talk to him.

What You Should Say and Some Responses

"How goes it, George?"

"It goes, but just barely."

"What seems to be the problem?"

"I only wish I knew. I guess *that's* the real problem. It seems the harder I work, the worse things become."

You nod. "There has to be an answer, and I'd like to help you find it. Why don't we start by comparing the way you're running the department and the way Pete Fisher did it. Apparently he did not have the same problems. Do you think the workload is greater now than it was when Pete was foreman?"

George thinks a bit. "Oh, about the same, I guess."

"What about the number of people? More or less?"

"I've got one additional person, but it doesn't seem to make much difference."

"Why doesn't it? What do you mean?"

"Well, all of the people were for Pete. They all seem to be against me. You'd think I worked for our competitor. There's more absence and lateness than ever. They don't follow instructions. They just don't seem to give a damn."

"You mean they gave a damn under Pete?"

"Yeah, they did. But I can't figure out why."

"Do you play favorites at all, give certain people preferred assignments because you like them better?"

"No." George answers firmly. "I'm especially careful about that. I bend over backwards to be as fair and impartial as I can. In fact, I'm not convinced that some of the guys can handle the work without help. If a job is tough and challenging, I do it myself. On other jobs, I try to help as much as possible. In fact if I don't follow up on a job, it doesn't get done right."

"What about cooperation?"

"Pretty bad. With the kind of cooperation I've been getting, if I didn't stay on their backs all the time, nothing would get done around here."

"George, have you ever considered the possibility that you might have things backward?"

George looks puzzled. "I don't get you."

"For one thing, there's such a thing as a foreman being *too* busy for his own good and the good of the department. You're oversupervising and overchecking because you feel you can't depend on your people. Maybe you can't depend on them because you are oversupervising and overchecking."

George frowns, but his puzzlement slowly changes to enlightenment.

"It's something for you to think about, George. As I see it, this could explain why you feel you have so much work to do. You are trying to do the work of four people simultaneously which is impossible. A good share of the jobs you're doing should be delegated. Most of the jobs your people are doing, they should be doing on their own. Only periodic followups on your part should be necessary to make sure jobs are on target. You don't want them to feel that you are continually looking over their shoulders."

Reasoning and Principle Involved

First line managers must supervise the work, not do it. When managers perform subordinate's work, they give the impression they don't have enough confidence in their subordinates to let them do their jobs on their own. Failure of a manager to delegate work simply overloads him or her, and robs the manager from the important function of supervising.

PROBLEM NUMBER 4

What to say to a supervisor about reassigning rather than laying off an employee.

The Situation

Chuck Vincent is 60 and has been with the company for many years. Although his performance has been declining a bit in the last year, it is not enough to be of concern. But other employees have begun to complain about Chuck, and lately he seems unable to get along with anyone. When one of your most conscientious employees came to you and reported that Chuck was making a pest of himself, and wasting her time in the process, you realize that something has to be done. You consult with Joe Brown, his supervisor.

What You Should Say and Some Responses

"Joe, I had a visit from Edith this morning. She wanted to talk to me about Chuck Vincent. You know, Edith doesn't waste much time on the job. She complained that Chuck has been making a habit of interrupting her work to talk religion and to try to get her to join his church. She said he is so square and virtuous that he's getting on her nerves."

"Yes, I know about that. She mentioned it to me a few days ago and probably figured I wasn't going to do anything about it. Half a dozen people have been on my back to get him out of their hair. He's been griping that people don't treat him with the respect he's entitled to, and he's continually lecturing people about one thing or another."

"Has he always been this way?" you ask.

"No, that's the odd part of it. He never bothered anyone until recently."

"Did something happen to change him?"

"Not that I know of. He's still on the same job he's had for the past five years. He's getting top rate for his classification, so I'm sure that's not the problem."

"What about the jobs he's been given to do? Are they difficult or complex?"

"No, if anything, most of his assignments have become easier. All I can think is that he's just becoming cranky and irritable as he gets older."

"How's his health?"

"OK, as far as I know. He seldom complains about not feeling well and he has a good attendance record."

"I see by the work schedules that most of the work he's been doing has been as part of a team. Is that right?"

"Sure. There's nothing wrong with that, is there?"

"Probably not. But from what you've told me, he may be bitter because he hasn't had any kind of a promotion for about five years."

Joe shrugs. "Chuck told me he figures he knows more than anyone else in the department. He also said he's entitled to a job in keeping with his training, experience and expertise. I agree that he has more experience than anyone else, but he's gone about as far as he can go. There are no higher level jobs for him to advance to."

"Joe, what do you think we should do about Chuck?"

"I talked to him at least three times about how he is bothering people and wasting both his and their time, but I can't seem to get through to him. To be honest with you, I can't stand the guy and neither can anyone else. I'd like to get rid of him."

"I suppose that would simplify matters, but do you think that would be the right thing to do? You know, Chuck is 60 years old and has spent most of his life with the company. In addition to that, his record over almost all of that time has been above average."

"I thought about that, but he's causing me and other people in the department a lot of trouble. Maybe Chuck was an asset to the company at one time, but in my opinion, he's a liability today."

"Let's look at the situation more closely. How many *employees* actually complained about him?"

"Well, I guess there are only three I can think of. Since they are griping about him repeatedly, it adds up to a lot of complaining, but only three people in all."

You smile in agreement. "That makes the idea of getting rid of him even a worse decision. As I see the situation, there are two ways to minimize or alleviate the problem, and neither of them involve laying off Chuck. Terminating him now when he's close to getting his pension is completely out of the question, especially in view of his good record and long service. Even if we considered early retirement, he would have about two years to go.

"I have a hunch that his present performance and actions have nothing to do with his age. Rather, he's unhappy with his status and the fact that he's not going anywhere with his knowledge, training and experience.

"Joe, you may be able to do something about this by varying the jobs you give him, consulting him on job-related problems, and giving his ego a boost at every opportunity. After all, he probably knows more about the operations than anyone else in the department. You ought to be able to put some of that knowledge to work.

"The other way I think we can handle this problem is even simpler. Every department in the company including yours, Joe, has projects and jobs that can be handled by one person alone. Instead of having Chuck working as part of a team, why not ask him to be a trouble-shooter and to handle special projects. The tougher the assignment, the better, as long as he's capable of handling it. You could play up the importance of these projects and jobs, even publicize one occasionally on the bulletin board.

"I wouldn't be surprised that doing this would go a long way to help matters. If Chuck is more or less on his own, he wouldn't come in contact with other people as much. That would cut down or eliminate the complaints we've been getting. What do you think?"

Joe visibly perks up and smiles. "It makes sense to me," he replies. "I think it's certainly worth a try."

Reasoning and Principle Involved

Understanding human nature, being perceptive, knowing what makes people tick, and having empathy are invaluable in coming up with answers to why some people act as they do. Effective managers know how to match people with jobs and work situations which will turn out best for both the individuals and the company.

PROBLEM NUMBER 5

What to say to an employee to whom you want to temporarily assign different work.

The Situation

This morning you found that there was no work for your welder, Herb Powell. He finished the backlog of welding jobs yesterday and there was no repair or new construction work to be done. Since your company is nonunion, you checked the backlog lists of other crafts in your department in search for work that you could assign Powell. When you found there was a big painting backlog, you approached him with the intention of assigning him a few painting jobs.

What You Should Say and Some Responses

"Herb, the welding jobs are all up to date, but I'm glad you're available. We've got a big painting backlog since we started the plant cleanup project, and two of the painters have been out sick. I'd like you to fill in there for a day or two until we get some welding jobs for you."

"That's not for me. I'm a skilled and experienced welder, and that's nonskilled work. I quit doing that kind of work years ago."

"This assignment won't affect your status as a welder or your pay rate. It's simply a matter of filling in where you're needed. At the moment, I have no welding jobs, and we're way behind in painting the shop and plant."

"I'm not questioning that," Herb replies. "All I'm saying is you should assign one of the lower ranked people to that kind of work, like a helper or a utility worker."

"Who I assign to what job is for me, not you, to decide. I've got to keep our operating expenses of the department to a minimum. I can't afford to have you sitting idle waiting for work when there's painting work to be done."

"That's not my problem," Herb remarks.

"It soon will be if you don't get going on this painting. You either do it or I'm suspending you for three days without pay. Which will it be?"

Reasoning and Principle Involved

Management can never let insubordination go unanswered. Supervisors and managers are responsible for assigning subordinates work which they are capable of doing. If subordinates do not comply, they are subject to discipline.

Chapter 12

PROBLEM PEOPLE

In the following situations, note how the manager is able to recognize and take action on subordinate's personal problems, particularly as they relate to subordinate's behavior in the office or plant. Notice also that the manager is careful not to go beyond a certain point in what is done about those problems.

PROBLEM NUMBER 1

What to say to a supervisor concerning an employee who has a nasty temper which gets him into trouble.

The Situation

Joe Roberti, a squat, thickly muscled man of 35, has the reputation of being unable to control his emotions. He has frequently gotten into arguments with fellow workers in the past, and was also involved in a fist fight four months ago. His personnel rating, however, is better than average in that his attendance and productivity are very good. Last week, Joe became angry with a fellow worker and threw a screwdriver at him. Today, he got into a brawl with another worker. You ask Tom Swanson, Joe's supervisor, to come to your office to discuss what should be done about Joe.

What You Should Say and Some Responses

"Tom, tell me about that brawl that Joe Roberti was in. What was that all about and who started it?"

"What happened was that Alex Simpson borrowed one of Joe's

tools and forgot to return it. After Joe had looked for it for quite a while, he finally saw it on Alex's bench. Although Alex told Joe he'd forgotten to return it and apologized, Joe got all excited, accused Alex of stealing, and began calling him names. Alex told him again that he was sorry and to act his age. That's when Joe swung at him and bloodied his nose. Alex fought back and knocked Joe down. Then a couple of guys stepped in and stopped the fight."

"You're saying that Joe started the fight?"

"No question about it. Alex was simply trying to protect himself, and there were a couple of witnesses who saw and heard the whole thing."

"I understand Joe has a long history of temper tantrums and fist fights. Also, I heard that he threw a tool at one of the fellows last week. Why wasn't he fired a long time ago?"

"Well, except for his temper, he's reliable and more productive than the average."

"I don't consider that reliability, a man who can't control his emotions, who turns to violence at the slightest provocation. We don't need people like him working in this plant. Did you discipline him for that previous fight and the tool throwing incident?"

"No, I simply gave him an oral warning."

"Tom, I want you to give him a five-day suspension and a written warning for this latest fracas. Make it very clear that one more display of his childish temper is all it will take to result in his termination with the company."

Reasoning and Principle Involved

Employees who are unable to control their tempers on the job are a hazard to their company and the people with whom they work. Management, however, needs documentation before such employees can be fired for cause.

PROBLEM NUMBER 2

What to say to a supervisor about how to handle a feud between two employees.

The Situation

Harry Jones and Dave Wilson are two members of the production crew who simply don't get along. Although both do what they're told, and their performance is a little better than average, they continually are a problem to their supervisor, Bob Dennis. When you become aware that their feud is affecting the efficiency and productivity of the department, you ask Dennis to come to your office to discuss the problem.

What You Should Say and Some Responses

"Bob, what are you going to do about Jones and Wilson? I've heard that they haven't talked to each other for weeks. With some of the projects the department is handling, we've got to have close coordination and cooperation of everyone in the department. The Thompson job we're working on now is a good example."

Bob scratches his head. "Maybe I should get both of them started on it, and when another man becomes available, get him to take over for either one of them so that they don't get into an argument."

"That's one way of handling the problem," you reply, "but there is a lot of waste and inefficiency involved when you do that. It takes time to get started on a project, and replacing one of those guys, just when he's got the hang of it, adds up to a lot of duplicated effort and energy. It means giving instructions all over again and checking to make sure the project's going as it should. Then you also have to get the man who's been replaced started on another assignment."

Bob nods. "You're right, but what else can we do?"

"Those guys have known each other for a long time. They work together in the same department eight hours a day, five days a week, not to mention the overtime. They probably see each other and come in contact with each other more than with their relatives and close friends. Their not getting along and not talking to each other simply isn't right. Think of the stress they've put on themselves."

"I hear what you're saying, but I don't see what kind of action I could take. I can't discipline them for not liking each other. They're not hostile or belligerent, so I can't ask them to shake hands and be friends. It would be a different situation if they got into a fight on the job or something like that. If they can't get along, and refuse to talk to each other, it's their own business, isn't it? Don't you think it's kind of a personal matter?"

"No, and I'll tell you why. When individuals in a department don't get along, the first thing they do is stop cooperating with each other. That's just the beginning of a bad situation. Some people have a strange sense of friendship. The rest of the crew, or part of them, are apt to take sides in the controversy, favoring one man or the other so that team spirit suffers. Work is disrupted and efficiency is forgotten or overlooked in favor of misguided loyalties.

"In business and industry today, employees are valuable only to the extent of their attitudes and feelings about their work, performance, and fellow employees. One person alone doesn't make a whole lot of difference. It's teamwork and cooperation that count.

"My recommendation regarding Jones and Wilson is to do everything you can to learn the reason for the friction between them. And then use every effort you can to restore friendship between them. Life is too short, and the responsibility for accomplishment too important, to put up with kid stuff like that."

Reasoning and Principle Involved

Feuding employees are detrimental not only to themselves but to their work group and the company as well. When there is no cooperation and little teamwork, productivity is bound to suffer. The most constructive action a manager can take for all concerned is to bring the feud to an end as quickly as possible.

PROBLEM NUMBER 3

What to say to an employee who is guilty of horseplay.

The Situation

Ike Thompson, one of your utility workers, enjoys playing practical jokes. While his earlier pranks have been limited to his fellow workers, lately he has become more bold and included members of supervision when he felt he could get away with it. Recently you talked to him privately and warned him that horseplay would not be tolerated in the plant, and he should refrain from doing it. He replied that it was only clean fun. Today, you approached him to discuss a work assignment during a break period when he and two other workers were seated at a table. As you made a move to sit down on an empty chair beside him, he yanked away the chair at the last minute, causing you to tumble. Luckily, you were not hurt, but you were visibly angry.

What You Should Say and Some Responses

"Hey, why did you do that?" you say as you get up.

"What's the matter? Can't you take a joke?" were Ike's words when he saw you were angry.

"I can take a joke all right," you reply, "but only when it's funny. I think your sense of humor is on the sick side, Ike. I could have been hurt."

"Wait a minute," Ike says anxiously. "I didn't mean anything by it."

"Ike, come with me to the office. We've got to talk about this."

Ike meekly follows you to your office. On the way, he says, "I'm sorry, I was just trying to have some fun." You do not reply. After you close your office door, you again speak to him.

"What you did, Ike, was more stupid than anything else. But in my book, it was horseplay, and that's a punishable offense. Since I had warned you a few weeks ago that we will not permit horseplay in the plant, I'm now going to give you a three-day suspension and also a written warning."

Ike appears stunned. "It was only a joke. I didn't steal anything or set the place on fire."

"This might have been a lesser offense if you had pulled that stunt on another worker and not on me. While horseplay by itself calls for discipline, your actions also show disrespect for supervision. I hope you learn a lesson from this. If you continue with your practical jokes and horseplay, you can expect more severe discipline in the future."

Reasoning and Principle Involved

Management must take action when an employee breaks a company rule. Overlooking the offense and saying nothing about it is equivalent to condoning it. Disciplinary action is required because the incident can affect the person's future behavior, the department's morale, and even the company's relations with a union, if there is one.

PROBLEM NUMBER 4

What to say to a troublemaker who coincidentally is near retirement age.

The Situation

Alan Trump, 62, has been working for the company for more than 30 years and generally got along well with everyone. In the last year, however, he has become a stubborn, unreasonable and disruptive person. Now he is constantly harassing fellow workers, getting into arguments with them, and wasting their time. But in spite of his impossible disposition, he does a fairly good job and needs the income he receives. In an attempt to help matters, you recently assigned him a job where he had to work by himself without coming into contact with other employees. But that didn't solve the problem. He still irritated people on break and lunch periods, at starting and quitting times, and in the locker room. When employees continued to come to you with their complaints about him, you realized you had to take action; you called Trump to the small conference room to talk to him.

What You Should Say and Some Responses

"Alan, for some time now, I've been hearing complaints about you. People are telling me that you've been causing all kinds of trouble, that you're unreasonable, ornery and cantankerous."

"I do my job," Alan replies. "I don't bother anyone."

"I know that's not true because I've heard of too many instances where you've criticized people, got into arguments with them, and generally made a nuisance of yourself. I've talked to you before about this. Apparently it hasn't done any good. You've continued to be a trouble-maker."

Alan looks away from you and scratches the back of his neck.

"Alan, you're 62 years old and eligible for early retirement. If you took it, you'd be doing everyone around here a favor, most of all, yourself."

Alan is not pleased with your suggestion. "What would I do if I retired? I'd drive my wife crazy at home. It's bad enough on weekends. If I was home every day . . . ." He doesn't finish the sentence.

"We can't continue as we are. You're disrupting the whole operation, and we've got a lot of employees who refuse to put up with you."

"I'll change," Alan promises.

"I've heard that too often to believe it now. No, Alan, I respect your age and years of service, but I also have a responsibility to the company and to every person who works for me. I feel I've done everything I can to change things for the better. But we've reached the point where I must either dismiss you or have you take early retirement. Which shall it be?"

Reasoning and Principle Involved

Managers have many responsibilities to consider in making decisions concerning the company's objectives and employee's welfare. When an employee is disrupting an operation, and management has done everything it can to get the person into line to no avail, it's time to either dismiss or retire the employee, whether he or she likes it or not.

PROBLEM NUMBER 5

What to say to a supervisor who can't control his temper.

The Situation

Dave Reilly, your Production Department supervisor, has the temperament and build of an old style Army sergeant. When he gives a command, he expects the recipient to snap to and get moving. If he has one weakness as a supervisor, it is his temper. He has been known to fly off the handle when it is least expected. Reilly's biggest problem on the job is contending with Turk Craznik, a worker who could be exasperatingly slow moving at times. Most aggravating of all to Reilly was Craznik's defiant manner when receiving work assignments from him. When you learned that the two had had a serious argument over a tedious, time-consuming job that Reilly assigned Craznik, you decided to step in. News had passed fast through the plant that they were going to have a fist fight after work in a lot behind the plant. You summon Reilly to come to your office immediately.

What You Should Say and Some Responses

"Dave, I want to get to the point quickly. No supervisor can function effectively without the respect of his crew or staff." Before you can say more, Dave interrupts you.

"My people respect me. I feel pretty sure they think I'm a good supervisor. There's just one guy in the group who ain't worth a damn, and he's been causing me a lot of trouble."

"You mean Turk Craznik, I guess."

"Right! This has been going on for more than a year, and I'm working on getting him fired. I already have a couple of warning notices in his file."

"Dave, you're not going to succeed with that. Just an hour ago, I heard that you and Turk had agreed to have a fight at the end of the shift. Of course, management cannot permit that to happen, regardless of who instigated it. I have already arranged for the police to be here to see that the fight does not take place.

"But, more important, your willingness to settle a controversy on such terms is unthinkable for a member of management. As I was saying when you first came in the office, a manager cannot function effectively without the respect of subordinates. And today you lost that respect.

"I have notified the Personnel Department that this is your last day with the company. As soon as you have collected your belongings, you can pick up your final pay."

Reasoning and Principle Involved

Once a supervisor or manager loses the respect of subordinates, he or she can no longer lead them. To earn this respect, the leader must demonstrate competence, reasonable intelligence and, most of all, control.

PROBLEM NUMBER 6

What to say to a manager about how to handle a sexual harassment problem.

The Situation

Helen Simpson, office clerk, is a good-looking blonde in her early 30's who has recently divorced. She along with other women in the department work for Frank Read, supervisor of the office services group. Read, who is 40 and married, has a habit of leaning over Simpson's shoulder to check the mail she handles or to scan reports. In giving her instructions or an assignment, Read sometimes places his hand on her shoulder or arm, a practice Simpson finds objectionable. Also, he occasionally tells her sexually oriented jokes as if she were one of the boys. Read has never directly or indirectly propositioned her, although his attitude left no doubt that he would if she gave him the slightest encouragement. Still, Simpson was becoming more and more nervous because of Read's harassment, however limited it might be. This reached the point where she has considered quitting her job. Before doing so, however, she took her problem to Bob Stoll, Read's superior. Stoll, not familiar with such problems, comes to you for advice.

What You Should Say and Some Responses

"Bob, from what Helen Simpson told you, I would say that she has a legitimate complaint. Sexual harassment doesn't have to be blatant to be objectionable. Read's actions also seem to have had an adverse effect on her health. In addition, his attentions have provoked her to go over his head in coming to you to complain, something most people are reluctant to do. That indicates that she's probably being harassed. I say probably because you can't say positively without proof.

"I suggest you take three steps. First, talk with Read, presenting the situation without making any accusations. Act as impartial as you can, saying that you are bringing a problem to his attention for his own good. Second, tell Simpson that you talked to Read, and ask her to let you know if the harassment continues. I believe that your talk with Read will alert him to the trouble he could be getting into, and he will quickly bring it to an end.

"Third, if Simpson reports that the harassment is continuing, watch Read as closely and discreetly as possible. If you see he hasn't backed off, we'll have to give him a direct warning that he could be discharged. Of course, we would need a good case and evidence before we consider such action. I don't think it will come to that."

Reasoning and Principle Involved

Society in general and management in particular are taking action today on sexual harassment problems. If a woman feels she is being harassed sexually there's no reason she should keep it to herself. Actually, she has an obligation to report it because that is the only way management has to put an end to it.

Chapter 13

COOPERATION

In the following situations, note the many ways available to managers to promote cooperation and bring about good employee performance. Notice also that managers must be careful not to go beyond certain limits in what they do about the personal problems of employees.

PROBLEM NUMBER 1

What to say to an employee who blames his poor performance on the type of work he has been asked to do.

The Situation

When you transferred Ted White from the engineering to the maintenance section in your department, the quality and quantity of his work declined noticeably. Although White was only in his 30's, he had demonstrated considerable skill in diagnosing problems in equipment and machine operation. You told him there was a shortage of people with his abilities in the department and you needed him on maintenance work. But this apparently did not impress him. After his performance continued to be poor, you warned him that he would be disciplined if it did not improve. He made a half-hearted promise to do better, but his output continued to be low compared to the rest of the crew. You saw that you must talk to him again.

What You Should Say and Some Responses

"Look, Ted, I'm not pleased with the work you did on that pump this morning. You've done much better work in the past. So I'm warning you again. If you don't improve, I'm going to suspend you."

Ted protests. "I'm doing the best I can."

"No, you're not. Your present performance is way below standard, and you know it. Are you having any problems with the fellows you have been working with?"

"No, we get along fine. I just don't like the jobs you've been giving me. Don't you have any other work I can do?"

"No, I haven't. We finished that expansion project you were on, and there aren't any new installations in sight. But I don't understand why you don't like the jobs you've been working on."

Ted hesitates, then moistens his lips. "Those jobs are dead-end ones. You don't get anywhere with maintenance work. Everyone knows that."

"That's not true, Ted. Look at Pete Miller and Rich Hanson. They moved up in the company, and they did maintenance work at one time right in this department. Also, quite a few of our engineering managers started with the company in the maintenance section.

"If that's what's been bothering you the past few weeks, rest assured, you won't hurt your chances to be a supervisor some day by doing maintenance work. In fact, the experience will actually be very helpful. You'll understand better what is involved with plant maintenance and why the company needs good people on those jobs.

"Now, what do you say to getting back on the job and cleaning up those backlog maintenance jobs. I'm willing to forget that your good long term record was ever interrupted if you put an end to this nonsense and do the job you're being paid to do."

Reasoning and Principle Involved

When a good employee turns bad, discipline should be meted out only as a last resort. Management should always try to get the employee to cooperate some other way.

PROBLEM NUMBER 2

What to say to a group leader about how to handle an intelligent and brilliant employee who sometimes ignores instructions and does not cooperate.

The Situation

This morning your group leader, Andy Paulis, came to you with a problem concerning the behavior of one of his electronic technicians.

Frank Daily, the technician, was an excellent trouble-shooter and had the ability to simplify complex situations and detect malfunctions that weren't apparent to his fellow technicians. Well aware of his talents, Daily made the most of them in his own peculiar way. When asked to do minor or easy jobs, he often forgot them or gave forgetfulness as an excuse for not doing them. Also, he was frequently late when starting work and when returning from lunch. Since he considered himself more privileged than others and showed it by being arrogant and snobbish, he was generally disliked by the rest of the staff. In retaliation, perhaps, there was little, if any, cooperation on his part. This particularly bothered Paulis who asked you for advice on how to handle him.

What You Should Say and Some Responses

"From what you've told me, Andy, I can see that Frank Daily could be difficult to figure out. But let's think about him a bit. I believe you'll find we can come up with some explanations for much, if not all, his behavior."

"Good, I need that. He can be quite a problem," says Andy with a smile.

"First, Frank is very bright and talented. I'm sure no one in the department would deny that. He's truly a professional in his field. Second, he communicates well, a skill that not many technical people are noted for. When he works out a tough problem, for example, he presents his solution clearly, logically and completely."

"There's no question about that," Andy comments.

"Third, he's been in the department for more than 12 years, yet, although his intelligence and knowledge match that of most supervisors, he never got beyond the position of senior technician."

"Primarily because of his personality," offers Andy.

"Right," you say. "Frank is his own worst enemy. One of his biggest problems is his resentment of authority. I think he is often defiant because he subconsciously feels that he should be giving orders to you instead of the other way around. His being late, forgetful and tending to ignore instructions are, I believe, the way he shows that defiance."

"What you said makes sense, but how do you handle a guy like that?"

"That's the big problem, Andy. What you have to decide is whether he's worth the abuse you have to take from him and the problems he creates. If you think he is, then you've got to adapt as best you can to the situation. In my opinion, the more a person like Frank works on his own instead of as part of a team, the happier everyone will be. As far as infractions like being late and ignoring your instructions, at a certain point, you simply have to insist that he be more cooperative or the company will have to let him go. But I'd think long and hard about that before you make such a decision."

Reasoning and Principle Involved

Many professional people such as scientists, technicians and engineers, are different from other employees in that they feel they are highly skilled and knowledgeable; therefore, they resent any treatment that suggests they are thought of as ordinary workers. First line managers and staff managers should be aware that the key to getting along with them is to treat them as special people.

PROBLEM NUMBER 3

What to say to a female supervisor about how to handle a male employee who isn't cooperating.

The Situation

Although your company has females holding down key jobs in the office, Linda Bower is the first one to hold an important supervisory job in the plant. Linda was well trained and experienced when she accepted the job six months ago. But Linda's department has not been doing well the last three months when rated on employee attendance, productivity and product quality. Records have proved that the low rating was due to the poor performance of three persons. Two of these persons showed slightly lower productivity, and one showed much lower productivity than they had in the past. Since you feel it is important for Linda to succeed, you go to her office to talk to her.

What You Should Say and Some Responses

"Good morning, Linda. Working hard?"

Linda smiles. "I guess you could say that. It seems like there's always another problem to handle. But what can I do for you?"

"I was reading your department report yesterday, and saw that Al Wilson's productivity rating was very bad. That surprised me. I never expected to find *his* name on your 'poor performers' list. Al used to work in my department years ago. Although he never was a ball of fire, he always did what he was told, and was at least average in what he accomplished."

Linda frowns. "I've talked to Al and the others a number of times about their output, showed them the figures, and even told Al that he might find himself out of a job if he didn't change for the better."

"What did he say?"

"Oh, he promised to do a better job, but I sensed he really didn't intend to. I guess my problem is, what do I do now? Should I suspend Al Wilson along with those other two guys? That would really make me look good—not even a year on the job and she's disciplining three people, all at the same time!"

"I can see that you're on the spot. I've got a hunch about what the problem is, but I'd like to check it out before I say anything more. I'll get back to you soon, Linda."

"OK," Linda replies.

You decided to chat with a couple of department heads who either fed work into Linda's department or worked on her department's output. Without revealing the entire problem in detail, you asked about how they felt Linda was doing as a supervisor, and also if they knew Al Wilson. One of your informants described Wilson as a macho character and an egotist. Another said that Wilson and some other workers were overheard putting Linda down saying that a woman shouldn't try to be a supervisor. One worker also made the remark that she wasn't tough enough to handle it.

The next day you stop again at Linda's office. After greeting you, she says, "I hope you have good news for me."

After filling her in on your discussions with the department heads, you say, "Linda, it looks like being born female is your main problem."

Linda isn't surprised. "I don't know," she replies slowly. "Maybe I sensed that all along but didn't want to say it. I.didn't think people like Al Wilson still existed."

"Well, they do, and you're going to have to confront them when you run into them. If I were in your place, I'd lay down the law with Al Wilson without pulling any punches. I'd say, 'Al, your record speaks for itself. You're not doing an acceptable job and haven't done so since I've been your supervisor. Since your performance prior to that was satisfactory, and since your assignments are the same now that they were then, I can only conclude that your problem is me. Al, if you have trouble taking orders from a woman, let me know. I'll see if there's an opening in another department. You'll be doing both of us a favor. From my viewpoint, I insist on standard or better performance. From your viewpoint, that level of performance will save your job.'

"Do you see the advantage of such an approach, Linda? Instead of Al putting *you* on the spot, you'll be putting *him* on the spot. I have a hunch that he'll straighten out if approached in this way, and those other two guys will follow suit."

Linda looks at you thoughtfully. "That sounds good, and it may work."

"I think it's worth a try," you say as you leave her.

Reasoning and Principle Involved

Companies have a right to require adherence to the directions of those they have placed in positions of responsibility and authority, regardless of their sex. Women have been taking a bigger part in our modern society, handling many jobs and duties that formerly were handled by men. A refusal to comply with reasonable orders of supervision is a grave offense and can lead to discipline or discharge.

PROBLEM NUMBER 4

What to say to a manager to persuade him to give up one of his best people.

The Situation

You were asked by management to set up a new department in the company and see that a well-qualified person was selected to run it. Your first step was to call a meeting of department heads to get recommendations on who should be offered the position. Preferably, that person should be one who was in line for promotion and has the kind of intelligence the job requires along with good leadership capabilities. Most of the managers in the meeting had one or more outstanding people working for them who might possibly fit into the job except that they lacked the unique training and experience needed. Finally, one manager suggested Bob Conner, an ambitious and knowledgeable young supervisor, and one of the hardest working people in the plant. He had been a supervisor for about three years and was doing an outstanding job. Moreover, he was well liked by everyone including management. But Conner's manager, Ken Wright, was not so enthusiastic about his selection as the other managers were. You realized that Wright was on the spot and everyone knew it. Feeling that the meeting room was not the place to press the issue, you called the meeting to a close. The next day you went to Wright's office to talk with him.

What You Should Say and Some Responses

"Good morning, Ken."

Ken is uneasy as he greets you. "Hi, what's new today?"

You smile. "Nothing, really. I just thought we might talk a bit. Better here than at a meeting with everyone sitting in."

Ken grunts, knowing what you want to talk about. "Still looking for someone to fill that department head opening?"

"Yes, my boss gave me the assignment and wants somebody as soon as possible. The person selected can then help with all the other work required to set up the department."

"I understand, but why are you coming to me? We have a lot of departments in the company. There must be several people who could handle that job."

"Maybe so. But every time I look at the list of people who could be considered for the job, I come up with Bob Conner as the most ideally qualified. Is there someone I've missed? Am I wrong in seeing him as highly competent with the right training and background?"

Ken doesn't answer immediately. After taking a deep breath, he replies, "You're right about Bob. He's the best man I've got. There aren't many like him around."

"Then—"

"I know what you're going to say. Then why not give him up?"

You wait, not saying anything.

"You know, guys like Bob are hard to find. It took me a long time to train and develop him. But now if I'm out for a day or two, on vacation, or even tied up in a meeting, I know he'll take care of things and the department will still run smoothly."

"I guess you feel that he's indispensable?"

"Well, I realize that no one is indispensable, but Bob's about as close to it as you could be."

"It's commendable that you should feel that way about him, but did you ever look at his position the way he might? When a person is labeled as indispensable, that means he won't be considered for another job, and he can't advance or be promoted."

Ken concedes that you are right. "If anyone deserves a promotion, it's Bob. But letting him go will put me in a bad spot."

"I don't think so," you say. "Look at it this way. When you let Bob move up, you gain in two ways. First, you carry out your responsibility to him—to see that he's given the opportunity to better himself. Second, you elevate yourself in management's eyes—you've demonstrated that you can develop subordinates to take on bigger jobs and greater responsibilities."

"You may be right. But where does that leave me? I'll have a big vacancy in my department."

"True, but that should be only a temporary situation. It may be tough for a while until you have a replacement trained and developed to step into Bob's spot. That's why it's important to groom your people for things like that in advance."

"I know that, but I have no one else in the department who's even close to having Bob's skill and knowledge."

"That's rough," you concede. "It sometimes happens; what you need is a good, talented replacement from outside your department. I suggest you talk to one or more of the department heads who were at the meeting I held on finding someone to head up the new department. You know, several people were mentioned who had potential and deserve to be promoted. Maybe one of them would like to transfer to your department."

Reasoning and Principle Involved

One of a manager's major responsibilities is to develop and advance his or her subordinates. While most managers hate to lose their top performers, the likelihood of that occurring should alert them to make sure they groom other employees with potential for such positions.

PROBLEM NUMBER 5

What do you say to an employee who is interested only in his pay and doesn't try to better himself.

The Situation

Art Roth has been with the company about two years as a production department employee. Eager to make some money, he sought a job and had been hired by the company before finishing his high school education. But Roth has not applied himself on the job to his full capabilities. Neither has he shown any responsibility nor a willingness to do more than was asked of him. Yet he expected merit pay increases periodically and asked for them three times in the last year. Each time, you turned him down because of his low productivity and inattention to the job. Today he brought up the subject with you again.

What You Should Say and Some Responses

"I'm sorry, Art, but I still can't request a pay increase for you."

"I've been here more than two years now, and I'm not getting anywhere. What does it take to get ahead in this place?"

"You've asked me that before, and I told you. The opportunities in this company are as good as any place in the city. You've got to do a better job and to cooperate. Up to now, you've been doing a mediocre to poor job. We went over your record each time we talked. If you get on the ball, Art, you'll have as much chance to get a raise as anyone else."

"OK," Art replies. "I promise to really put out from now on."

That conversation took place two months ago. This morning Art comes to your office with a slight smile on his face. "How about that raise you promised me?" he asks you.

"Art, I told you two months ago that when your output shows real improvement, you'll be considered for an increase."

"That's exactly why I'm here. I've really been putting out. Take a look at my record."

You go to the files for the records and then review them with Art. "You're right, your work has shown a slight improvement over the past six weeks. Not very much, but it's a start. Keep it up, Art, and soon we'll sit down and talk."

"Soon? What do you mean soon? Why does a guy have to wait forever to get a couple of bucks out of this company? You told me to improve and I did. What more do you want?"

"Look, Art, you've been a borderline employee in this department for more than two years. It will take more than a few weeks of better performance to overcome your reputation of not doing any more than you have to. I think I've made myself clear. When I feel you're making progress and doing much better work, I'll talk to you about a better job and more pay. Until then the best thing you can do for both of us is to stop pestering me for a merit raise."

Art doesn't give up. "I can see that you don't care if I'm kept in a rut. I always had the feeling you've got a grudge against me. I'm through being a sucker for you and the company."

"What do you mean by that?"

"I mean that if you don't give me a break for working hard like I've been doing these past few weeks, I see no point in working my ass off.

From now on, I'm going to take life easy around this place. If you want a full day's work out of me, you're going to have to pay me for it."

"Does that mean you're threatening to slow down? If it does, my advice to you is not to try it. If you think you are being taken advantage of, see your Union representative. But whatever you do, I want you to understand that if you don't measure up to the work standards for your job, you'll be disciplined accordingly."

Reasoning and Principle Involved

All workers today are not happy with their jobs, their supervisors, or their pay. It's the supervisor's job to handle the problem employees and bring their performance to an acceptable level in terms of the department's operation. But under no circumstances can supervisors permit threats to be made and carried out concerning that performance.

Chapter 14

CREATIVITY AND INNOVATION

In the following situations, note how the manager relates the value and worth of creative employees to a company's profitability and growth when discussing creativity and innovation with subordinates. Notice also how important it is for supervisors to encourage and work closely with employees who have creative and innovative potential.

PROBLEM NUMBER 1

What to say to an employee who "doesn't have enough time to be creative."

The Situation

Your company has for many years promoted suggestion programs as a way of spurring employees to be creative and innovative. Recently, however, the program has lagged and not many employees are participating. To turn things around, the company announced a contest two weeks ago, stating that awards for accepted suggestions would be doubled. Management also asked department managers to talk to their people to encourage them to participate. Several years ago, Phil Reynolds, one of your Production Supervisors, had turned in more suggestions than anyone else in the department. Now, however, he has yet to submit one for the current contest. You decide to bring up the subject with him.

What You Should Say and Some Responses

"What do you think of the suggestion contest, Phil? Do you think it will bring in a lot of good ideas?"

"Well, I don't know. I guess a company needs to give such programs a shot in the arm now and then. Otherwise people lose interest."

"What about you? At one time you were one of this department's top contributors. Have you got anything coming up?"

"I've been trying to find something, but so far, no go."

"How are you going about it? Do you have a system or procedure?"

Phil rubs his chin thoughtfully. "Yes I do. I've been looking at the department's problem areas, places where we have bottlenecks and delays, and I've been trying to find a way to change work procedures or operating sequences to make jobs run smoother or easier. But up to now, I don't seem to be getting anywhere."

"Any ideas why not?"

Phil shakes his head. "I dunno. Maybe I'm not getting into the problems deep enough. When I tackle a problem area, I intend to make a thorough study and analysis of it, but I don't seem to get around to it."

"Do you have some particular changes in mind?"

"I'd like to simplify some of the procedures, eliminate some steps if possible, and avoid duplication. With materials, I always look for more economical and easier to handle ones."

"That's certainly the right approach. I can see you're motivated and you understand the basics of producing constructive change and innovation. But I'm wondering if you have the time to apply the basics properly."

Phil looks at you questionably. "I don't understand what you're saying."

"Let me explain. I know that in the last year you've handled a lot of special assignments, expedited production and seemingly have been at several places at the same time. It's pretty hard to do any creative thinking when you're rushing from one job to another, troubleshooting problems and keeping the process running smoothly. Possessing creative talent and a good imagination are essential ingredients for being innovative and coming up with good ideas, but they're not enough by themselves. Creative people also need a certain amount of time to think through an idea, reflect on it and review it. You don't seem to be able to find that time.

"Phil, I'd like you to begin delegating more of your duties and responsibilities. Try to free up a portion of your time for creative thought. I'm sure you'll find this extra time highly rewarding in what you can accomplish mentally."

Reasoning and Principle Involved

Ideas come easiest to people when they think and study problems under conditions which are most conducive to generating them. But blocks in the way of creative effort must also be removed. Time is one of those blocks.

PROBLEM NUMBER 2

What to say to a supervisor about how subordinate's suggestions should be handled.

The Situation

Your company's annual suggestion contest has just been completed. As you read the final report from the suggestion committee, you see that one of your departments ranked very low in the standings both in the number of suggestions submitted and the number accepted. What bothered you in particular was that this department usually did well in previous contests. Since the supervisor of this department has held the job less than a year, you ask him to come to your office and to bring along his file on suggestions turned in by employees during the contest.

What You Should Say and Some Responses

"John, I'm sure you've seen the final report on the suggestion contest. Do you have any idea why your department did so poorly?"

"No, sir. I've been wondering about that, but I don't have an answer. The people in my department all seemed to be pretty enthused when the contest was announced. And I know every one of them would have liked to win one of those prizes, but . . . ."

"But what?" you ask.

"Well, the first week we got quite a few suggestions turned in. Nothing looked very good, but at least there were many which meant people were trying. But after that, the flow simply dropped off."

"Any ideas why?"

"No, sir. I don't know. Most of the people just seemed to lose interest."

"I'd like to take a look at your suggestion file," you say.

John hands it to you, and you start looking at the individual forms. After a couple of minutes, you take one of them from the file and read it carefully. It concerns an assembly operation carried out in the plant. Instead of making temporary solder connections, the suggestor had proposed rivets, claiming that they would be stronger and less likely to break; solder connections periodically broke under the existing assembly procedure.

"What about this one from Clarence Pile?" you ask John.

"That idea was turned down because it was impractical. Although it looked good in theory, in actual practice the procedure would take twice as long as the soldering. Instead of saving time and money, it would have added to the labor cost."

"So what happened?"

John hesitates, then says, "As I said, it was discarded. I thanked Pile for trying but told him we couldn't use the idea."

"And that's all?" you ask.

"Yes, sir."

"Did you explain *why* the idea was impractical?"

"Well, as I remember, I told him the cost of labor would be too high."

"I see. How long did you talk to him?"

John wets his lips. "Not very long. As I said, the idea wasn't practical."

"The reason I'm asking you all these questions, John, is that I noticed the suggestion was submitted during the first week of the contest. This indicates that Clarence Pile must have been interested enough and enthused at the beginning to spend quite a bit of his time trying to dream up this idea, however unacceptable it may have been. I also noticed that this was the only suggestion submitted by this particular employee.

"Do you see what I'm getting at, John? Pile was obviously caught up with the suggestion contest to begin with, but soon lost interest. I wonder why?"

When John doesn't say anything, you continue.

"It doesn't require a lot of insight or inducement to spend time and effort on a suggestion that appears to have cost improvement potential. But it does take a certain amount of tact and diplomacy to respond to a poor idea. Most employees are reluctant to submit ideas, particularly if they aren't aggressive individuals or accustomed to making suggestions. The reason they are reticent usually is because they lack confidence. They don't see themselves as qualified to come up with worthwhile ideas.

"Under such conditions, how a suggestion is received and handled by management often determines whether more ideas are worked on and turned in. Do you see the point I'm trying to make?"

"Yes, sir, I believe I do."

"Sometimes the attention and time you give to a poor and impractical idea can be as important as the way you respond to a promising idea. For instance, take this idea submitted by Pile. Suppose you reasoned that giving him a negative answer or brushing him off quickly, while it would save time at the moment, could endanger his future creative output. The thing to do then, instead of merely dismissing the idea as impractical, is to make a big deal out of it.

"You could compliment Pile on his imagination, enthusiasm and good thinking. You could wind up convincing him that even though that particular suggestion could not be used, he had a fine mind, was creative, and would naturally come up with more ideas. As a result, Pile would be encouraged to keep submitting suggestions, some of which might pay off.

"John, the higher you move up in management, the more important your creativity becomes. People who have good ideas are rare, and a person who shows promise in the art must be treated carefully. Such a person could be very sensitive. The easiest way to discourage such a person is to ignore him or her."

Reasoning and Principle Involved

One of the common ways for a manager to turn down a suggestion is to say that it is impractical. But before the suggestion is brushed off, no matter how poor it may be judged, the manager must try to determine what the suggestor's reaction is likely to be as far as future ideas are concerned.

PROBLEM NUMBER 3

What to say to a section head about how to promote creativity among technical employees.

The Situation

Your development department has grown considerably in recent years, but you sense that something seems to be missing in how employees go about their work. You soon conclude that the group lacks enthusiasm and creativity. While everyone performs their assignments routinely and usually on schedule, they seldom challenge procedures or suggest how jobs might be done easier or faster. Since this seemed especially true in Ben Black's section, you checked his forms, work sheets and records to confirm your thinking. You found that many procedures hadn't been changed in more than five years. Today's projects and assignments were being performed the same as they were years ago. Feeling that such conditions are not conducive to progress, and that obsolete procedures could even be harmful, you ask Ben to come to your office to discuss the situation.

What You Should Say and Some Responses

"Ben, I've been wondering about our work procedures in the department. For a group of skilled people engaged in development work, many of whom are professional, it seems like we're too machine-like in how we carry out assignments. What do you think? Is this a problem we should be concerned about?"

"I'm not sure about that. Why would we have a problem if everyone does his or her job competently enough most of the time?"

"The problem is that the operations have become too routine, people are performing too much like robots. We're too status quo. We may be missing the boat because we're in a rut."

"I see what you mean. I know we're not getting many suggestions or new ideas, but I wonder why."

"In my opinion, people are not naturally creative. Ideas do not come to them automatically—they have to push themselves to get them. I think that although most of our people are doing their jobs well, they've become bored with what they're doing and they're not using their imagination as much as they could."

"Maybe so, but what can we do about it?"

"There are several things we can do. As I see it, the main reason that operations are becoming too routine is overspecialization, people being restricted to only certain types of jobs. What I'd like you to do, Ben, is to give your people a variety of jobs, within reason of course. If you make assignments more diversified, it may add interest to the work. Also, encourage your people to question the procedures they've been following. There are bound to be better ways to do some of those jobs.

"Recommend that they talk to people holding similar jobs to theirs when they have a tough problem to solve, and warn them against being satisfied with the information and data at hand on those occasions. Tell them to refrain from discarding an idea just because it does not seem right when they first think of it. There are many ways you can spur people to get ideas."

Reasoning and Principle Involved

Managers should try to promote and develop creativity in themselves and their people. Creative people like their work and get satisfaction from it. As a result, they do better work and their company benefits.

PROBLEM NUMBER 4

What to say to a supervisor who needs advice on how to handle highly creative people.

The Situation

Walter Minter, a supervisor in the Development Department, has an engineering degree and over 10 years' experience in research and development. He is a firm believer in adherence to rules of procedure and behavior, and thus has little patience with people he considers eccentric or temperamental. Minter gets along fairly well with most of the people who work for him. However, Donald Lake, a young engineer, is an exception. Minter considers him a "character" and a "prima donna," mainly because of his work habits and his dress. Lake, in contrast, feels that he is a professional and should be permitted to complete projects as he sees fit; he also resents Minter's close supervision at all stages of a project. Lake usually wears bright shirts and dungarees. When one day he wore a shirt imprinted with an obscene slogan, Minter, highly irritated, came to you to complain about him.

What You Should Say and Some Responses

"You look like you're angry about something, Walter. Has something gone wrong?"

"It sure has. In fact, it's been wrong for quite a while. I just can't put up with this guy Lake. He just doesn't fit in our group."

"I've noticed that your personalities clashed now and then, and I've been meaning to discuss him with you. In my opinion, Lake is a bright young fellow and highly creative from what I've seen.

"I don't think his full potential is being realized in the department. Creative people want and expect personal freedom. They are often independent in their thoughts and judgments; they should be given latitude to pursue and develop new ideas if management can possibly let them do so. I can appreciate your irritation, but I have a hunch you're too uptight about him."

"Well, he might be creative, but have you seen the clothes he's been wearing? I think he's gone to unacceptable extremes."

"Yes, but it costs little to overlook oddities, and unusual dress might just be essential to creative functioning. You have to consider that Don Lake is in his twenties, we have no prescribed dress code in the department, and what he does is relatively harmless.

"If you want me to, I'll see if he can be transferred to another department. But my guess is that if you didn't bait him, check up on him, and instead gave him a little more freedom on the job, he would be much less of a pain in the neck to you."

Reasoning and Principle Involved

People who are creative sometimes present problems for supervisors because they behave and handle their work differently than other employees. Recognizing their traits and characteristics is essential to understanding and getting along with them.

PROBLEM NUMBER 5

What to say to a supervisor on how to persuade employees to get more ideas and turn in more suggestions.

The Situation

When your superior told you that the company would like to have employees be more innovative and creative, you decided to see what you could do in that respect. One approach you took was to check the records to see if employees who had won awards for suggestions in the past were continuing their winning ways. You learned that Paul White, a big winner a year ago, had not turned in another suggestion, much less had one accepted. This prompted you to talk to White's supervisor, Henry Rankin.

What You Should Say and Some Responses

"Henry, I feel that our company would be more competitive if our employees were more innovative and creative. I realize, of course, that truly creative employees are rare, that perhaps only 5 to 10 percent of the people have natural talent along these lines.

"This led me to look into how the few creative people we do have are doing. What I did was to check the records of employees who had come up with good ideas and been rewarded for them. I wanted to see if they continued to turn in award-winning suggestions. To my surprise, one of your people, Paul White, has not turned in another suggestion after winning a $500 award more than a year ago."

You wait a few seconds to see if Henry has anything to say. When he remains silent, you go on.

"In my experience, a company generally has two types of employees. The individuals who take their jobs for granted are one type. They follow instructions without questioning them as a rule and do what they're told to do. They may think a bit about the work procedure and how they are following it, but this is far from being creative thought. Perhaps nine out of ten employees fit into this class.

"The individuals who think about their jobs as they do them are the other type. Their thinking goes beyond the routine of adding figures, checking grammar in their writing, and putting paper in files. These persons question each job step before doing it. They continually ask themselves: is this the simplest, fastest and best way? Is this step really necessary? Could this step be combined with another? Henry, are you following me?"

"Yes, I am."

"Creative people, those who are capable of submitting cost-cutting and money-saving ideas usually come up with them from the way they do their work. It's just second nature to them. Furthermore, it would be abnormal and unusual for such a person to have just *one* good idea in his or her system. Such a person can usually be expected to have several ideas, providing, of course, that he or she is encouraged to do so."

You pause a bit, but Henry waits for you to go on.

"Paul White's suggestion was a good one. Even if simple, it was original and showed that he was a creative individual. I would have bet at that time that he would turn into a highly creative and productive employee, one who would go far in the company. Yet today, more than a year later, it turns out that the first suggestion he submitted was also his last one. That is what's bothering me. I wonder if he's been receiving the kind of encouragement and help that creative people need to keep them producing suggestions and ideas."

Henry is on the spot, and he knows it. But he is smart enough to level with you. "I guess the answer to that is obvious. If I had given White the help and encouragement he should have received, he probably would have come up with more ideas this past year."

You smile and say, "I couldn't help but feel that way. But what's past is past. What I'm more concerned about for the future is how you could avoid this kind of thing from happening again with White or any other employee who might have creative potential. When an employee shows inclinations and talent along this line, and has the desire and ability to think imaginatively and come up with something original, that capability must be fed and cultivated on a regular basis.

"Henry, I want you to make a special effort to pinpoint the potentially creative people in your group and begin to encourage and work closely with them to generate some ideas. Most people are timid when it comes to turning in suggestions. They feel they're not qualified to compete with the research and development people, the engineering and systems pros, who are paid to make improvement and changes in procedures. What you have to do is turn around such thinking in your people.

"Your people don't have to be intellectual or highly educated to be creative. Nor do they have to be born that way. Although creative people have certain traits which distinguish them from others, those characteristics can be developed with determination and practice."

Reasoning and Principle Involved

Supervisors and managers must do everything in their power to encourage and promote creativity. The difference between a mediocre supervisor and an excellent one often lies in the quality and quantity of ideas he or she dreams up and develops, and inspires his or her subordinates to produce.

PROBLEM NUMBER 6

What to say to a staff manager who runs into trouble when introducing a new procedure.

The Situation

The cost-estimating procedure your engineering department has been using is tedious and time-consuming. You were therefore pleased when an innovative young engineer, Bob Ronson, turned in a suggestion on a procedure for estimating costs that was clearly superior to the existing one. You explained the new procedure to your staff manager, Bill Sassman, who agreed with you and said he would take steps to have his engineers begin using it. After Sassman had put the procedure in writing and credited Ronson for originating and presenting the idea, he distributed copies of the procedure to his staff, stating that, effective at once, it would replace the former procedure. However, the staff engineers protested so vehemently that Sassman had to agree to consider changing back to the old procedure. He came to your office this morning for advice.

What You Should Say and Some Responses

"Bill, I can understand why you are disappointed with the reception given the new cost-estimating procedure by your engineers. I still believe, however, that it is superior to the procedure you've been using."

Bill nods and says, "What I don't understand about this is that if you and I both see Ronson's procedure as a much better one, why would the staff engineers object to it? They're professionals with a lot of experience. Is it possible they don't see the procedure's advantages?"

"No, I don't think so," you say. "My guess is that their turning it down has nothing to do with the advantages of the procedure itself."

"That's beyond me. If they feel that Ronson's procedure is better, why wouldn't they go along with it?"

"I can think of three reasons, any one of which could apply. One could be they resent not being consulted regarding the change. The second could be they resent the fact that the idea came from the newest and youngest engineer in the department. And the third could be that the advantages of the new procedure weren't pointed out, particularly from their viewpoint. Don't forget, the old procedure works and they're used to it. It isn't easy for many people to adjust to a change.

"If you had discussed the new procedure with the engineers in advance, it probably would have made a difference. If they were given the opportunity to get involved in it and made some contributions to it, their response might have been more positive.

"I'd suggest that you now try to correct these mistakes. It's not too late to bring them all together and ask for their input. Also apologize for trying to ram it down their throats. Lastly, suggest they try the new procedure for a month; say you'll revert to the old system if it doesn't work out."

Reasoning and Principle Involved

Managers must realize that sometimes it is just as important to sell a new idea as it is to create one. They should ask their people for comments and suggestions when they are considering a change. By showing they are concerned with acceptance, and that they want their people's approval, they are more likely to get both.

PROBLEM NUMBER 7

What to say to a new supervisor to help him promote creativity in a department.

The Situation

One of your older supervisors, Horace Tilton, decided to take early retirement. When replacing him, you saw that this would be a good time to initiate corrective action in how the department was managed. Horace was an autocratic, stubborn and narrowminded person who had stifled creativity and innovation, a situation you wanted to change. You ask Perry Deming, your new supervisor, to come to your office to discuss the problem.

What You Should Say and Some Responses

"Good morning, Perry. How are things going today?"

"Pretty well, I guess. Of course, I'm keeping close to Horace to learn as much as I can about the job. Starting Monday, I'll be on my own."

"I realize that you're new and inexperienced, and I want you to know that you can talk to me whenever you want to. If you let me know how much help you want, I'll try to give it to you."

"I can tell you that now. I'll need all the help I can get."

"OK, let's talk about the job a bit. You worked for Horace from time to time. How much do you know about his way of running the department?"

"Not too much. I only worked for him on a temporary basis a couple of times, so I had no real chance of learning how he operated. He seemed to be a capable supervisor. I saw that he had good control of the workers and didn't permit any horseplay or fooling around. I guess I respected him."

"What about work assignments and instructions? Did he spell out the work clearly? Did you always know what you were supposed to do or how you were supposed to do it?"

"Yes, I never had any problem that way. Horace really knows his way around. He leaves nothing to chance."

"What about his personality, Perry? Do you think he is well liked?"

"I can't say. I never was crazy about him, but I had no complaints either. While he's got a reputation for being tough, he's also fair. But he never was easy to talk to."

"I feel that not communicating well is a serious matter with a supervisor. I also heard that he wasn't too popular with his men. Maybe you can confirm this.

"Here's what I'd like you to do, Perry. When you take over the department on Monday, arrange to have a private talk with each of your people. That's always a good course to follow when you start a new job. Talk with them about their work, get better acquainted, and give them a chance to get gripes off their chests. While you are doing that, look for reasons why they turn in few suggestions. In fact, you might even ask them this question directly.

"You know, Perry, when a new supervisor takes over, some people will go out of their way to be helpful and cooperative to get on the supervisor's good side. You never know. People might say things to you they never would have said to Horace."

Perry follows your instructions and reports back to you the following Wednesday.

"How did it go?" you ask him.

"Pretty well, I think. I got some interesting information. Horace would never win a popularity contest, but the workers respected his abilities. Most of them said, however, that he's tough and cantankerous. He doesn't like to rock the boat or make any changes. Remember what I said about his being difficult to communicate with? Well, most of his people agreed that was true."

You nod. "Good work, Perry. As for being non-communicant, I can't think of a worse way to inhibit creativity. When your boss won't listen to you, any inspiration you might have is quickly killed. What did they say when you asked them about their suggestion output?"

"One fellow told me he once turned in a suggestion. Horace said that it wasn't a bad idea, but the way he had arranged the job was more efficient. Another guy suggested a procedure change but Horace wasn't interested. He said that the present procedure had been in use for a long time and worked—why look for problems and complications?

"It looks to me like Horace wanted things one way only, and that was his way. How does it look to you?"

"Perry, I couldn't agree more. All you have to do now is prove to these people that you're really receptive to new ideas, and then look for them to roll in."

You pause a bit, reconsider, and then resume.

"But there's only one thing I'm worried about. Horace got these people into the habit of not thinking creatively. It might be difficult to get them out of it."

"Yeah, I see what you mean. What we need is an incentive of some sort."

"Right! Maybe a contest of some kind."

"Like what?" Perry asks.

"Well, the guys are accustomed to the yearly suggestion programs. Their minds have been fixed to turn them off. This has to be something special. And I think I've got it. How about a 'Bust the Status Quo' contest?"

"What do you mean?"

"Challenge your people to improve the procedures that they've been following for such a long time. An award would go to anyone who finds a better way of doing the job than is outlined on the job sheets, specification forms, or in the manual. Prizes would be awarded in proportion to savings involved.

"If upper management OKs the idea, you could run this special contest in conjunction with the annual suggestion program which comes up next month. How does that sound to you?"

"'Bust the Status Quo.' I think you've really got something there."

"Not me—we! We both thought this thing out."

Reasoning and Principle Involved

Companies look to their first-line managers to promote creativity and innovation among employees. In addition, one of the main responsibilities of a supervisor is to make sure that no potentially promising idea of a subordinate is ever permitted to slip by without serious consideration and assessment.

Chapter 15

LOYALTY

In the following situations, note the many ways that employees may be disloyal to their companies. Notice also, that when a manager feels or learns that a subordinate is disloyal, the manager should first make the person realize that he or she is disloyal and then ascertain how such realization affects the person. If the person doesn't care, the manager must decide whether or not the company should continue to employ him or her.

PROBLEM NUMBER 1

What to say to a supervisor who has shown disloyalty to the company in public.

The Situation

When your assistant approached you with a peculiar look on his face, you knew that something unusual had happened. He told you that he had learned why a new employee, one who seemed to have great potential, left the company after being on the job only a month. Your assistant was told by the ex-employee that a supervisor, Al Schmidt, repeatedly had put down the company both on and off the job, stating that it was a poor organization to work for. While you found this hard to believe, you decided to try to confirm it and therefore summoned Schmidt to a conference room where you could talk to him in private.

What You Should Say and Some Responses

"Al, you've always impressed me as being a competent supervisor. You know your job, you run a tight organization and you seem to handle your people well. In addition, you've never indicated to me that you were unhappy or dissatisfied with your work in any way."

Al appears nervous. Instead of saying anything, he waits for you to continue.

"This morning I learned that Perkins, that young fellow who was with your group only a month, left because you told him this is a lousy company to work for, that management doesn't know what they're doing, and that it's hard for a guy to get ahead here. Is that true, Al? Did you knock the company in front of Perkins? Did you tell him it is a lousy place to work?"

Al shifts about uncomfortably. "Yeah, I guess so. I just had a bad day when nothing went right. I was kind of fed up with things."

"Do you really feel that way, that this is a bad place to work?"

Al shrugs. "I suppose so, once in a while. Don't you ever feel that way?"

"No, I never have. If I did, I'd look for another job. You know, Al, if you're not happy with a job, nobody's going to hold you back from looking for employment elsewhere."

Al suddenly becomes wary. "I didn't want to cause any trouble. When you think about it, this company is no better or worse than others. It's just that every once in a while, you feel low and wonder why you put up with things. That's normal, isn't it?"

"I can't disagree with you on that. It happens to everyone. But when you have a supervisor's job, you're a representative of management, and that means keeping such feelings to yourself. If you don't do that, you're being disloyal."

"I suppose that you can look at it that way."

"It's the only way to look at it," you say firmly.

"You're making a big deal out of this, aren't you?"

"That depends on what you mean by 'a big deal.' That's all for now, Al. I'll be talking to you later."

You end your talk with Al at this point because you want to find out how much bad-mouthing of the company he has been doing in front of others. After returning to your office, you ask your assistant to talk to the men in the plant to see what he can learn. A day later, your assistant reports that Al's periodic words of frustration were even more serious than you had feared. According to some of the other employees, Al is just biding his time at the company until he finds another job. Other employees said that Al saw himself as a topnotch manager, and thought that company management was too dumb to recognize it.

After you received this additional information about Al, you ask him to come to your office again.

"Al, I never fire an employee without first making an effort to reform the person or eliminate the problem. But in your case, there's more than one person involved."

Al frowns but sensing the worst, doesn't question what you're getting at. You quickly go on.

"When a man supervises people, his actions and behavior have a great effect on *their* actions and behavior. In your case, we need no better evidence than Perkins' leaving the company. What worries me more is the effect of your attitude on the rest of our employees.

"No supervisor can carry out his responsibilities and duties without loyalty. There's not one supervisor in our company without some kind of weakness or deficiency. Most of these, with hard work and conscientious effort, can be overcome in time. Disloyalty might be the one exception. It involves the character and style of an individual's make-up.

"Al, I don't want to have someone, particularly a supervisor, working for the company who lacks the integrity to be loyal to the people he works for. I have informed the Personnel Department that this is your last day with the company. You can pick up your final pay as soon as you have collected your personal belongings."

Reasoning and Principle Involved

When a supervisor vents personal complaints and dissatisfactions to subordinates, and runs down the company or its products, subordinates will never again have much respect for him or her. Loss of respect seriously undermines a supervisor's effectiveness.

PROBLEM NUMBER 2

What to say to an employee who threatens to leave the company.

The Situation

Sidney Falk is a valuable employee to you even though he has been with the company for only six months. Falk is a hard worker and is very ambitious. Hired as a mechanic to troubleshoot and repair machines, he understands equipment and is able to quickly diagnose a malfunction. Today, Falk came to you and asked for a raise. He also said he would leave the company if he doesn't get it. However, the company has just announced it lost money in the previous quarter and is presently trying to cut costs. Also, according to company policy, employees cannot be granted pay increases until they have completed one year of service. You weigh all the factors and eventually decide that you shouldn't attempt to bypass company policy in order to hold him.

What You Should Say and Some Responses

"Sidney, I want you to know that I and my superior think very highly of you. You've done an excellent job for the company in the short time you've been with us. But you may have heard that the company lost money this last quarter. Management is now trying to cut costs and get the company back in the black. Under these conditions, it would be very difficult to get you a raise."

Sidney frowns. "Well, that may be true, but the small amount of extra pay you could give me wouldn't be noticed. This is a fairly large company and it should be able to easily handle it."

"Yes, the company is large, but when a decision is made to cut costs, management looks for every possible way to do it. We don't want to lay off any employees for one thing. We would probably ask some people to take cuts in their pay first.

"But there's something else that blocks my giving you a raise at this time. According to company policy, employees cannot be granted pay increases until they have completed one year of service. I believe you've been with us about six months."

Sidney doesn't give up easily. "If you don't give me a raise now, I'm going to follow up on an opening I heard about at Wilks Company. My pay there would be more than what I make now plus the raise I'm asking for."

"I'm sorry, Sidney. But if I were in your shoes, I'd pass that up at Wilks. If you continue to do the excellent work you have been doing here, you should have an excellent future with us. I would like you to think about that before you make a move. Also, if you keep up the good work, you'll probably be one of the first to get that raise when the company is doing better."

Reasoning and Principle Involved

There is no question that many employers take good employees for granted and often fail to appreciate them until it's too late. On the other hand, it is not uncommon for employees to leave a job for a year or two and then return. They may learn that the company wasn't so bad after all, or that there were more opportunities for advancement with the company than they had originally realized.

PROBLEM NUMBER 3

What to say to a subordinate who continually talks about looking for a better job.

The Situation

Several times in the past few months, you were told that Neal Thompson, one of your supervisors, has been saying to both his fellow supervisors and his subordinates that he isn't satisfied with his present job in the company. He has also been heard to say that he doesn't see any chance for advancement and is therefore looking around for a better job somewhere else. Since you feel that a supervisor should not be making such statements, you tell him you'd like to talk to him in your office at the end of the work day.

What You Should Say and Some Responses

"Neal, it's been reported to me that you are telling people that you are dissatisfied with your job. Is that true?"

Neal hesitates, then slowly replies, "Well, yes, I thought I would advance much faster than I have. Also, I don't think the company is paying me what I'm worth."

"Complaints about your job, me, or the company made to anyone other than me are marks of disloyalty to me. Loyalty should be one of your prime responsibilities as a supervisor.

"If you don't consider loyalty important, then I must decide between two courses of action to take. I either give you another chance which means you stop complaining publicly and adjust yourself, or I decide you'll never be a help to me, and the sooner I replace you, the better for everyone."

Neal immediately becomes alarmed. "Gosh, I didn't think that anything like this would happen. I was just spouting off."

"This is a serious matter, Neal. I have always felt that when an employee is unhappy with his or her work, the employee will not do a good job. Both the employee and the company lose in such a situation. If you want to continue working for the company, you and I must find a way for you to gain satisfaction from your work. If you want to quit, I won't stand in your way; but as long as you work for me, you must be loyal to me."

"OK," Neal replies meekly. "I won't be doing anymore griping publicly. But I'd like to talk to you about my future with the company when you have some time."

"All right, Neal. Although I didn't intend to have performance appraisals with my supervisors until next month, I'll plan to talk to you Monday or Tuesday. I'll let you know later what time we can get together."

Reasoning and Principle Involved

When a manager feels that an employee is being disloyal to him, her, or the company, the manager must first make the employee realize it and then determine how such realization affects the employee. If the person doesn't care, then the manager must decide whether to continue keeping the employee. Performance appraisal meetings are good for discussing attitudes and feelings about the company and the job.

PROBLEM NUMBER 4

What to say to an employee who tries to take advantage of the company.

The Situation

Helen Ross is a young technician recently hired by your company. She graduated from a university well known for its excellent engineering curriculum. Since Helen expected to start with the company at a higher level job than the one in which she was placed, shortly after starting as a technician, she began to put off jobs and assignments that didn't require the use of her technical training. She also showed a reluctance to do "dirty" work even though it was expected of her as part of the project she was working on. Her disloyalty was reflected when she told another technician that how the company does was of no concern to her; she was interested only in work that would give her the experience to enable her to go into business for herself some day. Because of this attitude, other technicians in your department have begun to avoid her. They prefer not to work with her on department problems and vice versa. You see that you cannot permit this situation to continue.

What You Should Say and Some Responses

"Helen, I've observed that there seems to be some antagonism be-tween you and the other technicians. Are you having any problems with them?"

"Well, not particularly. One or two prefer to work by themselves But that's all right with me. I feel that I'm better qualified to handle some of these processing problems anyway."

"How do you mean?"

"Well, my engineering training puts me above some of the other technicians. And that reminds me—some of the assignments you've given me could be handled by a high school graduate. You know I've got a degree in Industrial Engineering."

"Yes, I know that, and I've been trying to give you challenging work. But there are many relatively easy problems that must also be handled. Your job as an engineering technician includes working on those problems, and I expect you to handle your share of them. I appeal to your loyalty to the company to accept such assignments."

"Oh, I'll do them, but I prefer work which will enable me to get ahead."

"It's normal to feel that way. But I would like to see you volunteer for jobs which would help the company and not only yourself."

Helen shrugs but doesn't say anything.

"Helen, I believe that the way you are handling your job is hurting you as well as the company. When you shun your fellow engineers and technicians, you cut yourself off from an important source of knowl-edge and also diminish your on-the-job learning experience. If you become a good team member, you will get help from others on your projects. This, of course, is to your benefit.

"Your value on the job depends not only on your talents and abili-ties, but also on your willingness to use them in a way that will be most helpful to the company. The most important requirement of your job is to satisfy the company to the very limit of your ability to do so. That was why you were hired.

"I want you to start spending part of your time in the production areas learning the operations and offering your help when you think it could be used. I'm going to watch for this during the next month. I also expect to see you working more with other technicians."

"What about my regular work? I won't have time for it if I do all these other things you're suggesting."

"Yes you will. I would like to talk to you again tomorrow after-noon, after both you and I have had some time to think about your future. I believe that if we did some planning, your performance would improve and you would also take a different viewpoint toward the company. When people get involved in planning, they become motivated, the work becomes more interesting, and they also get more satisfaction from it."

Reasoning and Principle Involved

While managers must demand loyalty from subordinates, planning and management by objectives promote and encourage it. When subordinates are involved in the planning function, they feel a commitment to carrying out the plans they helped to formulate. Management by objectives is a currently recognized and practiced procedure for performing the functions of management. It involves setting job responsibilities and performance standards for each job in a department. Although each subordinate has specific objectives, all subordinates work toward a common goal, directed by the manager.

PROBLEM NUMBER 5

What to say to the employee who criticizes the company.

The Situation

Your sales clerk, Paul Duffy, is now serving his second term as the Union vice president. He is a very aggressive individual who never hesitates to say what he thinks on any subject, including store management. He is strongly in favor of the rights of workers, and speaks out just as strongly against big business. When a new clerk, Benny Klein, was hired recently, you were very pleased with Benny's initial attitude toward the job and with the way he handled the work you assigned him. Lately, however, you've noticed that Paul has been advising him against developing good work habits. As a result, Benny does considerably less work than originally. Yesterday you overheard Paul telling him to slow down and making a disparaging remark to him about management. Near the end of the day, you tell Paul you'd like to talk to him in your office.

What You Should Say and Some Responses

"How did things go today, Paul? Has our sale brought in a lot of customers?"

"Yeah, I was pretty busy this afternoon, but now things have slacked off. What did you want to talk to me about?"

"Paul, I'm concerned about your attitude toward management and the company. I overheard some of your remarks to Benny Klein yesterday. They weren't very complimentary to management."

"I just wanted to make sure he didn't kill himself by working too hard."

"What do you mean by that?"

"Well, some of these new guys don't realize that the company is out to get everything they can from the employees without paying them decent wages. I simply wanted to point that out to him."

"That simply isn't true. The company pays equal if not higher wages than any other company in this type of business in the area. You should know that from having participated in the last Union–Management negotiations. Your attempt to reduce the productivity of Benny is a step in the wrong direction. The company needs loyalty from the people who work for it."

"That's a lot of b.s. All the company thinks about is making a big profit so they can pay management big salaries."

"Paul, all our employees should be concerned about the company's problems, its profitability and its future growth. Loyal employees can make a company, and disloyal ones can break it, especially when the company deals with services to the public.

"If employees in a store such as ours are down on management, and show it by doing only what they must do to get by, customers will soon be turned off. The number of people patronizing the store will drop and so will sales. In such instances, disloyal employees will eventually hurt themselves—they'll be asked to work fewer hours or may lose their jobs because they're no longer needed.

"I don't want to hear any more remarks from you about the company or the faults of management. If you don't like the way the company is operated, you can leave. If you continue to be disloyal to the company, you can expect to be disciplined."

Reasoning and Principle Involved

Some employees do not understand that loyalty is a mutual issue. They tend to be concerned only with the company's loyalty to its employees, rather than their own loyalty to their company. An employer is expected to show its loyalty by its willingness to help employees meet personal needs and by providing benefits. Employees can show their loyalty by doing a fair share of the work and cooperating with fellow workers, supervisors and management.

Chapter 16

AUTHORITY AND RESPONSIBILITY

In the following situations, note the important relationship between authority and responsibility. Managers should want their subordinates to have all the authority that they need in order to meet their responsibilities and accountability effectively. Notice also that managers often find it difficult to get subordinates to accept more responsibility.

PROBLEM NUMBER 1

What to say to two managers who can't agree on who should be responsible for handling a production order.

The Situation

Several departments in your company overlap in their capability of handling the manufacturing steps involved in processing production orders. This condition became reality when the company recently diversified and broadened its product line. In addition, many of the operations involve assembling of parts, an activity which is common to most of the departments. Consequently, when a large order came in a week ago from the Acme Company, you saw that it could be assigned to Department A managed by Tom Wolfe, or Department B managed by Dick Hall. You assigned it to Tom's department because you knew that Dick's department was two employees short and anticipated losing another. However, Tom came to you this morning saying that his department was not the best one to do the job and that Dick's department would be a better choice. You ask both managers to come to your office to resolve the problem.

What You Should Say and Some Responses

You waste no time in getting into the problem. "Tom, what's this all about? Why can't you handle this Acme order?"

"Well, we tried to do the job, but it hasn't worked out. I think Dick's people are better qualified to do this kind of work. They have more training and experience, because they've been doing similar work. In addition, they've got the facilities and layout to handle it. We never should have been assigned that job to begin with."

Dick immediately responds.

"But it was, and we both know why. My department is already overloaded with work. We've been trying for three weeks to get a couple of experienced machine operators without any luck. To make matters worse, one of my people is retiring next Friday.

"Another thing, Tom, is that your department's location is much better than mine for this order. You're closer to the materials needed and closer to where the assemblies have to be delivered when you're finished with them. That all adds up to less labor and lower costs."

Tom quickly speaks.

"From the standpoint of space, we're worse off than you are. Also, I don't think manpower shortage is a good excuse. You'll need more help if you take on the job, and you'll get it."

"Help means people," Dick replies. "Where will we put them? Move some of them into the office?"

At this point, neither Tom or Dick seem to have anything more to say. Both are unhappy and seem apprehensive, wondering what you will say.

"What's the big argument about? Why?" You direct the questions to both men. Tom speaks first.

"I'm trying to protect my department. I don't want to botch up the job or run up the costs."

You make no comment on his remarks. "You, Dick?"

"I feel the same way, I suppose," Dick replies.

You nod and look at both men. "Well, I guess that's a start. But what about the company? Did either of you consider that? Here we've got a confirmed order at a fixed price. Is the company going to lose money or make money on this order?"

Neither man answers.

"You're supposed to be two of my best managers. What happened to the training and experience you're supposed to have?"

Turning to Tom, you ask, "How do you decide where a job should be run?"

Tom knows the answer, but isn't eager to give it to you. "You consider all the factors involved and how much each costs. Then you total all the costs. The job should be run where it can be done most effectively at the lowest possible cost."

"Is that how you considered and evaluated the Acme job?"

"No sir, but . . . ."

"Let's hold up the 'buts' for a minute. What about you Dick? Did you estimate the costs of the Acme job?"

"No, sir."

You nod. "Since neither of you took the time or made an effort to think out how the job should be run and what the costs were likely to be, the objections you made have little significance. Do you agree?"

"Well, yes," Tom says, "but . . . ."

"All right," you say. "Let's talk about the 'buts.' In my opinion, a 'but' is usually nothing more than something in the way of achievement. Dick, your department is overloaded with work and short on people and space. Tom, yours is without the right facilities and experienced people for the job. I'm not saying these aren't valid factors, but the trick is to put a cost on each one. After that, you can work on the roadblocks. People, space, facilities and such can always be resolved if the calculations and estimations are right.

"Working together to make the company profitable is what's important. An individual is important and a department is important only as much as their goals tie in with the company's objectives."

You smile at both men and say, "This is an excellent opportunity for you fellows to work together as a team. Work out the costs for the Acme order as you've done with other orders. Then we'll get together to talk some more."

Reasoning and Principle Involved

Management decisions should not be based on personal preferences or department interests. They must concern the company and its objectives, and these generally relate to overall costs and the making of a profit.

PROBLEM NUMBER 2

What to say to a supervisor about why he should delegate some of his work.

The Situation

Ed Wilson, your supervisor in Department B, is as hard working and conscientious as they come. Only 24, he is one of the youngest management persons in the plant. But your instincts tell you that he is a bit unsure of himself. Each time you suggested he have lunch with you, he has turned you down saying he is too busy. Also, he spends many hours working overtime and still manages to be one of the first supervisors on the job at the start of the day. After you observed he was spending more than 12 hours a day on the job plus Saturdays, and taking very little time for lunch or breaks, you decided to have a heart-to-heart talk with him.

What You Should Say and Some Responses

When you get to Ed's department, you see he is working on a machine that has broken down. "Hi, Ed. I'd like to talk with you a few minutes."

Ed looks unhappy with your suggestion. "Gosh, I'm all . . . ."

"I can see you're all tied up, but this is important."

Ed frowns, but he talks to a machine operator nearby. "Pete, do you think you can fix this yourself?"

Pete replies, "Yeah, I'd like to give it a try."

"OK." Ed wipes his hands on a rag and turns to you. "What's up?"

"Let's go to the conference room where we won't be bothered and can talk in private."

Ed looks puzzled and then alarmed. "Did I make a mistake? Has someone complained about me?"

"No. Nothing like that. But there's something that bothers me and I'd like to talk to you about it."

Ed becomes more and more nervous, so you quickly get to the point.

"Ed, I want you to be honest with me. How is the job going? Are you having any problems?"

Ed hesitates, then says, "OK, I guess," but he doesn't seem sure of himself.

"All right," you say. "I'll be honest with you. I talked to some of the security people here at the plant, those who are here both early in the morning and late at night. I know that you're putting in more than 12 hours a day here. Why so much?"

Ed fidgets, and lights a cigarette with trembling fingers.

"There's a lot of work to be done, and jobs don't always run right. Someone has to follow up and see that the work gets out."

"But does that mean you have to do it? You've got some good people working for you. What about them?"

"Oh, they're doing their jobs, but when there's trouble, or problems . . . . Well, I feel I've got to take care of those things."

"How long do you think you can keep this up?"

"As long as it's necessary."

"Ed, it's my job to give you help if you need it, and that's what I want to do. That's my responsibility just as getting out the work is yours. The first thing I'm going to do is to point out to you that you're exposing yourself to burnout and serious health problems if you continue to try to maintain your present style of managing.·

"Every manager including first-line ones must learn to delegate some of their work, and most successful managers are skilled in doing it. I don't think there's any question about your need to do it. That's evident with all the overtime you've been working.

"Ed, you must certainly practice delegation if you have hopes of moving up in the company. Your skill in delegating could be the deciding factor in whether you can handle greater responsibilities and a bigger job; getting things done through others is the sign of a successful manager.

"If you are hesitating to delegate because you feel you must do a job yourself to have it done right, such an argument is false. If you feel that a subordinate can't do a job as well as you can, consider whether it's really necessary that the job be done that well.

"I'm going to briefly give you the steps to follow so you can start delegating. First, you must decide what part of your work you can delegate. An obvious choice is a job which another individual can do as well or better than you can. Save for yourself those jobs which require the experience, skill, and training which only you possess.

"Second, delegate to more than one person if you possibly can. Select the person to whom you're going to delegate a specific task by suiting the task to the person. By spreading assignments among all your people, you enable each to demonstrate their potential as well as gain recognition for getting a job done.

"Third, be clear and concise when delegating. Clarify what decisions you are delegating and what you are reserving for yourself. Recognize that delegating fails when the person to whom you have delegated a task fails to perform it or makes a decision beyond the scope of authority granted.

"Fourth, tell other people about your delegation. If you fail to let people know what and to whom you have delegated, you make it difficult for your helpers to get cooperation and to avoid resentment when making decisions.

"Fifth, follow up on your delegations. Even though you may have delegated some decision-making responsibility, you still have the total responsibility. You must keep up-to-date too, on *what* you have delegated. Stay on top of these things by asking that your people report to you from time to time.

"Ed, I left for last some important advice. When you delegate your work you must be careful not to go overboard. Some of your duties and responsibilities should *not* be delegated. Management expects you to handle such matters as planning, scheduling, policy formation, coordinating, control and supervision. If you give those away, the company won't need you."

Reasoning and Principle Involved

Delegating is not easy for many managers. Since they feel a bit uneasy when they do it, giving them advice and tips on how to delegate is always worthwhile. There's more to this art than most people realize.

PROBLEM NUMBER 3

What to say to a manager who gives you responsibility without authority.

The Situation

Your manager, Carl Swanson, has made you responsible for the productivity of your hourly people. This responsibility includes meeting the minimum acceptable standards in both quality and quantity of work performed. However, one of your people, Bernie Wells, has consistently failed to meet those standards despite all your efforts to help him do so. Wells is too old for the kind of job he holds, and is too set in his ways to conform to the newer production techniques and requirements. Thus, whenever you present your monthly production figures to Carl, they always are low for Bernie and for others whose output depends on his productivity. Today, Carl tells you he expects better results from your department. You feel you must respond by making clear your position on this problem.

What You Should Say and Some Responses

"Carl, the only way I'm going to be able to get more production out is to replace Bernie Wells with someone who is more productive."

"Why don't you correct his deficiencies or inadequacies?"

"I've already done everything I can in that respect. I'm assigning him only that work which represents the least he can do in order to justify his filling that job. I've explained to him carefully what he's expected to do and tried to motivate him. In addition, I've trained him properly to do the job satisfactorily and provided him with all the necessary tools and equipment."

"Well, then, why doesn't he produce like the rest of your crew?"

"He's too set in his ways. He won't accept our latest equipment acquisitions. A good example of this is his refusal to use the computer. You know the computer plays a big role in our operations these days. I intend to either fire him or have him transferred, and then replace him."

"You simply can't do that. Bernie has given the company many years of loyal service. He's always tried to conform, and he deserves special consideration. You've got to do the best you can with him. But you've got to get your production up. Your department isn't looking very good these days."

"Carl, I feel you are being unfair with me. You are holding me responsible for meeting our production quotas without the necessary authority to provide people to enable me to do it. While I'm willing to respect your wishes to keep Bernie in my department, I cannot accept criticism for his inadequacies and deficiencies which are mainly responsible for my inability to run this department the way I want to.

"I like my job and I feel it's a privilege to be working for you. But I cannot accept the blame for something which is not my fault. I enjoy working for the company, and prefer that I work for you. But if this situation doesn't change, I'm going to apply for a transfer to another department."

Reasoning and Principle Involved

Managers who are assigned responsibility should make sure they have all the necessary authority for meeting the related accountability. They should assume that they have that authority unless and until they are informed that they don't.

PROBLEM NUMBER 4

What to say to a supervisor to encourage him to accept more responsibility.

The Situation

When you left on vacation a week ago, you asked your supervisor, Rob Keller, to handle your work during your absence. Among other things, only a few important customer orders in process were on schedule and you expected they would be shipped on time. When you returned, however, you learned that the Spencer order was two days overdue on being shipped. You immediately called Keller to come to your office to find out why it is late.

What You Should Say and Some Responses

"Rob, what's the problem with the Spencer order? I heard it hasn't been shipped."

Rob frowns. "Yeah, I'm sorry about that. I know it's two days late. But, what the heck, we've been behind schedule before, and two days . . . ."

"I know it's only two days. But this was a special order, and the Plant Manager gave his personal word that it would be shipped on time. It seems that the customer needs this shipment badly."

"Gosh, I didn't know about all that. I didn't realize it was that important."

"I know," you say. "That was entirely my fault. To me, the job seemed simple, easy to run, and right on schedule when I took off last Friday. It never occurred to me anything could go wrong. What happened? Did you run into trouble?"

"We ran out of the polystyrene sheeting. A new shipment was supposed to come in but it didn't."

"Rob, that's no big problem. You could have substituted the acrylate sheeting or some other stuff. We've done that more than once in the past."

"Well, I kinda figured that. But I wasn't completely sure that it was OK, and I didn't want to take any chances. I tried to check it out with Burton because he is familiar with some of our sheeting applications, but he wasn't sure either."

"When did all this happen?"

"Tuesday afternoon. I thought about trying to reach you, but decided against it. By the end of the day, I figured there'd be only one more day's delay before you got back. We just stopped working on the Spencer order and began another job in its place. It's not that we didn't have anything to do."

"Why didn't you call the Spencer company? One of the managers there would have been able to clear a change with you. After all, it's their construction specs that we go by."

"I thought about doing that, but I didn't know if it would be all right for me to call a customer directly. I've never done that."

"There's no reason why not. Also, you've made substitutions before. You could have done that on your own."

Rob quickly looks at you. "I've never made a substitution without your authorization," he says. "That's what I wanted to do, but I was afraid to take the responsibility."

You nod. "OK, I understand. I will certainly see that you have the authority to act for me the next time I am absent."

Reasoning and Principle Involved

Managers must always double-check everything before an anticipated absence to make sure subordinates know what to do in any situation that might arise. Managers can't automatically expect subordinates to do something without first carefully defining and describing the extent of their responsibility and authority. When managers give subordinates the authority they need to make decisions and the independence to make them without fear of criticism and reprisal, they avoid the kind of indecision and anxiety that lead to temporizing and delay.

PROBLEM NUMBER 5

What to say to a supervisor on how to get workers to take on more responsibility.

The Situation

When studying the Plant Operations report of your company, you see that your department did not perform up to your expectations. There were two operations in particular where productivity continued to decline over the past three months. Both of these operations are under the supervision of John Talbot, a bright young fellow who, about four months before, had taken over the job. Wanting to get more information, you call John on the phone and ask him to come to your office to discuss these operations. You also ask him to bring his job assignment records with him.

What You Should Say and Some Responses

"Come in, John, and sit down."

"OK," was all that John says. He is unable to hide his uneasiness.

"Relax, John, you're not going to lose your job. But there's nothing like paying a bit of attention to a problem before it gets completely out of hand. I guess you've seen the latest Plant Operations report."

"Yeah, I saw it all right," John replies.

"What do you think? Did you expect to see such low figures for your area?"

"No, I was really disappointed. I've been working like hell to turn that downward trend around and get the figures up. Instead they seem to keep dropping."

"Do you have any idea why?"

"No, I just can't figure it out. I've been reviewing all the projects we're working on and they all seem to be going as expected. I've checked to see if we had any unusual expenses, and there has not been any. I just can't pinpoint the problem. So far as I can tell, I've been doing everything I should."

You nod. "Let's go over the Plant Operations report to see if we can find an answer. Maybe we'll come across something."

"OK," John says, as he moves his chair closer to your desk.

Looking over the report together, you skim over parts that are not relevant. Then you reach one which you had previously check-marked as one to be investigated.

"Here's something," you say. "The output of this Master press has dropped off considerably in the last few months. I believe you've got Hank Wills on this machine. How is that press running? Any problems with it?"

"No. Oh, it's occasionally down for one thing or another. But no more than any other machine."

"What about Wills? Does he have any problems with the operation? Does he completely understand the jobs he's been getting?"

John opens his job assignment file for the press and you read the list of jobs that Wills has handled over the past three months.

"Aren't some of these jobs kind of tough and complicated?" you ask John.

"They're about average," John replies. "Of course, Wills is not one of my best operators, I'll have to admit that. But I don't want to baby him. I figure that the only way he'll learn to accept his fair share of responsibility is by doing those jobs."

You nod, but make no comment.

"John, what about Matt Brown? He's running the "B" machine. His output is low and the number of his rejects seems to be just as bad as Wills'. Do you have any idea why?"

"No, other than that Brown's another slow one to show initiative. I've been trying to make him more self-sufficient. But I guess it hasn't worked."

"What kind of projects have you assigned him?"

John opens the file on the "B" machine and shows you the projects that he has given Brown the last few months.

"For a guy who you say isn't too sharp, you seem to be tacking a fair amount of responsibility on him."

John shakes his head in agreement. "Like I said, I don't believe in coddling people. I believe that the only way you can get a person to learn to swim is to throw him in the water."

You neither agree or disagree with John's remarks. Instead, you say, "Taking these two guys as the department's worst performers and the ones who seem to be dragging down the department the most, do you have any plan on what to do about them?"

"Only that I'm trying to give them special attention and to follow up their work closely."

"Do you think they're falling down because they've got a poor attitude, because they're not doing all they could?"

John looks skeptical. "Well, I don't know about that. I have the feeling that they're short on self-confidence. My hope is that as they get more and more into the habit of assuming responsibility, they will get used to it, and also more confident."

"How did they do before you took over as supervisor?"

"Neither one of them really put out much. Pretty mediocre, I guess."

"But they apparently stayed at a standard level according to the records," you say. "They seem to have grown a lot worse since."

"Yeah, I guess you're right," John agrees. I've been trying to up-grade them, but it doesn't seem to be working out. I always had the feeling that they were babied, the job made too easy for them, before I became their supervisor. That's why they never became responsible. But I'm trying to change all that."

"I see. Tell me, John, do Wills and Brown work alone most of the time?"

John thinks for a moment before answering. "Yeah, they do. Why do you ask?"

"I believe I see a reason why the department has low productivity problems. I have the feeling that you are taking some of your weaker and less capable people and trying to knock some responsibility into their heads. If Wills and Brown can't measure up to the rest of your group as seems apparent, many of those jobs are too tough for them to handle on their own. As a result, they either take too long to do the job because they're not sure of themselves, or they create a lot of rejects and waste.

"You might be able to get them in the habit of taking on more responsibility by pairing them with dependable people they can count on when you assign them a tough project. I suggest you try this a few times until you see signs they have developed more self-confidence."

Reasoning and Principle Involved

Every organization has its leaders and its followers. When a manager tries to force followers to take on more responsibility, he or she can expect to run into difficulties. It's better to assign followers simple jobs until they gain confidence, or assign them to work with a leader until they gain experience and confidence.

PROBLEM NUMBER 6

What to say to a manager who tries to sidestep his responsibility.

The Situation

A machine which your department manufactured last week had to be scrapped because it was made to the wrong specifications. Hearsay around the plant was that the supervisor, a young fellow only six months on the job, was at fault. According to the two craftsmen, White and Hanson, who built the machine, the reason the mistake occurred was because Chuck Ramsey, their supervisor, gave White poor instructions about what to do and how to do it. From what Ramsey told him, White assumed that the materials and tolerances to be used for the job were the same as those used for the Acme machine that he built about four months ago. This design, however, has since been declared obsolete. But White claims he was not aware of that and Ramsey did not tell him. You decide to have a talk with Ramsey about what happened.

What You Should Say and Some Responses

"How are things today, Chuck?" You smile to help relax the situation, and then ease yourself into a nearby chair.

"OK. What's new with you?"

"There's some disturbing talk around the plant about why we had to scrap that machine that White and Hanson built. I would like for you to tell me what happened."

Chuck appears uneasy and his face begins to flush. He fidgets with the pencil on his desk before replying.

"White knew that the Acme design was obsolete," he says. "He just forgot about it."

"How do you know he knew?"

"Well, a couple of weeks ago, I told our file and records clerk to put the specs and drawings in the inactive file. If he had to go to the inactive file to get the specs, he must have known that the design was obsolete."

You ask Chuck a few more questions, but he becomes more and more nervous and answers them in a vague, uncertain manner. Eventually you say, "No sweat, Chuck. I just thought I ought to talk to you about this. Thanks for your help."

You return to your office, wondering why Chuck was so nervous and why he was so vague when answering some of your questions. To follow up, you ask your assistant to talk to the file clerk about the transfer of the specs. However, nothing is learned from this because the file clerk does not remember that particular file. A day later you again go to Chuck's office.

Chuck greets you, more nervous than ever. This time, however, instead of insisting it was all White's fault, he admits that maybe his instructions weren't as clear as they might have been. He also concedes the possibility that the Acme specs and design had not been moved from active to inactive as they were supposed to have been; or that having been transferred, they could have been inadvertently returned to the active file.

"Still, there was no reason to assume the Acme job had anything to do with this job," Chuck protests. If White wasn't sure of what to do, he should have come back and asked me instead of guessing."

You make no immediate comment on that, but pause a bit before again talking to him.

"Chuck, you've held this manager's job for about six months now, if my memory serves me. In that time, I can't think of a single error you've made. For a young fellow in a tough new job, that is highly unusual.

"While I feel you're an outstanding manager for your age and experience, I also sense you're a bit over-anxious and insecure. People like that sometimes adopt a fixed attitude toward mistakes. They feel that honest human errors are cardinal sins and to be avoided at all costs. If they are involved in a mistake or a slip-up, they fear the worst. As a result of such beliefs, they go to extremes to cover up, and wind up as perfectionists. If they are managers, they earn the resentment and bitterness of their subordinates.

"If you are to continue as a manager who is respected by his people, Chuck, you will have to change your attitude and outlook on mistakes. Also, you must understand that a subordinate's errors are in part, at least, your responsibility."

Reasoning and Principle Involved

Most people on the job can't stand the person who never admits he or she could be wrong. The major problem with this attitude is that it hinders the determination of causes when errors are uncovered. It also makes taking the necessary action to avoid repetition difficult.

PROBLEM NUMBER 7

What to say to a manager who bypasses you by giving assignments to your people.

The Situation

The advertising agency you work for has a large number of accounts under contract. You and one other supervisor head up the two divisions in charge of the accounts. Both of you report to Clyde Mercer, an aggressive, competitive individual. He was responsible for the agency acquiring several new accounts last month, two of which were assigned to your division. Yesterday, Mercer bypassed you and went directly to the people you had put on the new accounts. He asked one of your account executives to immediately make a market research study, and he asked another to make some sketches for approval. You learned of the first incident when your subordinate came to you for help, and you ran across the other when passing by the account executive's desk. You feel that you must clarify your position and responsibility with Mercer, so you watch for an opportunity to talk to him when he isn't on the phone.

What You Should Say and Some Responses

"Got a few minutes, Clyde?"

"Well, I'll be leaving soon. Can you make it short?"

"I'll try. Yesterday afternoon, Bob Fisher, my exec of the Robinson account, came to me with a question on the market research study you asked him to make. I know that you are deeply interested in that account and . . . ."

Clyde interrupts you at this point. "Yes, I am. I picked up that account just last week, and I promised the president of the company that we'd give it our close and immediate attention. I meant to tell you that I had talked to Fisher, but I guess I forgot."

"Clyde, I know you mean well, and that we have to work quickly to satisfy our clients, particularly the new ones, but I knew nothing about this market research study when Fisher came to me. When you bypass me by asking my people to handle assignments, you undermine my authority as well as confuse my people.

"This makes it difficult for me to give them assignments because they feel strongly obligated to put your requests ahead of everything else. I would appreciate it if you talked only to me when you want a job done by my people. In that way, I will know what jobs they are working on. Also, I will be able to contribute to the cause as well as follow up on the project."

Reasoning and Principle Involved

Some managers will bypass their subordinates and then tell them about it afterward. Reporting after the fact apparently relieves their conscience. In small companies or in closely knit organizations, managers are prone to do a lot of bypassing and not much is thought of it. This can lead to trouble when there are differences of opinion or when managers at different levels are inconsiderate toward one another. Most managers in large organizations, however, agree that requests to get work done or jobs handled should follow the chain of command.

PROBLEM NUMBER 8

What to say to an older employee who has lost interest in the job.

The Situation

Mary Peters has worked in your company's information center ever since it was created. When she started on the job at the age of 45, she was an enthusiastic and energetic person, still interested in broadening her education and welcoming the many requests that daily were made for her services. However, you noticed that Mary seems to have lost interest in the job during the last six months. She moves slowly now and sees little reason to pick up the tempo when helping people who come to her desk for information, even when a line begins to form. Mary never arrives early in the morning and is the first person to leave in the evening. Since Mary's lack of interest in the job has made her a handicap in serving employees, particularly the technical and professional ones, you recognize that something must be done about her lack of performance on the job. After thinking about it at length, you decide to change Mary's duties and responsibilities. Late one afternoon, you go to the information center to talk to her.

What You Should Say and Some Responses

"How did the job go today, Mary?"

"Oh, pretty good, but I'll be glad to see 5:00 o'clock roll around."

"Well, just one more day and you'll have two days off. I've noticed that you haven't been working Saturdays lately."

"Yes, that's right. I've got a lot more important things to do on Saturday, such as visit my children and my grandchildren."

"I suppose you look forward to doing that."

"Yes, I do."

"Mary, I'd like to talk to you privately for a few minutes. Can we go into one of the study rooms where we won't be disturbed?"

"Sure, there's one that's empty."

You and Mary go to the study room. After you close the door, you turn to talk to Mary.

"I'd like to change your job a bit, Mary. With the change I'm thinking about, your job would be a lot easier for you. You would not be under pressure to quickly provide the scientists, engineers and other technical people the information and data they request. I can imagine that those requests for help can be quite stressful, particularly at the end of the day."

Mary appears alarmed and apprehensive. "What did you have in mind for me to do?"

"You would do staff work and also some planning. You would have acquisition and procurement responsibilities along with filing and cataloging work. The good thing about this is that you would be able to handle such jobs at your own pace."

"I'm not so sure I'd like that type of work. Some of it would be strange to me."

"Yes, that may be true at the start. But, I believe you would pick it up quickly. It's an opportunity for you to take a greater interest in all the functions of the information center. This will lead to more loyalty to the department and the company. In addition, I think you will gain more satisfaction out of your job."

"Well, I don't know," Mary replies.

"Mary, it's very normal for people to slow down on the job as they get older, and I'm sure you've begun to experience that. But the information center is obliged to provide fast, efficient service for the company's employees. I'm certain you agree with this."

"Yes, I know that's important. But . . . . I just don't know what to say."

"There's an alternative to what I've proposed. You could take early retirement. I don't know if you've done any planning for the day you retire, but you know it is inevitable. Your decision on when to do this hinges on your financial status, your feeling of security, and your outside interests and hobbies. You've told me you like to be with your family. Maybe you'd like to do some traveling in the next few years.

"Mary, I realize I've sprung this on you very suddenly. I know you'd like some time to think about what I've proposed. You can either remain in the department performing staff duties, or you can take early retirement. I'd appreciate it if you'd let me know what you decide to do in a week or so."

Reasoning and Principle Involved

The problems that can arise with older employees include a diminished interest in their work and decreased performance, among others. Managers can deal with these problems in a variety of ways, but should always show respect for older workers. Offsetting those drawbacks is a wealth of knowledge and experience, assets that all companies need.

PROBLEM NUMBER 9

What to say to a manager who tries to pass her responsibilities on to you.

The Situation

You and Elaine Fisher are managers of the sales clerks in a large department store. Elaine's responsibilities include women's wear, jewelry and cosmetics, among others. You handle men's wear, hardware, sporting goods, and similar items. In addition to supervising the clerks, both of you work closely with buyers and advertising people. Both of you also take and report inventories. Elaine passed some of her inventory responsibilities onto you shortly after she became manager a few months ago by asking you to work with the buyer in ordering women's shoes. She explained that since both women's and men's shoes are procured through one buyer, you would not be inconvenienced much by doing it. Caught off guard and wanting to help an inexperienced manager, you agreed. Today, Elaine came to you asking if you would also work with the buyers of jewelry. This time, you told her you would think about it and get back to her later. After thinking it over, you head for her office intending to say no to her request.

What You Should Say and Some Responses

"Elaine, I've been thinking about your request for me to work with the jewelry buyers, and I've decided this would not be the right thing for me to do. This is your responsibility, and not one that I'm prepared to take.

"I believe that doing this would lead to problems for both of us. Management would some day learn of it and we would both be in hot water. You know, job descriptions with this company are very specific on matters such as this. Besides, I'm sure you can handle the job because the procedure is very similar to that you are following with the other buyers. Why don't I work on it with you once or twice until you catch on? Of course, you will have to make the final decisions."

Elaine should have no recourse but to accept your offer. After you have made arrangements for that and are ready to leave, suddenly remember something.

"Oh, I almost forgot to tell you. I've referred the buyer of women's shoes back to you. You know, I was handling that part of your job only until you became more experienced."

Reasoning and Principle Involved

Solving problems for peers can stifle their growth and it can diminish a manager's effectiveness. The manager who makes too many such agreements will find less and less time and energy available for his or her duties.

Chapter 17

HONESTY

In the following situations, note how important honesty of employees is to conscientious managers while some employees are less inclined to treat it as a serious matter. Notice also, that managers should look for more opportunities to inform employees of the personal risks they take if they ever become involved in plant pilferage and theft.

PROBLEM NUMBER 1

What to say to a supervisor on what should be done to discourage employees from stealing company property.

The Situation

In every manufacturing plant, some tools and materials are lost or mislaid each month. The situation at your company is no different. But in the last few months, the amount of tool loss normally experienced has steadily grown to the point where it can no longer be tolerated. You ask the supervisor of your engineering and maintenance department to come to your office to discuss the problem and decide what to do about it.

What You Should Say and Some Responses

"As you know, Bob, we took the physical inventory of the department's equipment, materials and tools last week. At the same time, the book inventory has been run off and reported by the data processing department. I've been studying both inventory reports; there are too many differences between the book and the physical."

"What you're saying is that the book is bigger than the physical. But we can't be making that many errors in taking the inventory, can we?"

"No, unfortunately," you say. "The stuff is either vaporizing or someone is taking it out."

"Do you really think someone is stealing it?" Bob asks.

"I hope not. But we're facing a situation we can't afford to slough off. Look at some of these shortages."

You show Bob the list you made of the most serious shortages. Among them are small motors, expensive adhesives, micrometers and all sorts of small tools.

"I can see that most of these items are either useful around the house or can be resold easily."

"I was thinking the same thing," you say.

"What do you think we ought to do?"

You rub your chin thoughtfully. "There are several things we can do, but all of them are unpleasant and distasteful."

Bob nods. "You mean like having the guards at the gatehouse check lunch boxes, the security people make locker inspections, conduct lie detector tests, and that kind of thing?"

"Yes, and that's not the worst of it."

"What do you mean?"

You hesitate. "I'd rather not say, Bob. Hopefully, it won't come to that."

"Well, if you want to know how I feel about it, what it amounts to is putting your own people on notice that they're under suspicion, that you feel one or more of them are dishonest. These people are the ones I work with day in and day out, every day of the year. How do you go about telling someone that you no longer trust him?"

"It's not an easy job. I have to agree with you on that. But there's another side to this situation that must not be overlooked. Until the person or persons are uncovered, the entire department is under suspicion. When you greet Paul, Harry, Mary or Bill in the morning, can you be sure one of them isn't the guilty person?"

Bob takes a deep breath. "No, I guess not."

"In addition to that, how long do you think our company, or any other company, could remain in business if it continued to experience losses like this month after month? Under the circumstances, wouldn't you say that not only company management, but every employee, should be concerned about this? The thief isn't only stealing from the company; he or she is jeopardizing the job security of every person working here.

"I know you feel that it's an indignity to have your person, or even your locker searched, and requiring employees to undergo a lie detector test is, to say the least, a sign of distrust. Also, hiring an undercover detective to spy on people with the objective of finding the crook in their midst is about as sneaky as you can get. I can't argue that, Bob.

"But unfortunately, there's nothing else we can do. This situation has existed too long already. The time for action is long overdue, and we have no choice but to take it.

"I don't like this business any better than you do, Bob. In fact, at times, it makes me sick. But sometimes you simply have to do what has to be done, like it or not.

"To start, I'll ask the guards to make spot inspections at the gatehouse. I'd like you to conduct a locker inspection with no advance notice as soon as you can get some security people to help you. If these strategies don't bring results, we'll have to try something else including hiring a detective."

Reasoning and Principle Involved

It's very disheartening to a manager to discover that a presumably trustworthy subordinate turns out to be dishonest. Yet it's a trauma key people in government, business and industry are forced to endure. Managers must decide when to trust and when to mistrust. When the evidence proves almost conclusively that someone is dishonest, they must check up on everyone, unpleasant and distasteful as the job may be.

PROBLEM NUMBER 2

What to say to a supervisor about an employee who is stealing from the company.

The Situation

Don Foster, a lead man in one of your maintenance groups, is ambitious, sharp-witted and clever. He is also money-hungry. Experienced and smart, he functions as one of the department's best problem solvers. Since he is especially knowledgeable with tools and equipment, his supervisor, Ken Morris, frequently sends him to local suppliers and hardware dealers to purchase tools and materials. Also, if the company has a service contract with an outside firm, Foster generally is assigned to deal with that firm. These practices enable Foster to supplement his regular income by padding expense and overtime records. In addition, he often sells scrap items from the plant to dealers, falsifying the record and taking part of the receipts for himself. However, other maintenance employees know about his dishonesty because he brags about it. One of them resented it so much that he came to you and related a recent incident in which Foster pocketed $50 of the company's money. Having this information, you summon Morris to your office.

What You Should Say and Some Responses

"Ken, I just heard some disturbing news from one of your people. I was told that Don Foster recently sold some stainless steel pipe and fittings to a scrap dealer and made himself $50 on the deal. What do you know about this? Did Foster get a kickback?"

Ken appears ill at ease and doesn't seem to know what to say. "He may have. I'm not sure, but he probably did."

"What disturbs me more than the money," you say, "is your failure to control this transaction and to permit it to occur. If Foster steals from the company this way, he probably does so in other ways."

"That may be true, but it never amounts to much. He does a lot of important jobs for the company, and is considered sort of 'special'. I usually give him more freedom to buy and sell equipment and tools and to work with our customers on service jobs than I give other people."

You become very firm after hearing Ken's explanation. "I want that to stop as of now. I don't care how special you think he is. Every transaction must be tightly controlled. If it's hard to control, I want you to handle it yourself or assign someone you trust to do it. Permitting any employee to get away with dishonesty, petty or not, is simply an invitation for everyone in the department to do the same.

"I'm going to put a notice on the bulletin board stating that any employee caught stealing from the company will be dismissed, and I intend to see that this rule is enforced. If you're unable to do it, I'll find somebody who can."

Reasoning and Principle Involved

There is no question that loose ethical standards encourage dishonesty. Managers can never permit dishonesties to exist in how employees handle their responsibilities, regardless of how petty they may be.

PROBLEM NUMBER 3

What to say to the employee who borrowed a company tool and did not return it.

The Situation

Employees at your plant occasionally complain about the pilferage of personal assets. Thus management is touchy and sensitive about theft. Not surprisingly, then, there was quite a stir when an expensive piece of testing equipment was found to be missing. Since the missing wattmeter was used infrequently, the electrician who discovered the disappearance had no way of telling how long it had been gone. Management posted a notice on the bulletin board that if it was returned, no further action would be taken. A few days afterwards, Charley Davis, a long-time employee in the maintenance department and an electrician with an excellent performance record, came to your office.

What You Should Say and Some Responses

As Charley approaches your desk, he appears nervous and worried. "You know that missing wattmeter?" he stammers.

"Yes, what about it?"

"I took it."

You are stunned and speechless for the moment. Looking up at him you say, "Gosh, Charley, did I hear right? Do you know what you're saying?"

The look on Charley's face is answer enough. His expression shows he feels miserable.

"What made you wait so long to tell me?"

"I was scared. I never thought the tester's disappearance would cause such a hullabaloo. I didn't even expect it to be discovered for a long time. We seldom use it."

"For gosh sakes, why did you take it?"

"I was building a short-wave radio at home and needed it to test some of the circuits. It took longer than I expected. I never thought I'd get in hot water over this thing."

"You know how sensitive management is about taking company property. What did you expect to happen?"

Charley's face reddens. "I didn't steal it. I just borrowed it. If I stole it, I wouldn't be telling you about it now, would I?"

"No, I guess not."

"This isn't going to get me fired, is it?"

"I don't know. You didn't actually steal it, but you removed it from the plant without authorization. Technically, that is the process of stealing. I don't think I have to tell you how management feels about that.

"Charley, you're not a crook, but you really pulled a boner. I don't know if this will cost you your job. I'm going to have to get some expert advice."

You consult with the Personnel Manager and the Manager of Security on this problem. In your meeting, you point out that Charley has an outstanding performance record over his ten years of service with the company. You also mention that he is a top-notch electrician and one of the best people in your group. You add that you would like to keep him as an employee if possible.

The Personnel Manager acknowledges that Charley is returning the wattmeter voluntarily, and is not a thief. He adds that Charley is remorseful over the incident and realizes he's made a terrible mistake, one that he's not apt to repeat.

The Manager of Security comments that Charley's behavior was a serious violation of corporate security policy, one that should not be lightly dismissed. Severe discipline could be imposed as an example to other employees.

After considering and discussing all the factors related to this incident, the three of you decide to have the wattmeter suddenly appear overnight as mysteriously as it disappeared. You call Charley to come to your office to give him the news.

"Charley, I met with two members of management to discuss your situation. We decided that you should bring the tester into the plant very early tomorrow and put it in a cabinet behind some of our other testing equipment. Later in the day I will discover it when looking for something else. In that way, no culprit or crook would ever be named.

"We feel you have learned a valuable lesson from this incident, and with your past good record and many years of service, you deserve a break."

Reasoning and Principle Involved

The most human solution to a violation of corporate security policy may very likely be something other than severe discipline. A manager should always consider circumstances, records of performance, and other influencing factors when deciding what should be done concerning matters of personnel behavior.

PROBLEM NUMBER 4

What to say to the supervisor who strongly suspects an employee to have committed a theft.

The Situation

Two thefts have occurred in your department, both in the locker room. An employee's watch was stolen two weeks ago, and a wallet was missing last week. Although a thorough search had been made for the watch, no evidence was uncovered. The wallet, however, was later found in a trash can in the men's room. While licenses and credit cards were intact, $50 in cash was gone. This dispelled any possibility that the wallet had been lost and not stolen. After another week has passed with neither clues nor news on either theft, your supervisor, Al Johnson, comes to you saying he thinks the thief is Jack Jones, a young trainee in the Material Control Department.

What You Should Say and Some Responses

"Al, tell me why you suspect Jack Jones of being our thief."

"It's a long story, but I'm pretty well convinced. On Wednesday morning, I received a call from Mrs. Jones. She said Jack was sick with a virus and his doctor had told him to take the rest of the week off. I thanked her for calling and told her to tell Jack to make sure he has a doctor's note when he comes back to work on Monday.

"Friday, one of the guys in the shop came to me and asked if I'd seen the morning newspaper. He said that there was an item in there about Jack being held at the police station for questioning about a robbery in Centerville three months ago."

"So Jack wasn't sick at all," you say.

"Right, but that isn't all. After I'd heard that, I did some investigating. I learned that when Jack was underage, he was caught in a store robbery and served six months in the reformatory. It looks like he got an early start on being a thief and has been one ever since."

"That may be true. And it may not."

"There's more," Al quickly replies. "Today, when Jack reported to work, I asked him how he felt and also asked for a doctor's note. He said he forgot to ask the doctor for one. Then I told him that I knew he wasn't sick and instead had been held at the police station. I asked him why he lied to me, and also what had happened. He got angry and said that it was none of my business. He has a lawyer who advised him not to talk about it. He also said he had been taking a lot of gaff from the cops, and didn't have to take it from me as well."

"The picture certainly doesn't look good. But don't jump to conclusions. Even if he happens to have information about that robbery in Centerville, it doesn't make him a crook."

"That's true," Al replies. "But it makes him a suspect. Most of the guys in the plant are hot about those two robberies last month. And you know he was one of the guys with more than 50 bucks on him when he was searched after that wallet was stolen.

"I think you should fire him. After all, we didn't have any stealing before Jack Jones began working here. He served time for stealing before, and he's in some kind of trouble that's related to stealing now. Let someone like that loose in a plant, and you don't know who the next victim might be. The way I see it, the safest thing is to get rid of him, especially now that I've got him cold for lying about being sick."

"I can understand the way you feel," you say.

Encouraged, Al goes on: "The question is, *can* we get rid of him? If we tried to fire him for lying about being sick, could we make it stick?"

You shrug. "Maybe, and maybe not. Actually, I'm not concerned with that. I'm not so sure it's the question or problem facing us. The real question, as I see it, is whether Jack Jones has done something that warrants firing him."

"He's a known thief," Al says.

"Six months in the reformatory when under age? Does that mark him as a criminal for life?"

"No, but . . . ." Al hesitates. "Do you think it's safe to have a guy like that around?"

"I don't know," you say. "I'm as concerned about that as you are. Yet, what right do you or I have to say he's guilty? Suppose he's innocent of this robbery the police have been questioning him about and our two plant thefts. Who are we to judge him? If our judgment is wrong, think of the injury and injustice we'd be doing him. Courts of law are provided to judge a person's innocence or guilt.

"Don't misunderstand me, Al. I'm glad you and I had this discussion. With Jack's history and the fact that he was one of the men to have more than $50 on him when searched, I can appreciate the conclusions you reached. But there's another side to the coin, and that is the system upon which justice in the U.S. is founded."

Al smiles. "I get you. The time to judge Jack Jones is when there's evidence that he's guilty, not before."

"Or innocent," you say. "That's about the crux of the matter."

Reasoning and Principle Involved

Although managers are always under pressure to uncover dishonesty and prevent theft from company employees, they should keep in mind that when a police matter is involved, it should be handled by security experts.

PROBLEM NUMBER 5

What to say to a pilferage witness who refuses to testify.

The Situation

Losses due to pilferage in your company have been growing and management has become increasingly concerned. It was recently decided that the company would have to make some concerted efforts to learn which employees were guilty. Today, your supervisor, Henry West, told you he had overheard a conversation while in a booth in the men's room. He heard Bruce Colgate, an electrician, tell another maintenance worker that he knew which employees were stealing equipment and tools from the company, and fencing them through a trucker who frequently picked up shipments at the loading dock. That's all West heard. You immediately ask Colgate to come to your office.

What You Should Say and Some Responses

"Come in, Bruce, and please close the door behind you."

"OK." After Bruce sits down, he asks you, "What did you want to see me about?"

"I've been told that you know who has been stealing equipment and tools from the company."

"Yes I do, and it amounts to quite a bit of money."

"I want the names of the people involved. I also understand that a trucker has been paying them off. Who is that?"

"Sorry, but I can't give you that information."

"Bruce, I want to assure you that your name as informant will never be revealed. Nobody knows why I asked you to come to my office, and nobody will. Management cannot permit this stealing from the company to continue."

"I understand that. I don't approve of stealing any more than you do, but I'm not the kind of guy who rats on the people I work with."

"You're not being loyal to the company with that attitude. We need your cooperation on this matter. I feel it's one of your responsibilities to give me this information."

"My responsibilities do not include becoming a squealer."

"Bruce, if you refuse to cooperate, I will have to turn this matter over to our security people. My guess is that the police will be brought in. This is a very serious matter because these thefts endanger all our jobs. Further, I feel that if you don't cooperate with either me or the police, it will probably cost you your job."

Reasoning and Principle Involved

Some managers see employee theft as an inevitable byproduct of conducting a business. Permitting theft to continue when it undermines profit objectives is intolerable, whatever management's philosophy on the subject.

PROBLEM NUMBER 6

What to say to an employee who refused to let a security guard search his clothing when he left the plant.

The Situation

Late yesterday, Harry Shaw, a guard at the plant gate, phoned you that one of your people, Pat Schmidt, had refused to let his clothing be searched when he left the plant. Shaw had been observing employees who were waiting to ring out at the time clock. While most employees were carrying their jackets, Schmidt wore his zipped to the top and it bulged excessively. Since the labor agreement at your company specifies that the guards had the right to conduct searches at will when workers left the plant, this had become a longstanding practice. Clothing usually wasn't examined. Purses, lunch boxes, and packages carried out of the plant were searched at random. After getting all the details of the search from Shaw, you consulted with the Personnel Department and then arranged for Schmidt to be sent directly to your office when he arrived for work today.

What You Should Say and Some Responses

"Pat, I talked to the Personnel Department late yesterday after you had left the plant. It has been decided that you no longer have a job with the company. Yesterday was your last day. You can collect your personal belongings how, and then leave the plant. You'll get whatever money is due you in the mail."

Pat acts stunned. "There must be some mistake. What in the hell did I do?"

"It's what you didn't do. When you left the plant yesterday, the guard, Harry Shaw, asked you to open your jacket so he could see why it bulged. You refused. The guard was within his rights in asking you to do that."

"I didn't have anything under my jacket. The material doesn't lay right sometimes. It looks like it's bulging."

"All you had to do was pull down the zipper and show him. You decided not to do that."

"Sure I did. Shaw had no right to search me. That's an invasion of my privacy."

"No invasion was intended. In Shaw's opinion, and that of other people in the area, the bulge was unusual. You obviously had something hidden there."

"Whoever told you that was mistaken," Pat insists. "Regardless, it's wrong to fire me. Everyone knows it's OK for the guards to check only purses, lunch boxes, and packages. You can't suddenly start checking something different."

"We can, and we have," you say. "Sorry, Pat, but you're through."

Reasoning and Principle Involved

When an employee flagrantly refuses to be searched, he or she is very likely stealing. Company guards would be neglecting their duties if they did not insist on a search. Also, to support management's action, in some situations, common sense takes precedence over rules.

Chapter 18

PAY AND PROMOTION

In the following situations, note how managers must convince employees that they are fair when handling matters involving pay and promotions. Employees will more readily accept their decisions if managers are honest with them, explain their words and actions, and show them that they are not biased or prejudiced. Notice also that managers should be sympathetic to employee complaints and should assure them that all employees are treated equally.

PROBLEM NUMBER 1

What to say to supervisors about the best way to excel and to get ahead.

The Situation

Management of your company is planning to organize a new small department to handle special orders. Your superior tells you that a capable supervisor is needed to head up the new department. Knowing that you have several supervisors in your department who might qualify for the job, your superior asks you to select one for the job. After studying your people and their records of performance, you conclude to consider either of two men for the job. You plan to interview Vince Miller and Jeff Davidson, and from what you learn, recommend one of them to your superior.

What You Should Say and Some Responses

"How are things going, Vince?"

"Real good. We're pretty much caught up with our orders. The Superior Company job was finished this morning."

"Good work! It's nice to know there's at least one section in the department without any problems."

"I wouldn't go so far as to say that," Vince replies. "Every now and then, a new one comes up."

"That seems to be the norm around here. Tell me, Vince, how are your people coming along? Bill Jackson? Harry Pott?"

"They're getting along fine and doing a good job. I can't complain about their performance. Why do you ask?"

"I was just wondering," you say. "I like to check on who's coming up through the ranks, so I'll know whom to keep in mind should an opportunity for advancement come up. I thought Jackson or Pott might be likely candidates for an assistant supervisor's or supervisor's job some time in the future."

Vince looks wary. "They're two of my best men," he says. "I wouldn't rate them as supervisory material, but they're good men in the ranks."

You nod thoughtfully. "Let me ask you something, Vince. Just a hypothetical question. I don't have to tell you how valuable and important you are to the company and how much management thinks of you. But suppose you decided to retire or go into business for yourself. Or suppose I left the company and the boss decided you should get my job. Would Bill Jackson or Harry Pott be qualified to take over your job as supervisor? Or would anyone else?"

You can tell that Vince doesn't like your question because he frowns and looks concerned.

"You mean right now? Right away?"

"Well, say within a month."

Vince looks disturbed. "I guess it would take longer than that," he replies.

"How long?"

"Maybe three or four months. Both of those guys are used to working on day-to-day routine jobs with everything pretty well decided for them. They have no supervisory experience. Besides, I have about six or eight jobs I handle myself that they know nothing about. The jobs are pretty complicated. It would take a lot of instruction and training to turn over those jobs so that they're done right."

"I remember talking to you about delegating some of that stuff."

Vince looks nervous. "Well, I meant to, but those jobs are pretty important. I feel a lot better handling them myself. That way I know there's nothing forgotten and no mistakes.

"Hey, what goes on? Are you planning to make some changes around here?"

"Not me," you say. "And if anything does happen, you have nothing to worry about. As I said, you're a valuable person to the company. I would say that your job is secure."

After leaving Vince, you head for Jeff Davidson's office. Essentially, you ask Davidson the same questions you put to Vince Miller. Davidson, however, is much more relaxed when responding.

"If I quit tomorrow, or were made a manager, Bill Moore would be qualified to take my job. So would Ralph Solter, for that matter. In my opinion, they'd both do an acceptable job as a supervisor. Of course, if I could have a week or more to give them some last-minute briefing, that would be a big plus.

"But I've been training and grooming those guys all along. I have always felt that, with luck, a more responsible job might present itself one of these days. And when it does, I want to be ready for it. I remember you telling me some time ago that the best way to prepare for opportunity is to train and develop people to step into your shoes at any time."

"Right you are," you say. "Apparently you've been delegating some of your work then?"

"Yes, I have," Jeff replies. "And I've also rotated jobs when I could. Most of the people in my group are familiar with most of the jobs that we do, Bill Moore in particular. If he had to take over in a hurry, he'd know what to do. What makes you ask? Are some changes coming up?"

"Nothing I can talk about now," you say. "But there's a strong possibility something could develop. If it does, I'll let you know about it."

Reasoning and Principle Involved

Not only is the training and development of subordinates the best way for a manager to excel and get ahead, but it's also a key to ensure job security. Regardless of how good a manager is technically, if he or she doesn't understand the importance of building people, the manager will probably never rise any higher in the company.

PROBLEM NUMBER 2

What to say to a supervisor who wonders if he is qualified for his job.

The Situation

Ray Pembroke is Department A's new supervisor, having recently been promoted from a supervisory job in Department C which consisted of only eight employees. As head of Department A, he has 24 people reporting to him. When he headed Department C, he had it running smoothly. Now he has problems of poor attendance, high rejects, and declining productivity of the department members. With the thought that he could use your help, you head for his office to talk to him.

What You Should Say and Some Responses

"Hello, Ray. Got a minute?"

"Not really. But I suppose now's as good a time as any. I've been expecting you ever since the monthly reports came out. Isn't that why you're here?"

"Yes, but that doesn't mean you're on the hot seat. If you have some problems, let's talk about them. You may be a bit short on experience, but I feel you have what it takes to work things out."

"Thanks, that's what I need to keep me going. But, honestly I sure as hell must be doing something wrong, or not doing what I should, judging from what's happening. But I just don't know what it is. I've been working my ass off, but I'm not getting anywhere. Everytime I put a fire out, another one flares up somewhere else."

"How about the number of people you've got? Are there enough?"

"I've got more people than the department ever had, a good assistant, and the workload's no heavier. If I were to put on more people, it would just make the productivity figures look worse. I can't figure out why there are more machine problems, quality control problems, and more waste than ever before."

"Are too many of your people dogging it or goofing off? Do you think they resent someone outside the department taking the supervisor's job?"

Ray shrugs. "Not as far as I can tell. Bob Johnson, my assistant, said he wouldn't have taken the job if it had been offered to him. Too much responsibility, he said. I guess he's pretty smart. At any rate, as far as I can see, no one else is qualified for the job. I'm beginning to wonder if I'm qualified myself."

"Of course you're qualified," you say as convincingly as you can. "The job isn't all that tough if you handle it the right way. Your predecessor never seemed to have much of a problem running this department. Come to think of it, you never had much of a problem running Department C."

"That's true," Ray replies. "But I can tell you this. Department C was a breeze compared with this department."

"You may be right. If so, all we have to do now is find out why.

Maybe we can make some kind of a comparison between them. You said earlier that problems always seem to be coming up in this department. Didn't you have any problems in Department C?"

"Yes, I did, but I always seemed to have time to handle them."

"Time could be the key, Ray. Try to remember, and tell me how you spent your time when you were running that department. How did a typical day go?"

As best he can, Ray tells you about his previous duties and responsibilities. He handled four special reports on his own because they were complicated and extremely important. This took about ten hours a week, leaving him plenty of time for planning, scheduling, making decisions and handling other supervisory responsibilities. Since he was conscientious and hardworking, the department was always well run.

"OK, now let's talk about this department. How do you usually spend your time?"

Ray makes a wry face. "Jumping from one problem to another, or so it seems."

"But what about special reports, key jobs and such things?"

"It's pretty much the same situation here. Two or three special reports are required for each section, and I handle them myself. The problem is that in this department, I've got four sections to worry about. Each one has its own specials, so I wind up with two or three multiplied by four."

"And you do them all yourself?"

"I have to, with most of them. They're complicated and they have to be accurate."

"Why don't you give some of that work to your section heads, or to some of your most experienced people?"

"That would never work. For one thing, they'd take forever to do the job. For another, I'd be worried about the accuracy. Besides, the section heads are overloaded already, and they're working overtime."

"OK, how come they're overloaded? They weren't overloaded before you became supervisor."

Ray lets out his breath. He doesn't have an answer to that question. You continue, "If the department was running smoothly, would they still be overloaded?"

"Probably not. A good part of their time is spent on problems that come up because things aren't going right."

"OK. I think we're getting somewhere. Have you ever wondered if some, or most, of those problems are developing because you're so busy working on those special projects and doing other jobs yourself that you don't have time for your supervisory duties like planning, scheduling, job simplification and troubleshooting?"

Ray rubs his chin thoughtfully. "Hmm," he says, quietly.

"From what you've been telling me, I think your problem is time utilization and a failure to delegate. You're trying to run a 24 person department the same way you ran an eight person department. It can't be done.

"Ray, a reluctance and failure to delegate authority and responsibility is a sign of insecurity. This is your problem, and it is also why you feel you are not qualified for your job."

Reasoning and Principle Involved

Many managers don't realize how many management and supervisory problems develop out of their failure to delegate. No manager should ever expect to be permitted to take on more responsibility or be promoted if he or she has not learned to delegate.

PROBLEM NUMBER 3

What to say to an assistant manager about who in the ranks should be promoted to a supervisor.

The Situation

Your assistant manager, Jim Allen, told you today that one of his supervisors, Ed Pinkston, had decided to retire at 64 instead of at 65 as he had originally intended. Allen was surprised and had not thought about who he would get as a replacement. Now he comes to you for advice.

What You Should Say and Some Responses

"So Ed is going to leave us. He'll be a tough man to replace, Jim."

"Don't I know it. I was really surprised and completely unprepared. Who do you think I should try to get to replace him?"

"I feel you should know who in the department is the most capable. At the moment, I can think of only two who, in my opinion, would likely do a good job. One is Marie Kohl and the other is Henry Falk. Marie's quick and efficient. She seems to know her way around here. As for Henry, he's got a lot of experience and knowhow. I'd suggest we take a look at their personnel records.

"Why don't you also ask Ed Pinkston about who he would recommend. After all, he's the one we're going to replace. His opinion should mean something."

After Jim pulled the records from the files, you and he individually evaluated Marie and Henry using a point system based on several factors relating to performance including attendance, initiative, enthusiasm, productivity, getting along with people, and others. Then you compared your individual evaluations. You scored 52 points for Henry and 40 for Marie. Jim's evaluation was very similar with 50 points for Henry and 42 for Marie.

"Jim, before we go any further, why don't you talk to Pinkston."

"OK, I'll see him this afternoon, and then get back to you."

He returns to your office the next morning. "Pinkston didn't hesitate one bit when I asked him who he would recommend. He immediately picked Henry."

However, you can tell that Jim isn't convinced that he should select Henry for the job. Turning to you, he says, "How the hell can we make Henry a supervisor? He's 60 years old. It takes a long time to learn that job to the point where you've finally got everything under control. Also, how do we know he won't decide to take early retirement himself when he becomes eligible at 62?"

"That's a good question," you say. "We have no way of knowing."

"Another thing I just thought of," Jim adds. "Before we decide one way or another, don't we have to make sure the person we select actually wants the job?"

"Good point. I can pretty well guess what Marie's answer would be, but Henry might figure he's too old to start taking on more responsibility at this time of his life."

"Should I ask him how he feels about it?" Jim asks you. You frown. "No, that might not be as simple as it sounds. You can't very well ask him if he'd be interested in the job and then, if he says he would be, pick somebody else if he's the best qualified and has the most seniority."

"I see what you mean. So what should I do?"

"I'm not sure. If we could somehow or other bring up the subject of Pinkston deciding to retire and get people talking about who will replace him, maybe we'll learn if Henry would like the job. But that might not be easy to do."

"Yeah, but I could have one of my group leaders bring up the subject in his presence and see if he makes any comment. I'll ask Joe to have coffee with the group at the next break."

Later that afternoon, Jim returns to your office. "Well, we lucked out on that idea. Joe just told me that there was a lot of speculation and joking going on in the canteen about who would replace Pinkston. It came out that there was no question about how Henry felt about that job. He wouldn't think twice if it was offered to him."

"That's good news. I guess we're making progress on this thing."

"Yes, but . . . . I'm still concerned about Henry's age. It takes months to become a good supervisor. By the time he gets the hang of it, he could be almost ready to retire himself."

You nod. "Jim, let me ask you something. How old are you?"

"I'll be 34 in August."

"If you don't offer the job to Henry, you'd be offering it to Marie Kohl, right? How old is she?"

"About 30, I'd guess."

"How do you know if, after being on the job a couple of years, she won't decide to get a job somewhere else, decide to leave town because her husband was transferred, or simply decide to stop working?"

"I guess I don't."

"Let me ask you another question: considering Henry's long service and good record, don't you think he deserves that promotion?"

"Definitely. There's no question about that."

"OK, then. I've felt all along that you really didn't have a problem."

Reasoning and Principle Involved

While most everyone consciously feels they are not prejudiced, sometimes they harbor prejudices without knowing it. Aside from the obvious advantages of experience and maturity, older people usually feel a strong responsibility to do a good job. Management seldom makes a mistake when they promote an older employee.

PROBLEM NUMBER 4

What to say to an employee who insists he should be promoted because of his seniority.

The Situation

Last week, one of the power house employees, Jack Cornwell, decided to go into business for himself. The employees in this department are classified into three Grades. Since Cornwell was in the Grade 3 group, a member of Grade 2 would be promoted to replace him. Two people in Grade 2 signed the posting indicating they would like the job. While the next man in line for the job based on service

was Art Boles, a 40 year old worker with more than five years seniority, you decided to bypass him and promote a man who had been
with the company four years but had a much better record. Soon after
you posted a notice that Cal Busch was awarded the job, Boles comes
to you with a copy of the latest union–management contract in his
hand.

What You Should Say and Some Responses

"What's the problem, Art? You look like you have a question about
the labor agreement."

"I sure do. It says here that 'when a vacancy occurs, the employee
with the longest seniority in the next lower classification shall be given
the first opportunity to fill the vacancy,'" Art reads. "I have at least a
year more seniority than Cal Busch, the man you gave the job. That's
discrimination—I should get the job."

"It's not discrimination, Art. Management has the prerogative to
award the job to the person who is best able to do it."

Before you could say more, Art interrupts you. "That's a lot of
bull," he retorts. I'm the next man in line for that job, and I should have
a crack at it."

"You should be thankful you still have your present job. I can show
you letters in your personnel folder that show you've been disciplined
for horseplay and poor attendance. In addition, I frequently see you
goofing off and taking longer than is necessary to finish a job."

"That has nothing to do with this. I'm as well qualified for the job
as Busch. If you don't give me a crack at that job, I'll turn in a
grievance that'll make your eyes water. According to the labor agreement, I should have the job."

"Art, I can save you a lot of time and trouble. For one thing, your
record in the department proves that your attitude and performance
aren't up to the standards that management expects of the company's
employees. For another, read the union–management contract again.
There's another clause in it that affirms management's prerogative to
determine promotions and raises with ability as much a qualifying
factor as seniority."

Reasoning and Principle Involved

Knowing the union–management contract or labor agreement as
it is sometimes called, and what it says about promotions, is a must for
all supervisory personnel. Since grievances are costly in both time and

money, supervisors must constantly work to reduce their number and frequency.

PROBLEM NUMBER 5

What to say to an assistant manager about how to select someone for promotion.

The Situation

One of your supervisors has accepted a position with another company. As manager of the department, you decide to ask your assistant to review all the personnel in the department to find a replacement. You suggest he consider the three group leaders as the most logical candidates. While your assistant, Ed Pursell, generally agrees with this, he asks you how he should decide which of the three people would be best for the job.

What You Should Say and Some Responses

"Ed, a good way to start is to think about the qualifications for the job, the capabilities and characteristics of a supervisor."

"I guess you're talking about the traits that are required for leadership such as intelligence, ambition, self-confidence, integrity, and so on."

"Right. You can add to those: reliability, courage, decision-making ability, and a willingness to accept responsibility for the actions of others. Is there anyone you can think of other than the three group leaders—Mike Wills, Bill Samson, and Wilbur Stone—who might possibly meet our requirements?"

Ed thinks a bit. "Linda Hurt?"

You shake your head. "I don't think she has enough experience, but she certainly has the potential. We should give her a couple more years."

"Yeah, I see what you mean. So I guess that means we narrow it down to Wills, Samson and Stone, unless you can come up with somebody else."

"No, I can't," you say.

"Then as I see this situation, you could almost pick any one of them. They're all top-notch people, and they're all in line for promotion. Any one of them could handle the job."

"Maybe so," you reply, "but only one of them could handle it best."

"I guess so, but how do you figure which one?"

"Let's go over their records and capabilities one at a time."

You and Ed begin reviewing the qualifications of the three men. Seniority is not a factor because all are long-time, experienced employees. In addition, all are loyal, ambitious and respected by other employees.

"It looks like Wills has the best education," Ed comments, "But I feel that Samson is the most intelligent."

"You're probably right about that, but Stone's experience looks more diversified."

"Say, I've got an idea. Do you think we could come up with some problems for them to solve, the kind of ones they're likely to run into as a supervisor, and then see who handles them the best?"

"Ed, that sounds like a good idea. And I see how we can do it without revealing what we're up to. I'll present the problems at a regular supervisor's meeting and ask them to give me a report on how they would solve them or what they would suggest be done. We'll then evaluate the reports to see who responds best."

Coming up with some department problems is easy for you to do. That Friday, after you had covered all the items on the agenda with your supervisors and group leaders, you present two problems to the people in the meeting. In concluding the meeting, you say, "I know how busy you all are on the projects we talked about today, but this is important to the department. I'm sure you can find some time between today and next Friday to give these problems some thought. What I'd like from you by Friday is a report on what you think should be done. If you have any questions or need help, let me know."

The following Monday, Wills appears at your desk wanting to discuss the safety problem you had presented. Wills has a list of questions to ask. He also expresses his doubt that it would be possible to come up with a practical answer, and he brings up several points you feel are rather superficial. After spending almost an hour with him, you reach the conclusion that he hadn't given the problem much thought before coming to you.

Other group leaders also come for help on both problems, Bill Samson included. In most cases, you sense they are probing for leads or solutions rather than trying to think them up themselves. Some group leaders, Wilbur Stone included, simply want guidance in understanding the technical aspects of the problems. You are able to clarify matters for Stone in less than 10 minutes.

On Friday, all of the group leaders turn in their reports. Some are lengthy while others are brief. Mike Wills turns in a better than average report, and Bill Samson's is also good, but in both cases, the thinking is mainly yours, not the group leaders'. Wilbur Stone's report is by far the most constructive of all. He came up with good ideas on the safety problem and some interesting suggestions and recommendations on the other problem. Overall, he showed excellent thinking and a creative imagination.

After the meeting, you and Ed get together to review the reports. Both of you agree that Wilbur Stone's report is the best of all those submitted.

"Does this mean we should pick Stone for the supervisor's job?" Ed asks.

"Yes, but not only because he came up with the most outstanding report. He showed unusual independence, initiative and capability in the way he went about doing it."

Reasoning and Principle Involved

In working out problems and making decisions, effective managers keep two objectives in mind. First, they do everything possible to achieve the most productive and efficient result that they can. Second, they make an effort to act on their own, learn from the experience, and save time for their superiors. True professionals don't go to their superiors every time a problem comes up or a decision must be made.

PROBLEM NUMBER 6

What to say to an excellent employee who presently has meager chances to be promoted.

The Situation

Frank Gomez is a compounder in a large company in Houston, Texas, that makes chemicals for the rubber and paint industries. After earning two years of college credits, Frank was eager to get out on his own and make some money, so he applied for a part-time job between school semesters. When he found that he liked the job and didn't want to go back to school, Frank asked to be hired permanently. Since he had applied himself well, and the company needed a compounder, he was given the job. That happened four years ago. Frank is still on the compounding job, but now is discouraged because he would like a better job and sees no chance to move up in the company. He comes to you to ask for advice. Since he has been an excellent employee, you would not like to have him leave the company.

What You Should Say and Some Responses

"How's the job been going, Frank?"

"Oh, I'm getting a little bored, I guess, doing the same thing day after day. I'd like to make more money, too, but I know I'm already at the top of the salary bracket for compounders."

"Do you have a particular position in mind with the company? What kind of work would you like to do?"

"I'd like to have some challenging work. I'd like to get out in the plant and work on the process or the equipment. It would be very satisfying, I think, to work on an energy conservation problem or solve a costly maintenance problem."

"I understand how you feel. In fact, that's the kind of work I did when I first came to the company. I'd like to help you to get such a position.

"The first thing you should do, Frank, is to complete your college education and get a degree in either chemistry, chemical engineering, or industrial engineering. I believe you've already completed some college work. Is that right?"

"Yes, it is," Frank replies.

"Our company is growing and undoubtedly will need people in research, development and engineering in the future. Since you have done well in your present position, you would certainly be considered for one of those jobs. Also, the company will assist you with your tuition expenses if the courses you take are those required for you to get a degree in one of those areas."

"That sure sounds good to me, but I can see that it'll take me several years to get that degree since I'll only be able to go to school part-time."

"That's right, but believe me, it will be well worth the effort. I strongly recommend that you do it. Why don't you consult with an advisor at the local university as to what courses you need and how you can enroll for them attending classes at night? Once you're on your way and have planned how you'll get a particular degree, come back to see me. Maybe we can find some ways to increase your responsibilities on your present job.

"You might also think about whether you would want to work toward becoming a supervisor. A supervisor's job would give you valuable experience, and if you do well, it could eventually lead to a higher job in management. I could help you move in that direction by providing you with learning opportunities while you hold your present job."

Reasoning and Principle Involved

When an employee has done a good job and deserves recognition, a manager should see that he or she gets it promptly. Good employees are often lost because management is too slow to take action. Sometimes a simple raise can make an employee feel that the job has more status than believed. Other times, management should help the employee to achieve his or her goal of moving up to a better job with the company.

PROBLEM NUMBER 7

What to say to an employee who complains to you of not receiving a salary increase.

The Situation

Shortly after you had conducted your performance appraisals with your accounting and purchasing section heads, you put through some salary increases for them. As happens in many companies, when the first payroll payment reflecting the increases was made, these increases became known throughout the office. One day after that, Dorothy Hall, section head in advertising came to you complaining that she had not received an increase.

What You Should Say and Some Responses

"Dorothy, I can understand why you're disappointed that you did not receive a salary increase with this month's pay, but . . . .

Dorothy interrupts you to say, "I've been with the company just as long as Sarah, my friend in the accounting department, and she got one. Also, I've been a section head almost as long. Besides, I'm just as hard-working as she is. Why didn't I get an increase?"

"Everything you say is true. However, last year the president of the company decided to stagger the performance appraisal periods of the section heads and assistant managers so that managers would not be burdened with all the reviews at one time. He also had something else in mind. Since salary increases usually follow the reviews, this meant that they would also be smoothed out and not put a drain on accounting and finance all at one time."

Dorothy calms down a bit with your explanation but still is not completely satisfied. "I will be getting an increase then later?" she asks.

"Yes, provided, of course, that you continue to do your usual good job, and the company doesn't suddenly experience financial problems," you say with a smile.

"When will I get it?"

"Since I am now conducting appraisals twice a year, that should be in about six months."

"Well, it doesn't seem fair, but I guess there's nothing I can do about it," Dorothy replies as she leaves.

An Alternate Approach

"Dorothy, several years ago, the company adopted a policy of considering the relationship between responsibilities and compensation. This policy has resulted in an arrangement of all management positions in our company in descending order of their contribution to the company's success.

"Every job, of course, is important to the company and, therefore, so is yours. However, company policy always has been to reward good work and service in each department according to the contribution made by that department to the overall profit and growth of the company. You can understand then, why the Finance Department, for example, has far greater responsibilities than the Shipping and Receiving Department."

"Yes, I can see that," Dorothy comments.

"My superior has told me that I may recommend only certain salary increases at this time, and that I must start with those jobs which are most important to the company. Under this policy, the advertising department positions will be reviewed in about six months. If you continue to do the same good job that you're doing now, I should be able to recommend an increase for you as soon as that is authorized."

Reasoning and Principle Involved

When answering complaints of unfairness in awarding salary increases, managers should point out the differences in both job importance and company policy. In addition, they should be truthful, make no promises they may not be able to keep, relate decisions to positions and not to individuals, and praise wherever this is justified.

PROBLEM NUMBER 8

What to say to an employee who receives less pay than expected after accepting a lower rated job.

The Situation

Your company is presently not selling many products. Management thus decided to shut down part of the production process and reduce the number of people in the department. It was no surprise to the workers then when a layoff list was posted on the bulletin board. Several employees had to decide whether to become unemployed and collect unemployment insurance or, if possible, bump themselves into a lower rated job. Your company's union–management agreement gave employees this option when higher skilled jobs were eliminated. With this choice to make, Mark Holly, a punch press operator, comes to your office to discuss his situation.

What You Should Say and Some Responses

"I guess you've seen the bad news, Mark. Is there anything I can do for you?"

"I sure hope so. Being over 50, I'll probably have a tough time finding another job outside the company. What are my chances of bumping into a lower rated job?"

"Let me check through the roster," you say. After you do this, you say to Mark, "the only job you're eligible for is as a utility worker."

Mark winces and swallows hard. "I've got no choice but to take it. I need a job."

"OK, I'll put through the transfer. You'll be on that job the first of the month, the day after your present job ends."

Mark starts the new job on schedule. He isn't happy with the change but resolves to make the best of it. However, when his first pay on the new job is given to him, he is very much upset. Instead of receiving the top rate for his new classification, he is paid the bottom, or entry level rate which is 75 cents per hour less. He immediately brings his check to you to complain about it.

"I'm sorry if you expected a bigger pay," you say to him. "But you have no previous experience as a utility worker. You have to start out at the bottom of the pay scale for that job like everyone else."

"That's not right. I've got more than 5 years of service with the company."

"As a punch press operator, not a utility man. I'd like to get you more, but that's the way the hourly pay rates are set up."

"I don't think I'm being treated fairly. If I have to, I'll take this to the Labor Department."

"You can do that if you want to, but you won't get any more. If the company went along with someone like you who has no previous experience doing utility work, and paid you the maximum rate your first day on the job, it would disrupt the whole rate structure. It's a completely new job for you, and you'll have to start from scratch.

"If the union takes your case to arbitration, the company will likely win it. The fact that we have a specific clause in the labor agreement covering just such a contingency virtually assures it. The clause specifies that when an employee bumps to a lower rated job, only his or her experience doing that kind of work can be taken into consideration."

Reasoning and Principle Involved

Most union–management contracts in effect today extensively cover conditions and pay contingencies involved with the bumping procedure. Managers and supervisors of hourly employees belonging to the union should be familiar with clauses in the contract covering pay of employees.

Chapter 19

DECISION MAKING

In the following cases, note the many types of decisions that today's managers are required to make, and that when making decisions, they must at the same time provide assurance and confidence that their decisions are appropriate to the circumstances. Notice also, how motivation to action is behind any decision. The skill of making decisions under pressure must be developed if managers are to be effective.

PROBLEM NUMBER 1

What to say to a supervisor about evaluating a probationary employee.

The Situation

When hiring hourly workers at your company, it's the practice to place a new one on probation for one month before making the person a permanent employee. This procedure gives the company time to evaluate the new employee's attitude and performance. It also enables management to decide whether to retain the person or dismiss him or her. Two weeks ago, the company hired Kenneth Starr to fill a vacancy in the Production Department. Supervisor Vern Watson interviewed him and also checked his references before approving the hiring. Today you call Watson to discuss Starr and how he is getting along during his probationary period.

What You Should Say and Some Responses

"Vern, how's your new man, Ken Starr, doing? I believe he's been with us about two weeks now."

"I don't know for sure. While he looks OK and seems to be catching on to the job real well, underneath I have an uneasy feeling about him. I can't help it. I had it from the day that I hired him."

You frown. "You know, I wondered a bit about him shortly after he began work. I thought, perhaps, I was being unfairly prejudiced against him because of his poor personality. But if a guy knows his stuff and does his job, what more can you expect?"

"Not a thing," Vern replies.

"OK, maybe we should stop looking for things wrong with him. He's probably nervous and ill-at-ease on a new job, especially when a supervisor's around. I've known people like that in the past. They feel insecure in the boss's presence. They act shifty and furtive, and can't relax."

Vern is quick to agree. "I know just what you mean."

Another week goes by. Then Vern comes to you to again talk about Starr. "There's still something about Starr that makes me uneasy, and it's bothering Bob Hanson, my assistant, too. We talked about it this morning; he feels the same way. A man should be judged on what he knows and how well he does his job, shouldn't he? I seem to be considering something else in evaluating him."

"You're being influenced by the way you feel—your instincts?"

"Yeah, that's it."

"Instinct is an interesting and fascinating subject. While I try not to let intuition affect my decisions, I have a lot of respect for my instincts.

"For some reason you're unable to put your finger on, you instinctively feel Kenneth Starr is not to be trusted, and your assistant feels the same way. Since your instinct I'm sure has been confirmed in the past, there is a good reason to rely on it."

A perplexed look appears on Vern's face. "So what should I do? Fire him based on my instinct alone? Because I dislike him personally? Because I don't trust him? If he does his job and stays out of trouble, doesn't he deserve the benefit of the doubt?"

You nod. "You're thinking very logically. I agree that no man should be condemned without condemning action on his part or until proved guilty of offenses. Be that as it may, with a new employee, you have a different situation. A man may start on a job and be a model employee for as long as his probationary period lasts. But if he's lacking in character, loyalty and drive, he shows it after he's fixed on the payroll. Getting rid of him then becomes a Herculean task."

"Do you think Starr fits that description?" Vern asks.

"At this time, I don't know. You can't know either. But you're apparently concerned with what your instincts tell you. I'm not saying you should rely completely on them and ignore the facts as you see them. Just don't sell your instincts short."

"Which leaves me what?" Vern asks.

"That's the question, and I admit it's a tough one. By the way, how carefully did you check Starr's references when you hired him?"

"I called his two previous employers. They OK'd him."

"Who did you talk to?"

"The Personnel Department in both cases."

"You might try talking to his immediate supervisors, if you can reach them. If they'll talk to you, you might learn something new. Also, I'd watch Starr as closely as you can the next few days while he's still on probation. See how he works when he thinks he's not being watched by the boss. If he's putting on a probationary-period act, you might spot it.

"If nothing negative turns up by the end of next week, and if you can't prove him guilty of any wrongdoing, he deserves the benefit of the doubt."

Vern does as you suggested and was able to talk to one of Starr's previous supervisors. This fellow was reluctant to say much about him except to say his work was satisfactory. Sensing that the supervisor was holding back, Vern said, "I won't put you on the spot, but I'd appreciate it if you'd answer one question. Would you hire Starr again?"

"No, I would not," the supervisor unwaveringly replied.

The reason for the supervisor's answer became apparent within the next few days, Vern tells you.

"As you suggested, I watched Starr from a distance when he thought he was unobserved. It was like two different guys employed on the same job. Starr was an eager beaver in the presence of supervision. Out of sight of supervision, he was a different person, obviously caring little about the company and about the quality of his workmanship. During these last three weeks, he was interested in only one thing— running out his probationary period in style."

You smile. "Then I guess there's no question about what you are going to do now?" you ask Vern.

"No there isn't, and boy, I certainly feel relieved."

Reasoning and Principle Involved

Instincts often play a big role in helping managers to make good decisions. When managers feel they are right but do not know why, they should question what appears to be facts to the contrary. More often than not, they may avoid making a bad decision.

PROBLEM NUMBER 2

What to say to a supervisor who made a poor decision.

The Situation

In your mail this morning was a report you had never seen before. Titled *Weekly Machine Downtime by Type and Model*, it had been prepared by your supervisor, Ed Tillis, and was comprehensive, indicating that he had put quite a bit of time and effort into it. Wondering what prompted preparation and distribution of the report, you ask Tillis to come to your office.

What You Should Say and Some Responses

"Good morning, Ed. How are you today?"

"Just fine, but busy as usual." Ed looks at you to learn why you wanted to see him.

You pick up the new report from your desk and read the title aloud. "Quite an impressive report," you say. "Why was this issued?"

Ed shifts uneasily in his chair. "Well, last week the Manager of Maintenance, Pete Fisher, came to me and said that he could probably save the company quite a bit of money if he knew which production machines were down the most for maintenance and repairs. He could assign his maintenance engineers to work on those machines first."

You nod to indicate you understand. "But this report isn't something you put out in a hurry."

"No, it isn't. In fact, this first one took me almost three hours. But after doing it a few times, I'll probably be able to get it out in two and a half hours or less."

"Two and a half hours, once a week?" you ask Ed.

"Yep," Ed replies.

"And just like that you agreed to do this for Pete Fisher?"

"No. I first told him I couldn't do it, that there was too much work involved."

"I see. But he insisted so much that you had to comply?"

Ed squirms before replying. "No, it wasn't like that. Pete said he wasn't putting pressure on me to prepare the report. But he asked me to think about it. He said the information was very important to him."

"Oh, I'm sure it is, or he wouldn't have asked for it. What made you decide to go along with him?"

Ed appears more at ease. "I figured I should cooperate, even if it would be a lot of work. You know, it's easy to say you don't have the time to do something. But as you yourself have said, if you really want to do something, you'll find the time to do it."

You smile. "I guess you've got me there, Ed. I can't deny saying that, but gosh, you're sharp enough to know that for every rule, there's another one that says just the opposite. It's true that if you want to do something, you can almost always make the time. Contrarily, knowing when to say no sometimes makes more sense than saying yes and doing an excellent job."

"Then you feel that . . . ."

"Think it out yourself. Pete Fisher asks for information he wants to use in assigning work to his engineers. Your first reaction is that agreeing to give it to him will be time consuming and costly. Still, you decide to do it. Why?"

"Like I said," Ed begins to reply, but hesitates.

"You didn't want to give Pete the idea you didn't want to cooperate. I can't find fault with you for that. But relations with other members of the company are rarely that simple. I'd be the last one to undervalue the importance of cooperation and teamwork. However, I don't care what rule you want to follow, or what promise you propose, to each I would add: *where practical and reasonable.* That's the point you overlooked. I acknowledge that you agreed to prepare this report with the best of intentions. But was that a practical and reasonable decision?

"I don't think you know, because you didn't give it enough thought, didn't take the time to find out. Had you investigated and checked it out thoroughly, you would have found that, however much Pete wants that report, he doesn't need it weekly. Once a month would be enough. If you had looked further into the situation, you might have learned that while preparing the report is time consuming and costly for your department, the data processing department could run it off with very little effort and at a fraction of the cost. Finally, if you checked on who needs the report in advance, you would have learned that the only person who can work with that data is Pete Fisher. You could have eliminated the time it takes to collate and distribute those extra copies, not to mention the cost of the paper."

Ed appears both embarrassed and stressed. He has nothing to say.

"OK, Ed, I guess I've been pretty rough with you. After all, you had the best intentions. I hope, however, you learn from this experience that it's usually easier to say yes than no. What you should do in the future, before you agree to do something that will cost you money, time, or materials, is to ask yourself some basic questions such as: How much will this cost? Will I have to sacrifice something as a result? What will happen if I refuse? Can someone else do this more efficiently or economically than me?"

Reasoning and Principle Involved

Too many managerial decisions are made where emotion rather than reason dictates. Although there are times when human feelings are an important decision factor, in running a department or company, ignoring logic and reason can be a serious mistake.

PROBLEM NUMBER 3

What to say to a supervisor about how to be decisive in carrying out responsibilities.

The Situation

Recently you partially overhead a conversation between your supervisor, Rich Burton, and an electrician, Tom Shaw. Earlier, you had learned that one of the production machines in the plant was performing erratically. Wanting to see for yourself, you went to the machine to observe its operation. When you arrived, Burton was talking to Shaw about the machine but had difficulty in telling him what to do. Not wishing to interfere, you left the area, making a mental note to talk to Burton later in the day. After lunch, you told him you'd like to talk to him a few minutes in your office.

What You Should Say and Some Responses

"Rich, I noticed that the Acme machine was periodically stopping in the middle of a cycle this morning. Did you find out what was wrong and get it corrected?"

"Yes, I did, but it took quite a while to discover the problem."

"What was it?"

"A relay in one of the control circuits was sticking. We did not find it right away."

"I thought it was standard practice with such a malfunction of that machine to look at the control circuits first."

Rich's face reddens. "Yeah, that's right. I couldn't make up my mind what to do, but when Tom said he couldn't find anything wrong with the programmer, I finally remembered."

"Rich, I've noticed that you're a bit unsure of yourself in certain situations. On occasion, you are not decisive when giving your people jobs to do and instructing them on how to handle a problem. You can learn to be more definite. Once you get into the swing of it, you'll find it easy to hold to the pattern.

"It pays to make minor decisions promptly in your normal daily routine. By disposing of them as quickly as possible, you will have more time to think about and work on problems that are major and more important."

"I guess that's pretty obvious," Rich comments.

"Try to be solid and firm when you make a decision. Don't be half-sure or leave any doubt of your intentions. I don't know whether you realize it or not, but workers prefer to work for a supervisor who knows what he's talking about and is sure he's making the right decision."

"I sort of sensed that with Tom," Rich says.

"Another thing, forget the alternatives once you make a decision. Don't waste time thinking about what you could or should have done. Also, put aside any thoughts that you might make a mistake. Such thinking weakens your determination to be decisive.

"Lastly, once you make a decision, carry it out. Until you take action, nothing happens and you aren't decisive."

Reasoning and Principle Involved

Reluctance to make decisions can seriously handicap managers and supervisors. People on the job expect their leaders to be decisive and in control. Workers become fearful, uneasy, and even unwilling to proceed when they sense that their supervisor is unsure of what direction to go or what move to make. A decisive leader commands respect and gets action.

PROBLEM NUMBER 4

What to say to an employee who procrastinates in reporting on his work.

The Situation

Dennis Shaw is a technician in the Development Department of a paint company where you are manager of the department. You made him responsible for testing new materials, diagnosing the cause of paint failures, testing competitive products, and periodically updating the department files. While Shaw is generally doing a good job, he has been putting off the writing of test and progress reports and failure analyses. Since this is one of the most important of his duties, you ask him to come to your office to talk about it.

What You Should Say and Some Responses

"Dennis, I haven't received a test report from you in more than two weeks. Are you having problems with your test work?"

Dennis smiles weakly. "No, I just haven't got around to writing them up. Although I've finished the tests on five or six different samples, it seems that something more important to do keeps coming up."

"What have you found to be more important?"

"Well, ah, oh," Dennis stammers. "I received some samples of competitor's products last week, and I figured I'd better get started on those tests."

You nod. "Yes, those tests are very important, but that does not mean you couldn't have reported on work you did more than a week ago. Am I right on that?"

"I guess so."

"Dennis, I know you don't enjoy the reporting and documenting part of your job. Many technicians, chemists and engineers don't like the writing and reporting work they are required to do. But when you don't keep up with those duties, you're simply procrastinating. You've got to write those reports sooner or later.

"People most frequently succumb to procrastination when they are faced with an unpleasant task or a difficult decision. Often a job seems more unpleasant too, when they are not convinced of the need for doing it."

"Oh, that's not my problem. I know that documenting and writing reports is important and has to be done. It's just that I don't like to write. Maybe it's because it's difficult for me."

"The best way to overcome procrastination, Dennis, is to tackle the difficult jobs when you are at your best—when your mind and body are fresh. Then go after the jobs with determination until you get them done. In your case, I'd suggest you do those reports first thing in the morning, before you get into what you feel is more interesting work.

"While recognizing that you are procrastinating is a prerequisite to overcoming it, another way is to promise someone you'll handle a matter within a specified time. When you have committed yourself, it is very difficult not to carry out your promise. Your conscience just won't let you put the job off if you know someone is waiting for you to act."

"I guess I should do that with those reports. I'll try to finish them tomorrow and the next day."

"Good! Another thing, if you are deferring several duties or jobs, decide that you'll handle the most urgent one first, and then do one or more a day until you finish them. With that approach, you'll get a feeling of relief as well as satisfaction at each completion.

"Dennis, once you have overcome a procrastination problem, it is much easier to avoid it in the future. You will have demonstrated to yourself that you are strong-willed and capable of doing what must be done."

Reasoning and Principle Involved

Procrastination is the biggest roadblock to achieving goals and getting jobs done. Since everyone procrastinates to some degree, we must learn how to overcome it if we are to be efficient and productive. Managers can help matters by knowing what to do when subordinates fall victim to procrastination.

PROBLEM NUMBER 5

What to say to a first–time manager about what factors should be considered when making decisions.

The Situation

Although your new office manager, Paula Connors, has been with the company more than eight years, she has been office manager for only three months. However, since her previous jobs were as receptionist, typist and secretary to a vice-president, she is well versed in office procedures. But these positions apparently were of little help to her with the human relations problems she faced last week. Paula comes to you early Monday morning, wanting to talk about her problems.

What You Should Say and Some Responses

"Do you have a few minutes so we can talk?" Paula asks you.

"Yes I do. Have a seat, Paula, and I'll close the door so we won't be interrupted."

"I had a rough time last week, and I don't know whether I handled my problems and responsibilities as well as I should have. I've been thinking about this over the weekend, and felt that I'd better talk to you today."

"I'm glad you came to me. I feel you're doing an excellent job, but I know you don't have a lot of experience as a manager. What problems did you have last week?"

"Well, to begin with, two of the girls in the typing pool have been feuding. Things came to a head last week and I had to step in and try to straighten matters out. Then I had a discipline problem to handle with a mail clerk. Also, I completed a study and made some recommendations on procuring new office equipment. I mailed you that report on Friday. Now the Engineering Department wants to know if I can give up some of the office space for a new department which they want to put in.

"It seems that I'm continually being asked to make important decisions, and many times I'm not sure I'm making the right ones. When I look back at the other jobs I had before I became office manager, I didn't have nearly as many problems to handle."

You smile and nod. "I understand what you're saying, but I'm sure that you're going to do all right. Management felt that you had the capabilities to make a good office manager when you were offered this job. With more experience, the problems which you are facing now and will face in the future will not seem so formidable. Also, right now I can tell you a few things about making decisions that should be helpful and will probably make your job easier.

"Experienced managers know that many factors must be considered when making a decision, especially if it is comprehensive. They have learned that the soundness of their decisions depends on whether they have given the proper weight to each of the factors they have considered. You can be more sure of making a good decision if you are careful to review what you decided to do before you act. Answering some questions about the decision you're about to make is a good way to do this.

"For example, you should make sure your decision is compatible with company rules and regulations. Did you consider timing and is it optimum? Is your decision based on experience and history? Does it deviate from past practice?

"Did authorized and interested personnel participate in helping you make the decision? Are they in agreement? If there are several steps to be taken, are they in the right order? Will the expected results of the decision be acceptable to those who must carry it out?"

"My gosh," Paula says, "there certainly are a lot of things to think about."

"Yes, there are," you say. "To go on, you must be especially careful in making disciplinary decisions. Determine, for instance, if a particular decision would be good as a general rule for everyone, even yourself. Also, would you make a certain decision if you knew it would be publicized around the company? Would you be willing to defend the decision in another department?"

"That's certainly interesting and helpful. You know, I worry about making a bad decision. What are the causes of bad decisions?"

"I think the best way to answer that is to consider what's involved in making decisions. You can easily get yourself in trouble with making decisions if you're not careful. Insufficient or poor information to work with, for example, leads to guessing—you may guess wrong. Bad information leads to false conclusions, so you decide wrongly.

"Sometimes you may not have enough time. If you had more time to get facts and consider them, you could increase your chance to make a wise decision. Fear of the situation and the consequence of the decision is another cause, because if you are scared and lack confidence, your decisions may be adversely affected.

"You might be concerned with risk, and be overcautious when the risk is great. Not enough authority can also be a problem. Responsibility without authority leads to weak, unenforceable decisions. Similarly, if you consider a matter not serious or important, you may not give it enough attention or ignore it entirely."

Reasoning and Principle Involved

Knowing when and how decisions should be made is basic to the art of decision making. But managers must also be aware of the many factors which influence decisions and their relative importance. Understanding what's involved in making decisions is of value to managers because it lessens the pressure on them when they must make them. It also enables them to avoid making poor decisions.

Chapter 20

STANDARDS

In the following situations, note how valuable standards are to management as a means of controlling quality and quantity. Effective managers work with subordinates to help them meet standards thus assuring that costs are minimized. Notice also that most employees want and even like standards because they need something with which to measure and compare their performance on the job.

PROBLEM NUMBER 1

What to say to a supervisor whose only interest is getting the work out on or ahead of schedule.

The Situation

Norman Rogers is presently the youngest supervisor you have in the Production Department. Hard working, sharp and quick, he is fairly independent and likes to handle things on his own. Rumors are, however, that he's not getting along with some of his people. The productivity rating of his section has declined in the last few months, and two of his people have requested transfers out of the section. When this month's production report showed no improvement in the section's rating, you decide to make a personal visit to his office without calling him in advance.

What You Should Say and Some Responses

When you approach Norman's desk, you find him studying the production report. "Good morning, Norman. What do you think of the figures?"

"Oh, hi, I didn't see you coming," he says with a smile. Then, sobering up, "I think you know the answer to that one as well as I do. To tell you the truth, these figures keep getting worse, and I don't know why. I've been busting my ass to get them up and not having any success."

"Do you have any idea what's wrong?"

"No, not a one. When I took this job, I decided to put everything I had into it, keep everybody hopping, and grind out the production in a minimum of time. I figured I couldn't go wrong. Do you see anything wrong with that?"

"No, at least generally speaking."

"OK, so that's what I've been trying to do. Keep everyone on the ball, keep all the operations running, and keep machine downtime to a minimum. I figured that if I could get that done, the section rating and productivity of the workers couldn't help but go up. But for one reason or another, it doesn't seem to work."

You nod thoughtfully. Then after a few seconds you say, "I see that Jim Smith and Linda Raber have asked for transfers."

"Yeah, that's right."

"Did they say why they wanted to leave the section?"

"No, all they said to me was that they wanted to try a different job."

"Maybe if I talked to them, with your permission, I could find out something. They might tell me something they wouldn't tell you."

"That's OK with me."

"All right, I'll give it a try, and let you know if I come up with something startling or revealing."

Although Smith and Raber have applied for transfers, both are still working in the section. When you talk with Smith, he is nervous and ill at ease. But after you assure him that you don't want to put him or anyone else on the spot, and that you are just trying to help, he settles down. He tells you then that he knows that Norman is trying to make the section look good, but he is going about it the wrong way. Your conversation with Raber is similar but goes much easier in that persuading her to open up is no problem. After Raber substantiates her co-worker's report, you see Norman again to tell him what you have learned.

"Norman, both Smith and Raber feel that you're interested only in getting the work out on schedule or ahead of schedule. They think you don't really understand the close attention to detail required in the section's operations. They claim that trying to speed up the process by taking shortcuts, neglecting quality checks, and bypassing control steps results in a lot of errors and rework. This causes the productivity of the workers to be low, and makes the section look bad in the eyes of management."

Norman listens intently while you are talking. Sensing that you have finished, he asks, "What do you think I should do?"

"To start, I agree with your thinking that a manager's primary responsibility should be with results and not the detailed steps involved with each job. But even though you need not be concerned with such details, you have to know enough about each project and job to set realistic standards on both quality and quantity of what is being produced. You should also know what it takes to meet those standards.

"If you tried to expedite jobs and projects without such knowledge, you would probably fail and worse, you would also lose the respect of your people.

"I sense this is what has caused Smith and Raber to request transfers. I feel sure that it has been the major reason for the drop in productivity of your people."

Reasoning and Principle Involved

Pushing people to do the work they should be doing after studying to prove they are capable of accomplishing it is one thing—pushing them without this determination and being unreasonable about it is another. The former procedure leads to economical and efficient operations, the latter leads to waste and inefficiency.

PROBLEM NUMBER 2

What to say to a supervisor who is seemingly unable to efficiently use her time.

The Situation

Jill Kemp is a conscientious and hard-working supervisor. An attractive woman, she began working for the company in the office. But after a few years, she transferred to the Production Department because she felt plant work offered better opportunities for a woman. Recently you learned that she is working overtime almost every night. Since excessive supervisory overtime is a symptom of inefficient management of one's time, you decide to ask her why she finds it necessary to work that kind of schedule.

What You Should Say and Some Responses

"Hi, Jill. How are you today?"
Jill looks up from her desk where she has been working on time

cards and attendance records. Her in basket nearby is full with memos, letters, work schedules, reports and various forms. "Oh, good morning," she says. "I'm fine. What can I do for you?"

"I hear you're one of the busiest people in the company," you say with a smile. "I'd like to help you become less busy if I can."

A sign of anxiety comes to Jill's face. "I always can use some help, but your offer worries me. Are you unhappy with the job I've been doing?"

"No, not at all. I think you're doing a good job, and I have no complaints."

"Then what . . . ?"

"I'm concerned that you're putting in too much overtime."

"I'm sorry, but that can't be helped. I ask my people to work overtime as little as possible, but sometimes I have no other choice. We're overloaded with work and the day just isn't long enough."

"I'm not referring to assigned overtime," you say. "What concerns me is the long hours you've been putting in yourself, and coming into the plant on Saturdays too."

"Oh. Well, sometimes I wish I didn't have to work all those hours, but the work continues to pile up. I keep telling myself that when I become more familiar with the job and get more organized, things will start to ease up. But there's no sign of that happening yet."

"I can't help wondering if you're doing more than is necessary because you're the first woman supervisor in the Production Department, and you're going all out to succeed."

Jill smiles. "I suppose that could have something to do with it. Still, the work's there and it has to be done. If I don't work those extra hours, I'll get further and further behind. That would make matters worse than they presently are."

"My boss believes that everyone, supervisors included, should be on a standard and reasonable schedule, that it's not good for the individual or the company to work the kind of hours you've been putting in. I feel the same way."

Jill has a doubting look on her face. "I wish I knew a way to avoid it."

"That's what I'm here for, to help you find the way. How about telling me about your workload. Can I see your schedule?"

Jill hesitates. "I don't have a schedule. I just have a list I keep adding to, but I never get to the point where I've crossed everything off. I've written so many Repair Orders in the past month that the maintenance people shudder everytime they see me coming. It's getting to the point where I can't wait for them to make an adjustment or a repair so I go out and try to do it myself."

As Jill was speaking, a machine operator came to her saying, "Jill,

I'm having trouble with the small punch machine; it's holding up the Superior order."

Jill turns to you. "See what I mean? This is a top-priority job. I'll have to take a look at it."

"May I see that list while you're gone?"

"Sure." She takes the list from a pocket of her work uniform and hands it to you.

You read the list noting items which range from a variety of machine and production reports due to machine adjustments and changing of tolerances for special orders that should be made. When Jill returns, she tells you that the punch machine malfunction problem is going to take longer than she had expected. "Can we talk again some other time?" she asks.

"Of course."

However, when you call several times in the next few days, each time she begs off, saying she is too busy with rush jobs to spare the time. Finally, you say, "Why don't we set up a fixed appointment for tomorrow no matter how busy you are? I really think I can help you."

"Very well," Jill replies.

This time Jill keeps the appointment. You review her work with her, a single job at a time, listing whatever she can remember to tell you about the way she spent her time during the past week. When the list amounts to two pages, you stop to show her your notes.

"Jill, the jobs that I X'ed are ones properly suited for a supervisor to handle. They are jobs that involve planning or managerial thought, or reports of a confidential nature that can't be given to line employees. All the other items are jobs which, in my opinion, you shouldn't be doing at all; they are jobs you should delegate to your people.

"When someone comes to you with a problem, instead of telling the person what has to be done, you do the work for him or her. Other jobs aren't supervisory jobs at all. They're the kind of jobs you should be training others to do."

"What you're saying is that I should be delegating more work and authority."

"Right! And the sooner you get started, the better. I'll be checking back with you in a few days, and I'll want a report from you on your progress on training your people. Also, I'd like to have you tell me what jobs you've delegated since our talk today."

Reasoning and Principle Involved

Although delegation is at the same time the most difficult and the most rewarding of supervisory skills, no manager can ever consider himself or herself successful until it is faithfully practiced. Skill in delegating can be the deciding factor in determining whether a manager can handle more responsibility and a bigger job.

PROBLEM NUMBER 3

What to say to a supervisor about monitoring subordinates' actual performance against their expected performance.

The Situation

You are concerned about the operation and output of the newly created Assembly Department in your company. Operating costs have been increasing over the past few months, and the department has failed to meet its production schedule several times. Harold Vincent is the supervisor of the department; he has about 20 people who perform many operations in making several products. Vincent has been the supervisor only six months, but he's generally well-liked by the workers having previously been a group leader in a nearby department. You go to Harold's office to talk to him about the department's problems.

What You Should Say and Some Responses

Harold is busy at his desk as you approach. An anxious look appears on his face when he sees you.

"Don't look so grim, Harold. I'm sure things aren't that bad."

"Yes they are," he replies. "You've seen the latest production report, I'm sure."

"Yes, I have, and I'm not going to pass those bad figures off as unimportant by trying to say you don't have a serious problem on your hands. You do. But maybe we can talk about it and come up with an answer."

"That would suit me just fine. Where do we start?"

"First, do you have any idea why your operating costs are going up and why your people haven't been able to consistently meet production quotas?"

"Those are two big questions. As far as I can see, your people seem to be doing their jobs, and we haven't had any absentee problems."

"What about production rates? What kind of standards do you have set up for the department?"

"Standards?" Harold seems mystified by the word.

"That's right. Guidelines and times to perform operations so that you can periodically monitor actual performance against expected performance."

"Oh, I see; well, uh, I pretty well know what kind of results and output to expect from experience and from history."

You nod. "Experience is important, but how do you use it to establish your standards?"

"I'm not sure I know what you mean."

"How do you know that the standards based on experience or history are accurate and practical or realistic?"

"Instinct. I can tell instinctively who's doing a good job and who's goofing off."

"While I wouldn't disregard instinct, on what do you base your conclusions?"

"As I see it, every department in the company consists of three types of employees. There are employees who are conscientious and do the best possible job they can, employees who do an average job, and employees who goof off every chance they get."

"Probably true," you say.

"I figure that the good employees more or less set the standards you'd like to have and maintain in the department. It's the poor and average people you have to watch and make sure they're doing their job. If you can get them to stay at their workplaces and machines, and keep busy, you'll have it made."

"So far as standards are concerned then, they're what you know and think they should be."

Harold moves uneasily in his chair before answering. "Yeah, I suppose that's right."

"So there are no written standards?"

"I've never had time to put such stuff in writing. I've been too busy with other things."

"How do your people know what the standards are?" you persist. "Do you let them know how much work you expect them to do and what results are unacceptable?"

Harold clearly shows he is nervous with your questioning. "I think they know that. After all, when a person goofs off and does not apply himself, he certainly knows it."

Harold then glances at his watch and says, "Can we continue this later in the day or tomorrow? An order we're running out there is behind schedule and I'm worried about getting it shipped today."

"Sure, Harold. Say, would you mind if I just browse around the department while I'm here? I might see something or get some ideas."

"Do I mind? Not at all. Go ahead."

"OK. I'll let you know if I learn anything."

Although you already thought you knew why operating costs were rising in the department, this might be an opportune time to confirm it. You go to a file containing drawings and reports, and remove one of the folders to examine its contents. Presumably, as far as anyone seeing you could surmise, you are looking for something. Actually, from the area of the file, you have a good vantage point to observe most of the activities in the department without appearing too obvious and putting people on their guard. What you see is both interesting and instructive.

Generally, the work pace is slow with many employees talking to each other while they work. But they are paying more attention to what they are saying than to what they are doing. Just as bad, some of the group leaders are failing to hold down the talkers, and even talking more than the workers they are supposed to be supervising.

Just before you decide to return to your office, you notice that Harold has begun working at a bench along with two other workers. A short while later, you phone Harold to tell him you will be coming to see him first thing in the morning.

As you enter his office the next day, Harold perks up. "Hey, did you latch on to something yesterday? Is there hope for me yet?"

"There's always hope, Harold, but it's all up to you. What it comes down to, I think, is that you may get away with supervising a few workers in an unplanned way and without guidelines and standards to help you keep control, but if you try this with quite a few workers or most of the department, you're almost certain to fail.

"Your problem is you're so busy putting out fires, you've got little time to figure out ways to prevent them. On top of that, you have no time to actually supervise your people. Most of them are pretty much left on their own.

"I'm setting up a meeting for you with the Methods Department of the company on Thursday. The objective of this meeting is to plan and adopt a procedure for setting standards for your department to help you and your people to use your time more productively."

Reasoning and Principle Involved

When leaders mismanage their time and their people's as well, they are committing one of the most serious and most common supervisory mistakes. Adopting and enforcing standards is one of the first steps which should be taken to handle this problem.

PROBLEM NUMBER 4

What to say to a new employee on why the company has established standards covering quality and quantity of the work performed.

The Situation

A new product your company recently began to manufacture is selling beyond expectations requiring that the company hire additional people to make it. Although all new hirees are trained for the work they will be doing, sometimes one or two people do not completely understand why the company has set standards for both the quality and quantity of their performance. Such is the case with Jack Thompson, a young fellow who had dropped out of school but still met the job's requirements and was hired. After a few days on the job, he comes to you with some questions.

What You Should Say and Some Responses

"How's the job going, Jack?"

"Good! I've been turning out more gizmos every day, but I don't completely understand a couple of things the trainer talked about last week."

"What didn't you understand?"

"Well, first of all, he said it was important that each employee meet the standards set up for his job. What did he mean by that?"

"In some companies, standards are referred to as specifications. They include and consist of levels of quality and quantity set for the various manufacturing procedures. A quality standard, for example, might cover the weight, size or appearance of the product or the workmanship of the employees. A quantity standard often refers to the time it takes you to perform a certain job or make a particular product."

"I see. I can understand the need for a quality standard, but why is a quantity standard necessary?"

"There are several reasons for quantity standards. For one thing, people on the job want to measure their performance against a mark or level. If people feel there are no standards, then they will set their own because they can't be comfortable without some means of pacing themselves. Of course, this applies to both quality and quantity of performance.

"When people are left to set their own quality and pace level, trouble develops because the self-chosen standards will vary from person to person. Depending on the person and the requirements of the work group, the standards can be too tight or too lax, resulting in conflicts. This can cause more trouble than it takes for the company to set standards and insist that they be met."

"I see," Jack says slowly. Then after thinking a bit, "You are saying that the company is using standards as a means of control. Right?"

"Right! Control of product quality would be difficult if not impossible without them. So would planning and scheduling in the case of quantity standards. One of my job responsibilities is to check for deviations from the standards, determine the reasons for the variances, and correct them."

Reasoning and Principle Involved

All companies must establish standards on quality and quantity of their products or service as a means of control. Supervisors and managers play major roles in seeing that employees meet the standards.

PROBLEM NUMBER 5

What to say to a supervisor who is too easygoing and permissive with employees.

The Situation

Rudy Underwood, newly appointed supervisor of Department C, is noted for his friendly, helpful manner in working with employees. When a mistake is made or an instruction is misinterpreted, he points it out to the employee involved, but goes to great lengths not to embarrass the person or make a big deal out of it. However, an excessive number of rejects and amount of waste have also been created in Department C in recent months. Fearing that there may be a connection between Underwood's permissive manner of supervising and the material loss, you send your assistant to the department to learn if this is true. After your assistant reports his findings which confirm your fears, you visit Underwood to talk to him about it.

What You Should Say and Some Responses

Underwood is working at his desk when you arrive. He looks up with a smile. "Hi, what can I do you for?"

"Hi, Rudy. A couple days ago, I noticed in the Plant Operations Report that your department is leading all others in the amount of waste generated. Do you have an explanation for all the rejects?"

Rudy's face clouds and he becomes very serious. "No, I really don't. Those darned rejects have been bugging me, too."

"We've got to get to the cause of the problem, Rudy, because those rejects are seriously affecting the profitability of your operations. If I can help, I'd be glad to."

"Thanks, but I don't know where to look and how to get started."

"Maybe we can work on that together. As far as you can determine, would you say that some of your people, say, one or two, make more mistakes than the others?"

Rudy thinks a bit. "Yeah, I suppose so. There are always some people who make more errors than others, but not to a high degree. It seems to vary from month to month. I don't know if it really means anything."

"Let's take last month. According to the report, your rejects for that month are higher than ever before."

"That's right. But they wouldn't have been that bad if not for the Acme order. Gus Johnson worked on it, running it on one of the automatic punch machines. He made a mistake in centering the pieces and ran scrap for more than a half hour."

You nod. "I can see how that would really hurt. Anything else?"

"Yeah. Elaine Mazur fouled up a special order. She read the specs wrong and made the base plates too small on an assembly. About 50 pieces were run before one of the inspectors discovered the error."

"Shouldn't Elaine have spotted that on her own instead of relying on an inspector to do it?"

"You're absolutely right! She was busy looking at the next job she had to do while the machine was running. It's a mistake that she won't make again, I can tell you that."

You nod. "Rudy, before coming to see you, I asked my assistant to confirm last month's reject figures. He had no trouble in doing that since everyone in your department was aware of the two incidents you just mentioned. He said that both Gus and Elaine had trouble in setting up their machines, and they were also confused with the specifications. Of course, that doesn't excuse them from checking the pieces they were making. But both knew that you were very tolerant of mistakes and misjudgments, and that you encourage people to go it on their own.

"My feeling is that you're inclined to go overboard in permitting employees to operate independently and learn on their own, even if they make some bad mistakes in doing so. While I am a strong believer in seeing errors as opportunities to learn, even the most worthwhile practice and philosophy can be overdone.

"Rudy, in my opinion, you should be checking the various operations in your department more closely. Good as self-improvement and self-development may be, supervisory guidance and assistance can be even more beneficial.

"It's also important to know your people well. You have to know their weaknesses and their strengths, their failings and their capabilities. Had you known Gus Johnson and Elaine Mazur better, it's likely those rejects would have been avoided. You would have helped Gus in setting up his machine and Elaine in understanding the specifications. And you would have made sure they both checked their work."

Reasoning and Principle Involved

If some managers feel that they should be easygoing and permissive with the performance of employees, they should realize that needless mistakes can be costly. While mistakes may be viewed as part of the learning experience, other ways of learning do not have such drawbacks.

PROBLEM NUMBER 6

What to say to a foreman who adheres too closely to the rules.

The Situation

Charley Parker, foreman in the Repair Department, is getting the reputation of being unfair and too critical of the people who work for him. Hard-working and serious-minded, he adheres so closely to the rules that it apparently never occurs to him to stretch or even break one on occasion when a situation warrants it. As a result, he is not especially popular in the department. Feeling that Parker's attitude and actions may be responsible for the department's recent poor performance, you ask him to come to your office to discuss the problem.

What You Should Say and Some Responses

"How are you doing, Charley?"

"OK, I guess." But Charley's face is a cross between sour and anxious.

"I asked you to come in so we could talk about how your people are doing. I've been reading the statistics on your department, and some of the figures don't look good. I see you're working a lot of overtime, and I guess that's because attendance is bad. But even with the overtime, your backlog of repair jobs continues to rise."

"Yeah, it's not a pretty picture. These guys simply have me buffaloed. I guess when you boil it down, it's a matter of motivation and morale."

"It usually is," you say. Then you wait for Charley to continue.

"You know, sometimes I think I've got a bunch of cold and unfriendly people working for me."

"Maybe you feel that way because you're cold and unfriendly to them. Coldness is usually a symptom of poor morale, and it's often accompanied by poor cooperation and a lack of teamwork."

"I'm certainly not getting much of either of those."

"Could that be because you're a tough disciplinarian?"

"I don't know. I think I'm firm but fair, but I believe in being tough. In my opinion, permissiveness can make a department's operations sloppy and inefficient. I believe discipline where warranted should be reasonably harsh and equal for everyone at fault."

"Charley, when I was talking to one of the Personnel Department people last week, she mentioned that you had suspended two of your people recently."

"That's right. Randy Turner for absenteeism and John Miller for being careless."

"I talked to both of those people shortly afterwards. Both of them resented the discipline. News like that gets around fast, and one of them even complained to me.

"Randy told me his poor attendance during one month couldn't be helped. His wife suddenly had to have major surgery, and he was needed at home both before and after to take care of the children when he was unable to make other arrangements. He also told me that prior to that problem, he had a better than average attendance record.

"When I talked to John about his suspension, he was quite upset. He said he was not a careless person. He said also that the expensive tool he damaged while making a repair was an accident that could have happened to anyone. He had never before been careless with either tools or equipment."

Charley quickly defends his actions by showing you the company manual covering rules and regulations for employees. The manual states that employees are subject to discipline for various infractions including poor attendance and carelessness.

"But do you think you should literally apply that regulation to everyone?" you ask Charley. "Randy and John are both better than average employees with good records."

Charley shows he is embarrassed. "No, I guess not."

"Charley, I want you to do some serious thinking about what we've been talking about. Equal discipline and fair-mindedness don't necessarily mean that the same punishment should be applied for an offense regardless of who commits it. As I see it, the company manual is best used as a set of guidelines and not "The Bible," if you know what I mean."

Reasoning and Principle Involved

Managers must be flexible when enforcing rules and imposing discipline on subordinates. Each incident and infraction should be considered separately. Circumstances vary and subordinates are different in their motives and deeds. If managers are closed-minded and unfair, they may turn off their people. This could result in much more serious misbehavior on their part.

Chapter 21

COMPLAINTS AND GRIEVANCES

In the following situations, note how managers must be patient with people when answering complaints and grievances. Also, they should try to handle such matters as promptly as possible since complaints almost always are serious matters to those who make them. Notice also that knowledge of the union–management agreement as it applies to the grievance procedure is of invaluable help to managers in settling disputes.

PROBLEM NUMBER 1

What to say to the supervisor who complains of being treated unfairly because he wasn't promoted.

The Situation

When a middle level managerial vacancy occurred recently in your company, you felt that either one of two of your subordinates were qualified to fill the position. One of them, Bruce Thompson, had been a supervisor in the company for eight years. The other, Clarence Jones, had been one for five years. After considerable study, you promoted Clarence to the job. When Bruce learned that he didn't get the job, he came to your office to complain about it.

What You Should Say and Some Responses

As Bruce enters your office, you can tell he is very unhappy by the look on his face. "I just heard that Clarence got the new manager's job. I've been around here longer than Clarence, and I'm better qualified for the job than he is. I think I've been treated unfairly."

"Bruce, I want you to know I feel you've done an excellent job for the company. It took me a long time to make the decision to give Clarence the job, particularly since I was aware that you have more service with the company than he does."

"Then why didn't I get the job?"

"I went over both of your records. Clarence has more diversified experience in that he was a supervisor in Department B before he came to our department. In addition, he impressed me with how he helped the company sell the computer to the employees when we brought it in last year. For those reasons, I felt he was better qualified for the job.

"If you continue to do a good job for the company, I'm sure that your chance for a better position will come. Our company is growing and expanding. There will continually be other managerial openings.

"I don't want you to feel you've been treated unfairly, Bruce. In my opinion, you definitely have not been. If you do not agree with me on this, I insist that you continue to do your job to the best of your ability. Also, I do not want you to tell anybody else that you were treated unfairly."

Reasoning and Principle Involved

Managers must always make employees aware that they have not been treated unfairly when they receive such complaints. But first they must analyze the assertion of such treatment and ascertain it to be incorrect. Following that, managers must make it clear they will not tolerate unjustified charges of unfairness.

PROBLEM NUMBER 2

What to say to an employee who threatens you with a grievance.

The Situation

Last week you issued a formal warning notice to Carl Dulles for poor attendance. Dulles, one of your employees, was having personal problems at home. He had discussed them with you and also assured you that the situation would be corrected. Ordinarily, since he already had been orally warned about his lateness, he'd be subject to a two-day suspension, but you didn't consider his case a common one. For one thing there had been legitimate hardship involved. For another, his performance and work attitude were excellent, and he had an outstanding record for years. Another of your people, Joe Toth, had a lateness record just as bad as Dulles. However, Toth was a marginal employee, at best, with a poor work and social attitude. He had a reputation as a troublemaker, and you had issued two letters to him in recent months for horseplay and fighting on the job. Today, Toth is late again. You lead him to your office to talk to him.

What You Should Say and Some Responses

"Joe, this is the third time this month you've been late. Why can't you get here on time?"

"What's the big deal? I get docked for the time, don't I?"

"Yes, you do. But I can't handle work assignments efficiently if I don't know whether you're going to be here or not. Also, there's too much lost time involved in finding work for you when you are late."

"Well, I'll try to improve. I was out late last night and I didn't hear the alarm go off this morning."

However, after being on time for three days, Toth again comes in an hour late. This time, you issue a two-day suspension notice along with a warning letter stating that if the lateness continued, it would lead to dismissal. Ten minutes after you give Toth the notice, he comes to your office accompanied by Don Smith, his union representative.

"What's up?" you ask them.

"Plenty," Don replies. "Joe wants to know how come he gets a two-day suspension for lateness, and Carl Dulles gets off without any penalty?"

"Dulles didn't get off without any penalty. He was given an official warning notice that's now on his personnel record."

"Big deal," Joe replies. "A warning notice doesn't cost a guy money. How come I didn't get that instead of the two-day suspension? I can't afford to lose that much money."

"You should have thought of that all those days when you showed up late to work."

"I thought you'd say that. But what about Dulles? He's been late just as much as I have. Why should I get a suspension when all he gets is a warning? I thought discipline was supposed to be equal around this place."

"It's supposed to apply, and it does. I try to be fair and equal when I discipline people."

"You're not being equal when you give one guy a warning notice and another guy a suspension for the same offense."

"It's not that simple, Joe. Discipline isn't something you apply by its number in a book. We're talking about two different people and two different situations."

"The only thing different about the situations is that you think they don't come any better than Dulles, and you've got a personal grudge against me."

"That's not true," you say, "and you know it. But if you want me to level with you, the way you sometimes act on the job, it looks to me as if you've got a grudge against yourself."

Don has been listening to your conversation with Joe, and now speaks up. "We're not getting anywhere with this. It's my responsibility to see to it that Joe gets a fair deal. I can't see that it's fair if he gets a tougher penalty than the next guy for the same offense. So you'd better take back that suspension. If you don't, Joe is going to file a grievance."

You shrug and show you're not concerned. "Joe has the right to do that, Don, but you'll both be wasting your time and mine. Joe wouldn't have gotten a tougher penalty than Dulles if it wasn't warranted."

"Then you're not going to withdraw it?" Joe asks.

"No way. As I said earlier, Dulles' situation is entirely different than yours, Joe. He is genuinely concerned about the problem his lateness is causing and the effect of the warning on his personal record. Your attitude is as poor as your attendance. You act as if you couldn't care less about the effect on the department work or the schedule.

"If the union insists on carrying this thing to arbitration, I don't think you'll have much of a chance of winning it. You see, Joe, your personnel folder has all the documentation to back up what I've been telling you."

Reasoning and Principle Involved

The importance of documentation cannot be underrated when management is required to take a grievance to arbitration. However, management should always try to avoid this step when threatened with a grievance by explaining fully why the proposed grievance has no merit.

PROBLEM NUMBER 3

What to say to employees who spend too much time on union business.

The Situation

Union representatives Harry Summer and Pete Hurt work in the Maintenance Department. This morning, Summer came to you for permission to meet with Hurt to handle some union business. He said the backlog of union matters they had to resolve was too long and some items had to be handled immediately. You gave Summer permission but told him not to make the meeting too long, saying that the backlog of maintenance work was too long also. More than an hour has passed and the men have not returned to their jobs. You go to the small conference room where such meetings are held.

What You Should Say and Some Responses

Summer looks up after you have rapped on the door and walked in. "What's the problem?" he asks.

"You fellows have been meeting long enough," you say. "The work's piling up. You're needed in the plant."

"We're not finished yet," Summer replies.

"Look, Harry, I gave you permission for a meeting, not for a full-blown conference. Don't abuse the privilege."

"OK, we won't be much longer."

After almost another hour passes without Summer or Hurt coming out of the room, you return.

"Harry, this has gone on long enough. If both of you are not back on the job within five minutes, you'll be in serious trouble."

Summer shows he is annoyed. "We're not wasting time or fooling around. This is important union business."

"The work is also important, and that's what you're being paid for."

"We'll be finished when we're finished," Hurt grumbles. "Take off and let us finish it."

"I'm telling you one more time. I want you both back on the job right now."

Summer refuses to comply. "As union representatives, we're responsible for doing this work and entitled to the time it takes to do it."

You do not continue to argue with him but leave the room. Instead, you have a disciplinary suspension typed for the two men. Twenty minutes later, you give them the suspension slips.

Summer acts amazed. "You can't do this to us. You can't suspend us for carrying out our responsibilities as union representatives."

"That's not why you're being suspended. You're being suspended for failing to follow instructions and do the work that's assigned to you. If you disagreed with my request to get back to your jobs, your only recourse was to file a grievance on the matter after carrying out my order."

Reasoning and Principle Involved

Attending to union business on company time is a privilege granted by management to union representatives. It is not a right. If permission to hold a meeting is granted, it is clearly within management's prerogative to terminate it if the representative's absence is adversely affecting the work and the company's operations.

PROBLEM NUMBER 4

What to say to an employee who complains about being given too much work to do.

The Situation

Betty Hanson works in the utility company offices where you are the office manager. She is doing an excellent job on the billing and customer service work you assign her. Although you have complimented her whenever she did unusually good work, she has complained when some of the work was difficult or she felt pushed to complete it quickly. Also, she has begun to compare the amount of work you give her with what you give the other girls in the office. As she was leaving after work yesterday, she came by your office to say, "Why don't you give more work to Linda and Cheryl? You're giving me too much and that's not fair." Rather than ask her to stay late to discuss the matter, you suggested that the two of you talk about it this morning.

What You Should Say and Some Responses

"Good morning, Betty, how are you today?"

"Just fine. It looks like it's going to be a good day."

"Right. Betty, after you've got things arranged at your desk, why don't you come to my office so we can talk a bit."

"OK, I'll be there in a few minutes."

After she arrives and sits down, you immediately bring up the purpose of your meeting.

"Before I left the office last night, I looked back at the recent assignments that I've given you, Linda and Cheryl. While I always try to distribute the work fairly, I'll have to admit that I've inadvertently given you more, but not much more, than I've given the other girls.

"I'm sorry about that. I guess I must have subconsciously felt that with your greater skill and speed, you'd handle those jobs better and faster than the other girls. I'll be more careful about that in the future."

"Thank you. It bothers me when I've got too much work to do. I guess I just get nervous about it."

"I can understand that. Most efficient people feel that way about their work, and you are the most efficient girl in the office. By the way, Betty, how do you like your job? Are you getting along all right with Linda, Cheryl, and the other people in the office?"

"Oh, the job's going pretty well. Right now I'm concerned with my husband. He might lose his job and have a rough time finding a new one. I guess that's putting me on edge."

"Let me know if that happens. Maybe the company can help."

"Thank you."

"And, Betty, be sure you talk to me whenever you have a problem or are unhappy about a situation or a turn of events. That's what I'm here for."

Reasoning and Principle Involved

Managers should always answer employee's complaints as promptly as they can. Employees may not do their work satisfactorily until managers do so. Complaints almost always are serious matters to those who make them. Sometimes an outside problem is the cause of a complaint. If a manager can find a solution to it, he or she can make a friend.

PROBLEM NUMBER 5

What to say to a supervisor about how to work with the union grievance procedure.

The Situation

When your company recently expanded its production process by putting on another shift, the Personnel Department went outside the company for a few of its new supervisors. One of them, Brad Wilson, previously worked for a smaller company, a nonunionized one. Since your company is unionized, you were not surprised when during his first week of training, Wilson came to you with some questions on the union grievance procedure.

What You Should Say and Some Responses

"Have you read the union–management contract, Brad? I assume the Personnel Department gave you a copy."

"Yes, I've got one. All I can say is it sure covers a lot of things. I've gone through it a couple times. Each time I do, it gets a little clearer."

"You'll probably have to refer to it frequently in the next few months until you learn everything it covers."

"I can see that, but I'm especially interested in the grievance procedure. I'm wondering how I'll get along with the union, and if I'll be able to handle a complaint."

"It may appear difficult, but I wouldn't worry about it. But it is true that to get along well with the union, you must know how to handle a complaint. Once you acquire this skill, you will be able to resolve differences of opinion on the job more easily as well as carry out the responsibilities of your job with more authority.

"Brad, don't consider a grievance as a personal attack on your authority. Instead, see it as a way the union communicates to management a complaint or the existence of a problem. With this viewpoint, you will not be resentful or antagonistic when you handle grievances. It makes for a more equitable solution of problems for all concerned."

"If the union turns in some grievances on me, I sure hope the company can win them."

You smile and say, "Winning a grievance is not as important as promptly settling it so that an employee can be productive with a minimum of dissatisfaction and loss of time on the job. The longer it is put off, the more unhappy and discontented the submitter becomes. If a grievance is promptly and properly investigated, the chances of outside arbitration being required are greatly decreased."

"What kind of grievance does the company usually get?" asks Brad.

"Although a majority of them fit one pattern or another, you can expect two to occur more frequently than others. The first kind is imaginary or arises from a misunderstanding. Of course, it is real to the employee, and a supervisor should accept it as such. You should still give a grievance your full attention no matter how illogical or impractical it may appear. And be especially thorough when investigating a grievance which seems to be far out of line—it may be the surfacing of a serious hidden problem.

"The second kind is simply the expression of an employee asking that he or she get a fair deal. The person may be wrong or not sure, but wants things checked out.

"You've got to give the employee the facts and a fair answer. Although you may have to say that he or she is wrong, the person will know that you took a personal interest and tried to help. If, however, you ignore or slough off the complaint, the employee will feel that it was not important enough to you. The disappointment and dissatisfaction resulting may bring you more trouble later."

"Does the company usually get a lot of grievances? What's the best way to avoid them?"

"Not an excessive amount, in my opinion," you reply. "Management never likes to receive grievances from employees. Yet, few companies which have unions are able to completely eliminate them, try as they may. This is not to say that a lack of grievances means that everyone is pleased on the job. When management receives numerous grievances, however, they must search for the reason or reasons. Angry employees are not productive. The company loses when employees are unhappy or feel ignored.

"A good way to avoid grievances is to discuss proposed changes in the work with the union before putting them into effect. Another way is to ask for the union's help and cooperation in solving problems and resolving differences of opinion as soon as they become known.

"Probably the most practical and realistic approach to reduce the number of grievances is to take a less rigid view of the agreement, to be more liberal when interpreting it. Both the union and management should recognize that situations and conditions involving people on the job change. The agreement must periodically be changed accordingly. If the agreement is looked upon as a guide for solving problems and reaching decisions rather than as a group of inflexible regulations, both the union and management may be more willing to concede on issues more often."

"I can see that I need to really study the agreement. But can you tell me what I should do in particular to avoid making mistakes? I would sure hate to have a grievance go to arbitration and cost the company all that time and money."

"A study of the grievances of employees that end in arbitration hearings revealed that about 90 percent of them reached that point because of mistakes made by supervisors. In my opinion, there are three serious mistakes that supervisors make.

"First, they too often make light of or brush off legitimate complaints. When an employee turns in a grievance, the matter is more important to him or her at that time than anything else. The employee will not be satisfied until the grievance is answered.

"Second, supervisors may try to handle a compliant without getting all the facts. This mistake occurs because they don't place enough importance on the matter to justify a thorough study of it. The problem is aggravated when the supervisor isn't aware of the true feelings of his or her people and hasn't been interested enough to learn their likes and dislikes.

"The third mistake is imposing severe discipline for a minor offense. The union often feels that discipline meted out by the supervisor is too severe. The problem of consistency must also be contended with. If you suspend one person for a rule violation, you can't give a simple warning to another person for the same offense."

Reasoning and Principle Involved

Knowing the union–management agreement and what it covers is a requisite for getting along with the union. The most important of this is the grievance procedure. Since employee grievances are costly in both time and money, supervisors and managers must constantly work to reduce their number.

PROBLEM NUMBER 6

What to say to an employee who complains that the company is taking advantage of him.

The Situation

In an effort to raise efficiency and increase labor productivity, you were asked by management to analyze your department operations to eliminate duplication and waste. Management also recommended that you combine certain jobs, make reassignments, eliminate specific jobs of some employees, and add jobs for others where feasible. In your department, instrument and electronic control repairs are made by electronic engineers as described in the job classification manual. One of the steps you take to improve efficiency is to relieve the engineers of selected repair work that does not require a high degree of skill. Such work can be handled by electricians. When George Porter, an engineer, learns of the change you made, he comes to you to complain about it. Porter is known for wanting to work as much overtime as he can get.

What You Should Say and Some Responses

"What's new, George?" you say as he approaches you.

"I don't think much of the changes in job classification you are trying to make. You're taking some of my work away from me. My job description says that repair work is to be handled by electronic engineers, not electricians. This change violates the contract."

"No, it doesn't. Nothing in the contract prohibits management from changing assignments to improve efficiency."

"You might be trying to improve efficiency, but you're taking advantage of me to do it. That's not fair."

"The changes that were made will raise the efficiency of the department and increase the labor productivity. One of the ways they will accomplish this is by eliminating needless overtime work."

When George sees he has not changed your mind, he leaves but returns a half hour later with Pete Henderson, his union representative.

"George has a point," Pete tells you. "Those repair jobs belong to the engineers because of precedent if for no other reason. You can't change employees' jobs unilaterally without getting the union's agreement."

"What the company is doing does not violate the contract," you say. "The engineers are overloaded with work, and the electricians have the time and capability to handle those minor repairs. Besides, experienced engineers aren't working efficiently if they take on jobs that can be handled as well by semi-skilled employees. Management is within its rights in making the change."

Pete shows he is angry. "If you continue to do this, you'll wind up with a grievance on your hands."

"Pete, you're fighting a losing cause. In most other cases that I know about where management's right to assign duties was challenged, arbitrators ruled for the company. I know that the changes that have been made to improve our department operations will be upheld."

Reasoning and Principle Involved

Management is obliged to improve efficiency and increase productivity wherever it can. There is a responsibility to the stockholders to do so. In addition, management should protect and secure the jobs of employees, improve the company's competitive position in its industry and help combat inflation.

Chapter 22

INSTRUCTING AND TRAINING

In the following situations, note the extent of the involvement that many supervisors have in training and instructing employees, and how they should communicate in order to make learning easy for trainees. Notice also that managers are very much concerned, as they should be, with the progress and response of employees to training.

PROBLEM NUMBER 1

What to say to the supervisor of a trainee who is seemingly not suited to the job.

The Situation

Frank Parson, hired a week ago, is a slightly built young man in his early 20's. A quiet, serious fellow, he has a habit of blinking rapidly when engaged in conversation. As with all new hirees on hourly jobs, he is on probation for a month, after which he is either released or becomes a permanent employee. When you first observed him working on an assignment his supervisor, Bill Torrance, had given him, it was apparent he hadn't fully understood Torrance's instructions, although he'd assured Torrance he had. On top of that, he seemed to lack the manual dexterity required to work with tools easily and efficiently. While you were aware that the company didn't have to decide his fate for another three weeks, you wondered what Torrance's opinion of Parson was at this time.

What You Should Say and Some Responses

"Bill, how do you feel about Parson? Will we be keeping him or letting him go?"

Bill scratches his head and is slow to answer. "Frankly, I'm having a hard time deciding."

"Meaning?"

"Meaning that I like his attitude and the amount of effort he puts on a job. But he's not very handy with tools, and there are times I get the feeling he's not very sharp. Yesterday I gave him a relatively simple job that should have taken about three hours. Parson took about twice that long to complete it and he also made two mistakes. But I have this to say about him: he conscientiously tried to do a good job and he worked hard at it."

You nod. "That's about the same impression I got of him when I watched and talked with him a couple days ago. On the other hand, we can use more people in the plant who are serious and hard working, and try to do the best that they can.

"The problem is, how do you weigh and balance those characteristics and inclinations. What bothers me is that with his kind of effort, his productivity may increase and he could develop into a valued employee. How many people have you known who have the brains and potential but fail because they're too lazy or lack the initiative to make something of themselves?"

"Plenty," Bill replies. "So where does that leave him?"

"I just don't know. At any rate, his probationary period still has three weeks to go. All you can do is continue to give him jobs and instruct him, and see if he shows any signs of improvement."

A week later, you again talk to Bill about Parson. "How's he doing, Bill? Any improvement in the last week?"

"Yes and no," Bill replies. "The other day I gave him a desk job that involved bringing our preventive maintenance records up to date. I figured it would take him about an hour, but he did it in about 35 minutes. My first thought was that he must have omitted some of the jobs. But I checked and not only was the job complete, he didn't even make a single error.

"Right after completing that job, I gave him some assembly and finishing work. He just didn't do well on that. He was awkward and slow and just couldn't catch on to the step sequence. I don't know what to say to him. He's been trying to put everything he's got into the job, and in my book, that counts for a lot. But unfortunately, his productivity is quite a bit below standard."

You wait a bit and then say, "Bill, as I see this problem, you're afraid to get this man fixed as a permanent employee because if he doesn't make it, you're stuck with him."

Bill nods affirmatively.

"I feel this is good reasoning," you say. "From what you've told me, and from what I've observed, I see Frank Parson as a clumsy, misplaced individual, however conscientious and well-intentioned he may be. You paint him as awkward and slow, unable to follow instructions no matter how hard he tries. At the same time, you reason that because he's got a good positive attitude, he's entitled to every chance he can get, that maybe, because he's motivated, he may turn out well.

"What you are ignoring or minimizing is that some people are awkward and inept by nature. They act as if they had two left hands and are also slow to respond.

"Another matter that should be considered is the small assignment he did where his performance was well above standard, the paperwork job. That may be significant. It could be that Parson would do well on a desk job in the office. No matter how hard he works on his present job, if he has to struggle and strain, he won't be good at it and will eventually hate it.

"My feeling is that he isn't suited to what he's trying to do. Keeping him where he doesn't belong would be a disservice to him, to the company, and to yourself. The biggest favor you could do for all concerned would be to let him go in the hope that he'll find a job that is right for him."

Reasoning and Principle Involved

If a person is not right for a job, keeping him or her on it would amount to a bad decision on the part of the manager. People should be assigned the kind of work they can do comfortably, confidently, and effectively.

PROBLEM NUMBER 2

What to say to the employee who wants special training that the company can't justify.

The Situation

When Joe Trent was hired by your company a year ago, he was a highly motivated individual who showed a lot of initiative and enthusiasm. Although he had not finished college, he was looked upon as a good candidate for a management job. But Trent's enthusiasm and drive lasted only about six months. Working as a machine operator, his output has steadily been declining even though you have talked to him about it several times. Early today, you gave him a job to do which you expected him to finish in about four hours. When you followed up just before lunch, the job wasn't even half done, and he apparently had been daydreaming. Your approach seemed to snap him abruptly out of his reverie. You warned him again that he was not meeting the work standards, and that if he didn't improve, he might lose his job. Late this afternoon, he appears at your desk with a nervous look on his face.

What You Should Say and Some Responses

Still irritated by his earlier behavior, you brusquely ask him, "What's your problem, Joe?"

"I'd like to talk to you if you have a few minutes."

Expecting that Joe has decided to resign, a sensible move in view of his standing in the department, you lead him to a small conference room where you can talk in private. Once you are seated, you ask him, "What's on your mind, Joe?"

Joe breathes deeply and then says, "I've been thinking about what you told me this morning. The way I've been going, I don't suppose I have much of a future with the company. But I want you to know that what's getting me down is the work."

"Joe, no one is forcing you to stay with the company. If you don't like the work, you can quit."

"No, that's not what I mean. I don't object to working here. What I mean is that the jobs you assign me are boring. You don't need any brains to do them. I think I've got enough intelligence to handle work that requires some skill and is also more interesting. After all, I've had almost a year of college."

"Are you going to college now?" you ask.

"No, I dropped out."

"I see," you say. "Look, Joe, I know that you've got a high IQ and are above average in natural intelligence. You also learn quickly. Those are the reasons we hired you in the first place. But people don't get higher level jobs unless they're trained for them, and they don't get special training unless they prove that they are qualified for it. What kind of higher level work are you trained and experienced in?"

"Nothing special right now," Joe replies. "That's what I wanted to talk to you about. I'd like to be taught how to operate the automatic drilling machine. I know that Watson is quitting pretty soon and his job will be open."

"You're right about that job opening, but two other fellows have told me they want the job. Why should I consider you for it instead of Bill Fisher, for example, who's been doing a much better job for the company than you have?"

"For one thing, I could learn the job faster than Fisher or any of the other guys. I could also do a better job than they could."

"Well, that's one man's opinion. But regardless, Joe, let me think about it. I'll get back to you later."

Feeling that you did not want to make a hasty decision on Joe's request, you take some time to think and reason on the matter. A day later you tell Joe that you are ready to talk to him about his request.

"Joe, I'm turning down your request to be assigned to the automatic drilling machine opening, but I want you to know why I made this decision. While I feel that you'd be the best man for the job, that would be true *only* if you applied yourself properly. I can't overlook your unacceptable performance the last few months, and I have no way of being sure that you wouldn't repeat this on a different job.

"I remember that you got off to a promising beginning when you first started with the company, but then you fizzled out. You began college but fizzled out on that also. I realize you've complained about your work being uninteresting, but every job has an element of boredom, and we all have to endure some of it.

"I often find that when I'm in doubt about a decision I have to make, my best bet is to rely on my sense of fair play and justice. With your performance the last six months, you've really done nothing to earn this opportunity. There are others who would also like that job and worked harder for it."

Reasoning and Principle Involved

Although there's no guarantee how anyone will work out over the long term on a new job, history has proven that the person who is steady and hard working has a much better chance of succeeding than the bright person who lacks the character and resolve to do the job that he or she is presently being paid for.

PROBLEM NUMBER 3

What to say to a worker who is not responding well to training for a new job.

The Situation

Your company conducts an in-house training program for employees. This enables new hirees and nonskilled workers to be trained for better, higher-paying positions in the company. Several people in your department are participating in the present program, one of them being Don Carlson, a stock delivery man in the Production Department. Carlson is training for the job of Quality Control Inspector. Unfortunately, his progress during training is way below standard. Halfway through the course, it is apparent to you that he isn't going to qualify. There is too much detail to be aware of and remember. Carlson is also having difficulty reading and understanding specifications and control data. After the instructor tells you he has failed his third consecutive test, you talk to him about it in your office.

What You Should Say and Some Responses

"Don, I've been told that you failed another test in the training program."

"Yeah, I did, but it was close. I'm not worried about it because I'm beginning to get the work better."

"The instructor told me you also did poorly in the field work."

Don frowns. "I didn't think I was that bad. Anyway, I'm going to study harder and do better."

"You told me that the last time we talked."

"This time I really mean it."

"OK, Don, I'll give you one more chance to make good. But if you don't do much better soon, I'm afraid that will have to be it."

Don thanks you and says nothing more. When another week passes with no improvement in his performance, you tell him that you are sorry, but you're going to take him out of the training program.

Showing his disappointment when he hears that, he says, "I'm doing the best I can."

"I know that, Don, and I'm not saying you're not trying. But you're simply not keeping up with the program and making enough progress."

"I didn't think I was doing that badly."

"Here are your records, Don. You've failed almost all the tests, and your field work ratings are very low. With that kind of performance, you'd never be able to cut it on the job. I'm sorry."

Don brushes off the records as not meaning much. "It's not fair to treat me that way. You're supposed to go by seniority in making promotions to better jobs."

"I agree. That's why you were permitted to take the training. You were the next one in line for the job. It's not my fault if you can't qualify."

Don becomes insistent. "I know I could qualify if you gave me the chance."

"You've been given the chance for a long time. I have no choice now. I'm taking you out of the program."

"You can't do that. I'm entitled to complete the course. If I don't qualify then, that's another matter. But I deserve a full chance to show you I can handle the job."

"No, I'm sorry, Don."

"I'm going to talk to my union representative about this," Don says as he leaves.

Reasoning and Principle Involved

When management has full documentation that an employee isn't responding to training, it is unlikely that the person will be able to perform satisfactorily on the job he or she is being trained for. Under such conditions, the company can't be expected to make an investment of money and time to give the employee additional training.

PROBLEM NUMBER 4

What to say to a manager about the responsibility of having a subordinate trained to handle some of his duties.

The Situation

It is customary for you to conduct a Plant Operations meeting with all department heads every other Friday afternoon. The agenda for this meeting is prepared by the Manager of Production, Keith Norris, who usually distributes copies one or two days prior to the meeting day. You have been very busy this week and were not aware that you didn't receive the agenda until you looked for it Friday morning. Then you remembered that Norris had reported in sick with the flu on Wednesday and had not returned to work since then. You immediately phoned his secretary and asked her to see that the agenda was prepared for the afternoon meeting. You also made a note on your calendar to talk to Norris about this omission when he returned.

What You Should Say and Some Responses

"How are you feeling, Keith?"

"Oh, a little weak, but I guess I'll live."

"As you probably know, we asked Norman Anderson, your Area B supervisor, to handle some of your duties while you were out. I believe he has filled in for you occasionally when you were out of the plant."

"Yes, I know. Mary, my secretary, told me this morning."

"Keith, we were in a tight spot on Friday. You hadn't prepared the agenda for the Plant Operations meeting and nobody knew how to handle it. When I called Mary, she and Norman searched your desk and files for it. They finally found the previous meeting agenda, but it had only a few notes on it."

Keith is obviously embarrassed. "Gosh, I'm sorry about that. I usually get that agenda out early in the week, but I was so busy with other things that I just didn't get to it. Then I caught the flu on Wednesday."

"I haven't told you everything," you say. "Both Norman and Mary spent the whole morning Friday working to get the report out. You know there's a lot of data and information that goes into it. In the meeting, it was apparent they didn't get all of it, and they made some mistakes besides."

Keith shifts uncomfortably in his chair but doesn't say anything.

"But that wasn't what bothered me the most about this fiasco. I was disappointed to learn that you did not have someone in your group who could get out the agenda in your absence. This is so basic, I thought I could take it for granted, particularly with the man who's supposed to be the top department head in the company.

"I guess I shouldn't take anything for granted, so I'm going to spell out for you what I'm talking about. First, you should make sure there is at least one person in the department, and preferably more than one, who is familiar with every job or procedure.

"Second, you should know that training people to do a variety of jobs makes their working for the company more interesting. They feel they are important to the company, especially when they are called upon to do something other than their usual work.

"Third, training your people to do other jobs is one of the best ways I can think of to develop and upgrade your people. That should be a goal of every manager.

"Fourth, training subordinates gives you an opportunity as manager to learn who catches on to new jobs the fastest, and who has the potential to move up in the company.

"And fifth, the practice takes you off the hook, and keeps you from getting into the kind of trouble you are in at this moment."

Looking directly at Keith, you ask him, "Do you understand?"

"Yes," Keith meekly replies.

"I don't want to harp on this incident, but having to work with an incomplete and somewhat inaccurate agenda on Friday made our meeting slow and inefficient. It also delayed some manufacturing decisions and actions. So I can't overstress the importance of avoiding such occurrences by anticipating their possibility and taking steps to make sure you're prepared for them."

Reasoning and Principle Involved

Managers can't be on the job everyday. Everybody takes a vacation or a business trip now and then, and few people are not ill once in a while. The answer to this problem is that managers must see that subordinates are trained to handle their superiors' duties and responsibilities when they are absent.

PROBLEM NUMBER 5

What to say to a supervisor about how employees should be trained.

The Situation

It is standard practice at your company to have new hirees for the Production Department trained by the supervisor they will be working for; the company does not have a training department. With the recent expansion of one of the production lines, there was a need for three more operators. They were hired and will report for work next week. Since you believe the supervisor, Walt Roger, is not aware that he will be expected to train these people, you ask him to come to your office to talk about it.

What You Should Say and Some Responses

"Walt, how's the installation going on the new line? Will we be able to start it fairly soon?"

"Yeah, it's looking good. According to the engineering department, all the mechanical work is complete, and the electricians will finish tomorrow. They've already operated a few of the machines and conveyors, and timed them out."

"Good! I've heard from the Personnel Department that three new people will be reporting in next week. They'll be getting a lot of orientation and information about the company and the plant from Personnel, but they won't learn much about the process. It will be up to you to train and instruct them on the job."

Walt smiles. "I figured I'd probably be involved with that. But how am I going to do that along with all my other work?"

"What I thought you might do is have Dick Holmes take your job as a temporary supervisor for a week or so while you're training the new people and also getting the bugs out of the system. How does that sound to you?"

"OK, but I don't know how good I'll be as a trainer. I've never done any teaching or trained anybody in my life."

"I don't think you'll have any problems with that. You're the best supervisor I have when it comes to knowing the equipment and the process. I'm sure the engineering people will help you with explaining how some of the new machines operate."

"I'm not worried about that," Walt replies. "It's what I should say and how I should explain things that worries me. I don't know the background of any of these fellows or their experience."

"I've had copies made of their job application forms and the information they gave to Personnel. Here are those records. It won't take you long to get to know them. Also, I thought I'd give you a few tips on teaching and training so you won't get into trouble on that score."

"OK, I could use all the help you can give me."

"First, I would recommend that you use an easygoing approach. This puts trainees more at ease and in a mood to learn. Also, I would try to speak their language. By using words they know and understand, you leave no doubt in their minds. Prefer short words to long ones, simple words to complex ones, and short sentences to long ones. Being brief and concise helps you to be clear."

"I shouldn't have any problem with that," Walt comments.

"When you start to describe a process or procedure, explain the simple things first. Save the difficult ones for later when the trainee's minds are better adjusted to learning. Along the same line, pause between steps of procedures and change of subjects to give trainees time to absorb the instructions. Let them think a bit. It helps learning.

"Walt, many of the new machines have been modernized. A good way to point out the new features is to compare them with the way the old machines used to operate. Some of the new hirees may have had experience with older machines. You can learn this from their personnel records. Learning is easier when the relationship to something familiar is pointed out."

"That's right," Walt remarks. "Maybe these guys will be familiar with some of our machines and equipment. It will be easier to train them if they are."

"It's a good idea during a training session to encourage feedback from the trainees. Get them to ask questions to determine if you are getting through and to find out what you should repeat and where you may need to place emphasis. If the trainees are reluctant to ask questions, ask some yourself.

"Another thing Walt, try to keep discussions and remarks positive. Put the record straight whenever you get a negative comment from a trainee. Your effectiveness as a trainer is always better when you stress the positive.

"Lastly, limit the number of ideas or points covered at a single training session. It's better to do a thorough job with a few ideas than an incomplete job with many. When time is short, be satisfied to get across one idea clearly and completely."

Reasoning and Principle Involved

Successful teachers and trainers have developed techniques in communicating that enable them to be easily understood. Such people are effective because they constantly work at being simple, concise and clear. They also recognize that employees are individuals with human emotions, and that they cannot be treated as machines.

PROBLEM NUMBER 6

What to say to a manager about how a new supervisor should be indoctrinated.

The Situation

Your company has embarked on a capital investment program which has required that the Engineering Department be expanded. The Manager of the Department, John Turner, saw that his project supervisors were overloaded with work and the starting of new projects was being delayed. After discussing the situation with you, Turner arranged for the transfer of an experienced project supervisor from another plant. The new supervisor, Harvey Crawford, started out well in that he understood the work and the standards that had to be met. He also enthusiastically accepted assignments and instructions from Turner. After a month on the job, however, Crawford began to have trouble in getting along with the other supervisors. In their eyes, he became brash and overbearing, apparently not caring whom he stepped on to get his way. Bothered by this turn of events, you go to Turner to discuss the problem.

What You Should Say and Some Responses

"John, I hear that Crawford isn't getting along well on the job. Rumor is that he's pretty aggressive for only being with us about two months."

"Maybe so," John says. "I guess he's pretty ambitious."

"I wonder if he was properly introduced to our way of doing things in this plant."

"Well, when I interviewed him I saw that he was an independent type of individual and not afraid to assert himself. So I haven't spent a lot of time with him. I sensed he knew his way around and didn't need much guidance."

"That could be the reason for his present disturbing behavior. While there's much that can be said for giving professional people freedom and independence in how they handle their jobs, I feel that this can be carried to extremes. Making sure that supervisors are indoctrinated carefully is important for a variety of reasons. One of the most obvious is to establish standards of conduct and performance over the long term on the job.

"Another reason why an indoctrination is important is that it enables the individual to make a smooth transition from one job to another. The individual may also need guidance and support at this new phase of his or her career.

"Lastly, proper indoctrination tells subordinates what is expected of them, which decisions they can make for themselves, and how far they can go in promoting themselves. Had these things been clearly defined for Crawford, in all likelihood his brash behavior, along with the resentment and noncooperation it brought on, would have been avoided."

Reasoning and Principle Involved

Although managers are well aware of the importance of breaking in new rank-and-filers so they get a good start on a new job, proper indoctrination of supervisors is also necessary. After all, supervisors have the responsibility of guiding and controlling the performance of several individuals, so getting them started right is certainly equally if not more important.

PROBLEM NUMBER 7

What to say to a supervisor who hasn't been forceful regarding your instructions.

The Situation

Last week you told your supervisors that you want them to correct the habit of some of their employees of arriving late in the morning and leaving early in the afternoon at the end of the work day. You said that you wanted the supervisors to see to it that all of their people were punctual at both times unless they had valid excuses. Beginning this week, you have been spot-checking adherence to your instructions and have discovered that the people working for one of your supervisors, Leonard Hall, have not been conforming to your request. By asking around, you learn that Hall has only halfheartedly talked to his people, and hasn't checked up very much on whether they are complying. Further, when he finds they are not, he either doesn't criticize them or admonishes them too gently. Wanting to straighten out this situation without being too harsh on Hall, you bring up the subject after you've talked to him about some other problem.

What You Should Say and Some Responses

"Say, Leonard, before you leave, do you remember my meeting with all the supervisors in which I told everyone that I want people to be at work on time in the morning and not leave early at quitting time?"

"Yeah, I do. I talked to my people about that the next day."

"In the last few days, I've checked all the areas and found that your people are lacking in that respect more than the people reporting to the other supervisors. Maybe you haven't been as forceful in your instructions to them as you should have been."

"Well, that could be, I guess, but I *did* talk to them."

"You'll have to tell them again, and I suggest you do it in no uncertain terms. Also, I want you then to regularly check up on them to show that you mean business.

"If some of them continue to break the rules, handle them in the usual way for those who consistently violate company policy. And if you can't seem to get one or more of your people to comply, come to me and we'll decide what we should do."

Reasoning and Principle Involved

When managers issue orders or give instructions to subordinates which they must in turn pass on to their people, managers must make sure that the subordinates understand that the orders or instructions must be carried out. If, for any reason, subordinates are lax in this respect, managers must insist on the subordinates' compliance.

Chapter 23

ALCOHOL AND DRUGS

In the following situations, note that many of the serious problems facing managers today are those having to do with employees' weaknesses. Typical of such problems are alcoholism and drug abuse. Notice also, that managers are not expected to solve such problems, but are advised instead to persuade the troubled employees to seek professional help.

PROBLEM NUMBER 1

What to say to the supervisor of an employee who is a problem drinker.

The Situation

Pat Ryan is known throughout the company as a heavy drinker. Yet he never drinks on the job. Although he has a poor attendance record, he sometimes goes as much as two months without losing a day. Since he does his work satisfactorily most of the time, his supervisor, Neil Williams, generally leaves him alone. As long as the drinking doesn't interfere with his work, Williams reasons, it is none of his business. Recently, however, the situation has changed. One day last week, after returning from lunch where he had been drinking, he ran rejects for a half-hour on his machine. After talking to him, Williams saw that he was in no condition to continue working, and sent him home. Today was a repeat performance of too much liquor at lunch except that the security guard would not let him back into the plant. After Williams arranged for Ryan to be taken home, he reported the incident to you.

What You Should Say and Some Responses

"Neil, what did Pat have to say for himself when you arranged for him to be taken home?"

"Not much except to say that he didn't feel well and shouldn't have come to work today. I neither accepted this explanation or rejected it. But since I talked to him about his drinking last week, what should I do now?"

"Why don't you get his personnel folder from the file. We'll look through it and then decide."

After you and Neil study it, you turn to him and say, "How do you feel about Pat? Do you think he deserves another chance? Or do you feel that he's had it?"

"Pat's a darned good worker when he stays in line. Except for these two messups, if I let him go, I would miss him."

You nod. "That's one thing to consider. He's a conscientious guy who knows his job. Another thing is that he's got a family to support, and jobs are not easy to come by these days."

"Yeah, and he's got almost ten years of service with the company. You can't ignore that."

"Neil, supervisory responsibilities cover a lot of things. While they're pretty clear-cut most of the time, every now and then you run into a situation where one responsibility seems to interfere with another. Like now, for instance.

"While a supervisor's first responsibility is to the company, at the same time, another one of your responsibilities is to your people. When they become employees, they place their careers and maybe even their futures in your hands. You're expected to train them and help them to grow, and you're responsible for their safety and well-being on the job."

Neil nods to indicate he understands. "Speaking of safety, working around machinery when you've had too much to drink can be dangerous."

"Absolutely!" you say. "But let's talk about what we do with Pat. As I see the situation, we have several options. For one, we could fire him. That's probably the easiest and fastest way out."

Neil quickly adds, "We could have a talk with him to try to get him to understand the seriousness of this thing and to give him another chance to reform."

"But you've already tried that," you say. "It doesn't seem to be doing much good."

Neil scratches his head. "I guess the only other option is to let the matter ride. In other words, do nothing."

"Doing nothing, of course, is an option. But there's still one other we shouldn't overlook."

"What's that?" Neil asks.

"How do you classify alcoholism? Is it an infraction or a disease?"

"According to the experts, it's a disease. Alcoholism is just like diabetes or heart trouble," Neil replies.

"Right! And what do you do with a disease to bring about a cure?"

"You prescribe medication or a treatment or surgery."

"OK. However, the situation must be handled with extreme care in an employee–company relationship. If the employee asks for help, the supervisor should be prepared to suggest going to a community alcoholic center or Alcoholics Anonymous. But it is the employee who must take the step toward rehabilitation. This way, the company does not become involved in treatment for alcoholism any more than it would for diabetes or heart trouble.

"The employee must recognize that he or she needs outside help and be motivated to get it. Loss of the job can motivate an alcoholic employee like nothing else. Refusing to agree that outside help is needed, and saying that he or she can stop drinking whenever he or she wants to is not rehabilitation. The employee merely says those things to get the supervisor off his or her back. An alcoholic employee is not able to stop drinking without outside help.

"Alcoholism is a complex disease with no one treatment that works with all people. There are possible slips from time to time that can occur with even the most motivated individual.

"I'd suggest you talk to Pat as soon as he returns, and give him the whole story. I can only hope that he will go along with you. Otherwise we may soon be looking for someone to take his place."

Reasoning and Principle Involved

Supervisors should hope that their efforts in combatting alcoholism will result in the retention of a valued employee. If the employee refuses or fails rehabilitation and is terminated, the supervisor nevertheless will know that he or she handled the problem in a dignified and compassionate manner, and brought it to an early conclusion for everyone concerned.

PROBLEM NUMBER 2

What to say to a supervisor who, you suspect, knows that one of his people is a drug dealer.

The Situation

You were disturbed yesterday when one of your people told you he had overheard a conversation in the men's room related to the use of drugs in your organization. The informer said that an employee mentioned that your supervisor, Allen Newsome, knew from whom cocaine could be bought cheaply, and the dealer was a company employee. Hoping there is no truth to what your informer said, but knowing that it cannot be ignored, you ask Newsome to come to your office.

What You Should Say and Some Responses

When Allen comes into your office, he appears nervous and uneasy, particularly after you ask him to close the door behind him. You waste no time in getting to the point.

"Allen, I heard something yesterday that bothers me very much. I was told that cocaine may be bought from an employee, one who works for you."

Allen almost jumps out of his chair, but doesn't say anything.

"Your best bet is to level with me, Allen. I don't think I have to tell you how serious this can be."

Allen wets his lips. "I don't know. There've been rumors going around, but I don't pay much attention to them. As long as the work is getting done, that's all I'm concerned with."

"You're telling me you know nothing about it?"

"That's right." But his face betrays his nervousness and discomfort.

You look at Allen searchingly. "Listen, Allen, because this is important. If you know anything at all, this is the time to speak up. While there are a lot of rule infractions and behavioral quirks of employees that you can temporarily let slide and wait out to see what happens, drug use or trafficking isn't one of them.

"Drug use in general, and cocaine in particular, can wreck not only human beings, but companies as well. Drug use is costing industry billions of dollars a year in lost productivity, absenteeism and accidents. If it's going on here in our company, we have to put a stop to it before it gets out of control. Do you understand?"

"Yeah, sure," Allen replies hesitantly.

"I'm going to ask you again; are drugs being used in your department? Do you know anything about it?"

Allen lowers his eyes and quietly says, "No."

"OK, Allen, that's all."

Two days later, Allen comes to you with a haggard look on his face. "I just can't go on any longer, because I know you'll eventually find out. Buck Tripoli is selling cocaine, and I have been using it. You'll probably want to call the police."

"Thanks, Allen. I suggest that you immediately start a rehabilitation program—I hope it's not too late because I know you want to keep your job. Buck Tripoli of course, will not be able to do that."

Reasoning and Principle Involved

While it may come as a shock for a manager to learn that drug abuse exists in the company, it should spur management to immediately take steps to eliminate it. Since most abusers will desperately want to keep their jobs, they should be encouraged to seek help for their problem.

PROBLEM NUMBER 3

What to say to a supervisor who is too helpful with employees.

The Situation

Bob Perkins has been a supervisor only six months, but already he has gained the reputation of always having the best interests of his people in mind. Being outspoken, sympathetic and empathic complemented his style to the extent that he was becoming too friendly with his subordinates. In contrast to Perkins, Frank Read, one of the best workers in Perkins' group, was quiet and reserved. Read was a steady, dependable employee who minded his own business and did his job without being conspicuous. So it was a surprise when you received a call from the Personnel Department reporting that Read had quit without notice. Soon afterward, you ask Perkins to come to your office. When he appears, you motion him to have a seat while you close your office door.

What You Should Say and Some Responses

"What's the story on Read, Bob? Personnel called me that he had quit but they had no other information."

"I'm not sure," Bob replies uneasily. "He's been having trouble at home."

"I had heard that but heck, Bob, he's been with the company for more than five years. A fellow doesn't suddenly quit his job when he has trouble at home. He must have some other reason. Did he talk to you about it?"

"About intending to quit?"

"About anything. Anything that would explain this."

Bob shrugs. "Well, we did talk a few days ago. I thought something was wrong and tried to find out what it was. I wanted to help if I could. Also, I felt he was drinking too much. I figured maybe if I stepped in, I could prevent things from getting worse."

"Did he ask for your help?"

Bob looks at the floor. "No, I guess my help was the last thing he wanted."

"How was his work going?"

"No complaints. Frank was one of the best men in my group."

"What about his attendance?"

"Pretty good, in fact, better than average."

"This thing that you were worried about—that he might be drinking too much—was he always sober on the job? Did you ever find him under the weather?"

"No. The booze never seemed to affect his work."

You pause a bit to think. Then, "What did you say to him in your talk?"

Bob appears uncomfortable. "Let me tell you what happened. I had seen Frank by himself at a bar the night before. He looked so down and alone, my heart went out to him. So the next day, I asked him to come to a conference room where we could talk informally and in privacy.

"I told him that I had been in trouble myself, and it didn't take a detective to figure out he was having a rough time. But Frank didn't say anything.

"So I tried again. I said that sometimes it helps to talk out your problems, and get them off your chest. But again he didn't respond. Then, I said, 'OK, if you don't feel like talking about it, that's your right. The last thing I want to do is pry into your business. But there's just one thing I'd like to say to you. Whatever your problem is, liquor can't help; it can only make things worse.'

"Well, Frank's face tightened up, but he still didn't say anything. It was very quiet for awhile. Finally he said very softly, 'Is that all?'

"I looked at him and said, 'Yeah, I guess so. But look, Frank, if you ever need help . . . .' Frank, however, didn't look back or say anything as he left."

You wait a bit to see if Bob has anything else to say. When he doesn't, you say, "It all seems such a waste. I really get upset whenever a talented, productive employee quits for some mindless reason that so easily could have been avoided. My guess from what you've told me is that you embarrassed Frank into quitting. In trying to be helpful where your help wasn't welcomed, you provoked Frank's resignation just as certainly as if you had fired him.

"Bob, for your own good and mine as well, I hope you've learned something from this. An employee's personal life should be your concern only when it affects his or her performance on the job."

Reasoning and Principle Involved

When help that's uncalled for and unwanted is offered and forced by a manager, it becomes something less than assistance. There are too many times when well-intentioned meddling can cause as much damage as indifference or neglect.

PROBLEM NUMBER 4

What to say to the foreman who wants to know how to handle a person he suspects is using drugs.

The Situation

Roger Kohl, one of your longest service supervisors, is a very conscientious and honest person. He is one of the leaders in promoting safety in the plant, and frequently discusses safety with his people. Being of this nature, he is particularly careful in seeing that the workers use the protective clothing furnished by the company and are alerted to the hazards of some of the jobs he assigns them. Also, he is always aware of their moods and feelings. Lately, he has noticed some unusual behavior of one of the young employees, Pete Smith. Suspecting that Smith might be using drugs, he comes to you to discuss the problem.

What You Should Say and Some Responses

"Roger, I'm glad you came to me with this problem. Whenever someone behaves abnormally or seems to be careless on the job, it's important to act immediately. This is especially true if you suspect the person is using drugs."

"From what I've read about drug users, Smith shows many of the symptoms. But what should I do?"

"Similar to handling alcoholism, a big help in rehabilitation of a person on drugs is getting the person to admit to the problem. The person whose job performance has begun to be affected by drugs should be told that he or she has to decide between holding the job and continuing on drugs."

"Are you saying that I should get tough with Smith?"

"No," you say. "You must be practical and levelheaded about drugs not to alienate him. Encourage him to discuss the problem and try to present the arguments against drugs, but be careful how you do it. Scare techniques usually are ineffective because Smith most likely has firsthand knowledge which can contradict them."

"It looks like I might have a tough time convincing him," Roger comments.

"Maybe, but maybe not. You might try talking about safety on the job. Tell him you'd sure hate to see him have an accident because he didn't see a hazard or wasn't alert enough to avoid it. Is Smith generally concerned about safety?"

"Not that I know of, but I can try promoting safety."

"Tell him also that a good way to start a withdrawal program is to see his family doctor who will either help him or refer him to an agency that can do so. As a supervisor, you can demonstrate that people can enjoy life and have fun without resorting to the use of drugs. Point out too, that the person who is enthusiastic and gets satisfaction from his or her work shows everyone that happiness and enjoyment can be realized without taking drugs."

Reasoning and Principle Involved

The problem of drug abuse cannot be solved easily, but success is possible if several elements of a withdrawal program are adopted. Most important, the drug user must be determined to overcome his or her dependence on them. Professional help, both medical and psychiatric, is usually needed.

PROBLEM NUMBER 5

What to say to a manager you suspect is having problems with alcohol.

The Situation

Glen Padulla is a store manager of the lumber company you work for. Since the central offices of the company are located with this company outlet, you frequently see both Glen and his department heads during the day. Padulla has been with the company for more than 20 years and generally has been a productive employee in whatever job he held. But lately, his department heads have been slacking off in both the quantity and quality of their work. Also, Padulla frequently has been coming to work late, and always with a different excuse. His face seems unduly flushed much of the time, and every once in a while you think you smell alcohol on his breath. In addition, you have noticed that the department heads seem to be talking among themselves more than their jobs seem to require. Concerned about the declining productivity of the organization, you ask Padulla to come to your office to talk about it. You want to give him a chance to improve conditions without bringing up the question of the suspected alcoholism.

What You Should Say and Some Responses

"Glen, I've noticed that your department heads' productivity has declined considerably in the last few weeks. Were you aware of this?"

"No. As far as I know, they've been doing their usual good job. How did you mean?"

"They seem to be wasting too much time shooting the breeze, talking about things other than business and generally loafing. I remember that this happened once before, about a year ago. You had taken three weeks of vacation, and things went to hell while you were gone. Their present behavior suggests to me you haven't talked to them lately about keeping up with their work."

Glen looks a bit sheepish and doesn't say anything.

"Have you been feeling OK, Glen?"

"Yeah, I'm all right. Why do you ask?"

"Well, I've noticed you've been late quite often in the last few weeks, and that isn't like you. Years ago, you used to be on the job before everyone else."

"I've been running into a lot of bad luck recently. Oversleeping, car trouble, misplacing my keys and that sort of stuff."

"I see. I guess everyone runs into those kind of problems now and then. But, Glen, if you're having any kind of unusual problems at home, I would like you to talk to me about them. Maybe something can be done to prevent such problems from having an adverse affect on your work."

Reasoning and Principle Involved

A good manager is always alert to the symptoms which might reveal that a subordinate is having problems with alcohol. The manager should, however, be careful not to accuse or even hint to the individual that an alcoholism problem exists. It's best to give the subordinate an opportunity to bring up the subject himself or herself.

PROBLEM NUMBER 6

What to say to a supervisor about how an employee who is failing on the job because of alcoholism should be handled.

The Situation

For some time, you have suspected that one of your accountants is an alcoholic. Al Foster is frequently absent on Mondays, and he frequently takes long lunch periods away from the office. Also, errors and mistakes have begun to show up in his work. You were not surprised, therefore, when Bob Steele, his supervisor, stopped by your office to talk to you about his poor performance on the job and what he should do about it.

What You Should Say and Some Responses

"Bob, I'm glad you came to me with this problem. Many companies today have programs for dealing with alcoholism of their employees, and ours is one of them. The immediate supervisor is the key to the success of any program of this type. You must act promptly when an employee's job performance drops off. If the cause is alcoholism, the situation can only get worse."

"There's no doubt in my mind with Foster," Bob says. "You can smell the alcohol on his breath when he returns from lunch."

"Companies which have employee assistance programs want their supervisors to encourage people who are failing on the job without clear cause to discuss the matter with appropriate personnel. The program consists of diagnosis, counseling, and treatment by professionals. Usually the alcoholic must first be talked to personally by his or her supervisor."

Bob appears concerned and uneasy. "Gosh, how do you bring up the subject? What should I say?"

"A good way to start is to say, 'Al, I've noticed that something is affecting the way you handle your job. I think I know what the problem is, but I can't help you until you tell me about it.' If Al is honest with you, all to the good. But it's likely that Al will say that he can handle the alcohol he drinks, and can stop drinking anytime if it is necessary.

"Whether or not Al admits to the problem of drinking, you must tell him that the company will not continue to accept the particular failures in job performance of which he is guilty. You must point out that failure to do better will eventually cost him his job with the company."

"I think I see what you're getting at," Bob replies.

"You see, Bob, an alcoholic values his or her job and will do almost anything to protect it. The problem drinker must believe that you are serious when you say that he or she must give up drinking or suffer such consequences. If the person doesn't believe you, you will probably not get results.

"Talking with and trying to help an alcoholic isn't easy. While you may feel sorry and want to be protective, covering up for the person doesn't help—you will only delay solving the problem. That's why I'm glad you came to me with this problem.

"Encourage Al to get professional help. You cannot depend on any promises he may make. Although he may mean well and fully intend to do better, having this disease may make him incapable of changing. He may also lie as well as offer all sorts of excuses. You should see these for what they are and realize they are of no benefit.

"Being patient and not losing your temper may be difficult but you won't get anywhere with lecturing, criticizing or scolding. Helping him requires the best you have in dedication and human relations skill, realizing that he probably is incapable of handling the problem without your or someone else's help."

Reasoning and Principle Involved

Many companies today have instructed their supervisors on the procedure to follow in working with their people on the alcoholism problem. A company must always take the stand that if an employee will not admit to the problem and is unable to improve his or her performance on the job, the failure will eventually cost the person's employment with the company.

Chapter 24

CHANGE

In the following situations, note how managers recognize that many employees do not readily accept change, particularly if it is of major significance. Notice also, that there are many facets to be considered when a change is to be made. The manager who sells a change before it is made has a much better chance of having it readily accepted.

PROBLEM NUMBER 1

What to say to a manager whose people are resisting a company-wide procedure change.

The Situation

Management of your company has decided that a computerized control system is needed to make the company more competitive. It is now scheduled for plantwide installation in a few months. The purpose of the system is to facilitate planning and scheduling, improve material control, reduce inventories, evaluate labor utilization, and better control maintenance operations, among others. The introduction of the system will take a considerable amount of effort and work on the part of many people. However, resistance of some employees to accept it has arisen. Even without understanding the system, a few of the people seem to feel that in some way they'll be hurt by it. Ben McGraw, Manager of the Engineering and Maintenance Department, comes to you to discuss the problem.

What You Should Say and Some Responses

"Well, Ben, we should have the new system running in a couple of months if we don't run into some major delays."

"Maybe, but I've already got some problems in my department. Two guys in the maintenance group are really against it. Harold Riggins and Bill Talbot never seem to miss an opportunity to badmouth it."

You shake your head knowingly. "That's to be expected. Most companies run into the same problem any time a new procedure or system is introduced. You always find objectors who are against the setup rather than for it. A lot of people don't like change of any kind, whether they understand it or not."

"The trouble is," Ben comments, "that guys like Riggins and Talbot have big mouths and their words carry a lot of weight with the rest of the group. What worries me is that they'll talk down the computerized system so much that others will begin to feel the same way about it. Is there anything we can do to counteract that?"

"Good question, Ben. What we'll have to do is come up with a way to promote it and show its advantages over what we're doing now. In one way or another, we'll have to also show that the system isn't going to benefit the company alone, but all the people working here as well.

"The problem is how to make the message believable. Coming from supervision or upper management, a few of the employees are apt to discount it as unbelievable."

"I agree," Ben replies, "but if we could get them to understand what we're trying to do, it could make a big difference."

"One thing that I'm planning to do is to bring all the employees together and explain what a computerized system is, how it works, what it will accomplish, the benefits involved, and why we need the system. I'm also going to tell them that we should have had a system like this years ago. As for why we didn't: because it costs a lot of money and requires a considerable investment and development time; and because a lot of training at all levels will be required to set it up properly and make it run right. Lastly, we've been hoping a better and more economical system would materialize.

"Of course, we've been hurt by the delay. Our objective now is to get started on schedule, and get the bugs out fast so it can operate smoothly and efficiently."

Ben nods agreeably. "That sounds good, but we'll probably have to do a lot more to sell them on it."

"Yes, we will. Have you had any orientation sessions with your people yet?"

"No, I thought I'd have the first one next week."

"What are you planning to say?"

"First, I'll talk about the entire system as you will have done, and then I'll explain specifically how it works in our department. After that, I'll give them an opportunity to ask questions. I'll also encourage them to get their doubts and gripes off their chests."

"While you can't stop them from griping and complaining, you may be able to reverse their thinking if you handle them right."

"How would I do that?" Ben asks.

"There are several ways," you say. "One is to get as many people as you can involved in the project. Get them to participate as early as you can in the planning and scheduling. While you're absolutely right in encouraging them to ask questions and tell you their worries, you might think about going a bit further with that.

"In planning how the computer will be used in your operations, you'll come across some problems and also some options. This is the place to get your people involved. Tell them about the problems, and ask for their advice and suggestions. They are the ones who are closest to the job and they may be better equipped to solve the problems.

"Give them a chance to contribute to the program. We know from experience that people tend to support ideas and procedures if they played a part in developing them. But the timing is very important. Always be sure to ask for suggestions before you make a decision, not after. If you simply pay lip service to involvement, you'll be found out."

Ben nods. "I've thought of a couple of problems already."

"Another technique you can use to help you to put the system across is to anticipate particular objections and arguments your people might have. Why would a person object to the system? What would the person be worried about? In our situation, the only valid worry an employee might have is that the person's lack of effort and resultant low productivity might be exposed by the system. For this person, the system presents a danger. But remember, he or she represents only a small minority of your people. For the people who work hard and for people who do extra work, the system will show this and give them the credit and recognition they deserve.

"Another thing, Ben. Be sure to point out how important this system is to the company in keeping it competitive in the industry. Many of our competitors already have such systems in operation. Our failure to do the same would put us at a serious disadvantage, endangering sales and making our jobs less secure. Job security is important to every employee, regardless of his or her level.

"Ben, every department in every company has one or two individuals who are the most popular and highly respected by a majority of the employees. Usually they're experienced and outstanding performers which accounts at least in part for why they're looked up to and respected. If you can take these people into your confidence, convince them that this is a good system, and gain their support, the chances are high they will do a better selling job for you than you could ever do for yourself."

Reasoning and Principle Involved

Persuasion is usually more successful when good salesmanship and logic are applied. A smart manager is aware of this and uses every tool available to him or her to convince people. The best approach is to make the interests of all concerned the goal.

PROBLEM NUMBER 2

What to say to an employee who protests the company's setting of fixed times for lunch and break periods.

The Situation

Maintenance employees at your company long have been given greater leeway than production employees on lunch hours and break periods. The generally established lunch hour for production employees is noon to 1 P.M. Although the official lunch hour for maintenance employees is from 1 to 2 P.M., this period was not strictly adhered to because of work assignments which might be finished before or after 1 P.M. As for break periods, maintenance employees were permitted to take them when it was most convenient, the thought being that the nature and press of the work would dictate the most suitable time. But as operations expanded and the maintenance department grew larger, you saw that permissiveness with regard to lunch and break periods was no longer practical. For one thing, too many employees took advantage of it to extend lunch and break times beyond the specified period. Also, it had become important to have all maintenance people working when production people were away from their workplaces to optimize machine running time. With those things in mind, you posted a notice on the bulletin board fixing the time that lunch and breaks should be taken, and stating that no deviation would be permitted. Within an hour, Walt Murphy, a mechanic came to you to protest.

What You Should Say and Some Responses

"Something seems to be bothering you, Walt. Can I help?"
"You sure can. What you posted on the board is illegal. Lunch and

break periods have been flexible for years and become standard procedure. You can't unilaterally change it. You have to negotiate that with the Union."

"Sorry, Walt, but I don't agree with you. It's my responsibility to run this department efficiently. I can no longer do that with the flexible setup. Besides, I'm not shortening or taking away any time on your lunch and break time. The same lunch and break periods still are in effect."

"No, you can't do that," Walt insists. "If you persist in going ahead with this, I'm going to file a grievance."

"Well, you have the right to do that, but you won't get anywhere with it. The labor agreement contains a 'rights' section that gives management the right to establish or change rules in a reasonable and nondiscriminatory way to maintain or promote shop efficiency. Flexible lunch and break periods were acceptable in the past, but conditions are different today."

Reasoning and Principle Involved

Many union–management contracts and labor agreements today give management the right to unilaterally make a change when efficiency is at stake. Literally, this means management has the right to run the business as it sees fit.

PROBLEM NUMBER 3

What to say to an employee about how he should suggest a procedural change to management.

The Situation

Frank Mellon is a buyer in the Purchasing Department of which you are the assistant manager. Last week he presented an idea to the manager, Bill Post, involving a procedural change in the department. Post turned it down. Convinced that the idea would save the company a considerable amount of money, Mellon comes today to present it to you.

What You Should Say and Some Responses

"Hi, Frank, how are things going?"

"Real good, especially since I've got an idea that will save the company at least $10,000 a year."

"Is that right? I'd heard you had a brainstorm, but I didn't know it was that size," you say with a smile.

"It's all written up in this folder. Take a look and see what you think."

Frank hands you a folder containing about a dozen sheets of paper. The sheets contain mostly handwritten blocks of prose and some charts and graphs, none of which are neatly arranged.

You quickly leaf through the sheets, and then look up at Frank. "This looks like quite a project."

"It sure is. I spent a lot of time on it."

"Bill Post's secretary told me you showed it to him, and he turned it down. That's hard to believe if there are really savings to be realized."

"Well, there's no question in my mind it will save the company at least $10,000 a year, maybe more. I've got documented evidence right here that proves it. Take a look."

You start to review the sheets in more detail. "This looks kind of complicated," you say, and then glance at your watch. "I've got a meeting I have to attend in 15 minutes."

"It's really quite simple," Frank says, refusing to be put off. "The idea is you set up a blanket order with the low bidder on a storeroom item, one that we use quite a few of. But you don't state a fixed quantity. Then when the storeroom runs out, the storekeeper simply phones the vendor and asks for so many to be shipped immediately. The savings comes about in that you don't have to go through the lengthy procedure of issuing a three-part purchase requisition and a six part purchase order each time you want a new supply. Think of all the time and labor you save, not to mention the forms. And think of all the different items in the storeroom to which this could apply."

You look a bit leery. "You may have a point, but I don't think the arrangements will be that simple. What about specifications and terms? What about discounts for purchasing in quantity?"

Frank smiles. "That's all covered in these sheets."

"That may be, but I can't look at it now. Like I said, Frank, I've got to go to a meeting. If you want to leave the papers here with me, I'll be glad to look them over later."

"That's OK with me. Maybe you can find out why Post turned it down. I'm still convinced it will save the company a lot of money."

"OK, I'll look it over and get back to you as soon as I can."

"Thanks," Frank says. "I'm anxious to see if you'll agree with me that it will really save the company a lot of money."

The next day you have an opportunity to look at Frank's proposal. You find it very poorly organized and prepared, and have to spend considerable time rereading it in order to understand it. For one thing, it is too wordy requiring that it be read several times to make sense. For another, much of the information is out of order and is also repetitive. That afternoon, you give it back to Frank.

"What do you think?" Frank asks with concern.

"I think you've got some good ideas, but they're pretty well hidden."

"Hidden? How do you mean?"

"There's no question that your idea is a good one, and could possibly save the company some money. But, Frank, your presentation is terrible; lousy may be a more descriptive word for it. It takes an expert analyst with lots of time to break it down, decipher it, and make sense of it. If there was a way to make a simple explanation difficult, you found the way to do it."

"So what should I do?" Frank asks.

"I'd say you need to redo it. It needs to be reorganized and above all, simplified. Simply presented, and in orderly sequence, the proposal could be very impressive."

Frank's face brightens considerably. "Do you really think so?"

"I wouldn't have said it if I didn't think so."

But now Frank becomes concerned. "I just don't have any experience with this kind of thing. Will you help me?"

"Sure," you say. "As far as I know, I have some free time tomorrow afternoon. Let's tentatively plan on working on it about 1:00 P.M. OK?"

"Yes sir," Frank says with a lot of enthusiasm.

As you planned, you spend about an hour with Frank, pointing out areas where the proposal would have to be revised and reworded. Two days later, Frank returns to your office and leaves the folder on your desk. It now contains the neatly arranged and typed proposal on only five sheets of paper.

"This is more like it," you say. "It's a big improvement."

"Thanks to you and your help. But would you do me one more favor?"

"What's that?" you ask.

"Since I already presented this idea to Bill Post a week ago and he turned it down, would you take it to him now?"

"No, I don't think that's the best way to handle it. Why don't I go with you? You can talk to him about it, and I'll back you up wherever I can."

Frank is pleased with your suggestion. "OK. That sounds like a great idea."

You phone Post for an appointment, explaining the situation. An hour later, you and Frank are seated together in Post's office. Post reads the new proposal with obvious interest, nodding now and then as he comes across an answer to a question he had in mind. Finally, he puts it down, turns to Frank, and says, "You know, it is hard to believe that this proposal is the same one, or even related to the one you made last week. What I looked at then was a hodge-podge, a real jumble. What you have here is a well–thought-out and properly organized presentation."

"Thank you," Frank replies.

Post continues. "Frank, when you approached me a week ago with your proposal, the timing couldn't have been worse. I was ready to leave for a meeting, after which I was scheduled to make a tour of a new installation with a Vice President of the company. Yet I never want to discourage the submission of suggestions and ideas from employees, particularly when one comes from a member of my department.

"So I thought I would take a quick look at what you had in mind. I figured that if it had possibilities, I could get into it in more detail later. Well, as I'm sure you learned, the quick look only confused me and turned me off. That's why I rejected it.

"However, things are different now, thanks to your persistence, Frank, and to the help of the assistant manager," Post says as he smiles at you.

Reasoning and Principle Involved

While ideas of employees are important to management, there's a great deal more to a good idea than the idea itself. The way it's presented to management could make a big difference. Timing is critical as is the quality and form of the proposal itself. Even the best idea, improperly or poorly presented, can fall flat.

PROBLEM NUMBER 4

What to say to a supervisor about how to sell workers on a new system.

The Situation

About a week ago, you held a meeting with your supervisors to tell them that a new system for determining the production output of the various departments of the company would be put into effect in about two months. You told the supervisors that once the system was in operation, management would be able to estimate and schedule production runs more accurately than ever before. In addition, supervisors would know their manpower and equipment requirements well in advance which should result in better personnel and machine utilization. Also, they would be able to distribute the workload more fairly among their people, and should be able to avoid most of the scheduling problems they've become accustomed to. You went on to explain that work standards had been revised and upgraded by the Industrial Relations Department to correct some of the inadequacies and inequities that existed. Today, one of your most conscientious and experienced supervisors, Harold Laney, comes to your office to ask if you had a few minutes to talk about the new system.

What You Should Say and Some Responses

"Sure, Harold, what do you want to talk about?"

"I thought I ought to bring you up to date on the rank and file's attitude regarding the new work measurement system."

"Management's general announcement to employees hasn't even been issued yet," you say.

"I know," Harold replies, "but whenever a major change is expected out of the front office, the word always seems to get around. Anyway, the rumors are flying fast and furious. The people who aren't convinced that the new system will cost them their jobs are sure that it will affect their work pace or cut their personal time. One of the girls said that it was management's intention to check up on employees' every move like kids in the first grade. Another guy says it won't be long before supervisors will be keeping track of how much time people spend in the restroom.

"And it's not just in my department," Harold adds. "I've been talking with some of the other supervisors, and they've been getting the same kind of comments from their people. The employees seem to be strongly against the system. They figure it's going to hurt them one way or another."

You nod thoughtfully. "That's not unexpected. Work measurement and performance evaluation systems are almost always received this way. There's usually a lot of anxiety and fear generated with such plans, but I didn't expect the resistance this soon. It's so easy to misjudge the power of the rumor mill. We'll have to take action to counter it at once.

"We figured that the promotion and selling of the system would be made simultaneously with the general announcement that was to be made in about a month. But now it looks like we'll have to move everything forward to counteract the damage done by the grapevine."

"What kind of selling job did you have in mind?" Harold asks. "And what can I and the other supervisors do to help?"

"You can do quite a bit. In fact, the failure or success of the system will be primarily up to you and the other supervisors. It's the supervisor who is closest to the operations who, with the willing cooperation and support of the workers will make a new system work. Without the cooperation of the crew, no system would have much of a chance."

Taking some sheets from your desk you go on, "Here's what the Industrial Relations and Systems Departments have planned to use to sell the system. I'll have these sheets run off this afternoon so they will be ready for distribution in the morning. I hadn't planned another meeting on the new system this soon, but considering what you told me, we'll have to accelerate this entire project. You can notify all the other supervisors that I am scheduling a meeting for 9:00 A.M. tomorrow.

"But now I'd like to give you a preview of what the selling program will consist of. I've found that when people anticipate a significant change, the details of which are neither known nor understood by them, they imagine the worst. The words *work measurement* imply to many people that the company will be checking up on them on the amount of work they do and what they don't do. Work measurement can also be a way of applying pressure on them to increase their output.

"Actually, this isn't the purpose of the procedure at all, and the selling program hopefully will put this across to them. Work measurement not only benefits management, but also employees at all levels. This is what we'll have to get across to our people, and we'll have to prove to them how they stand to benefit specifically. For one thing, it will make work distribution more fair and equitable. The employee who goofs off won't get a free ride on the back of other employees. Better planning and scheduling will increase efficiency, and will also relieve pressures and tensions brought on by too many rush orders and projects. We should have a more relaxed and healthy work group as a result.

"Being more efficient means more on-time deliveries and better customer service. Most employees understand that when our customers are dissatisfied, there is more stress on everyone, and everyone's job is a little less secure. Also, I'm sure that some of our competitors already have in use sophisticated work measurement systems. If we didn't do the same, we'd be at a distinct competitive disadvantage, and jeopardize all of our jobs.

"Another important selling point we want to make is that an accurate work measurement system helps the employee who wants to move up on the job by showing management what he or she can do. With such a system, productive work is revealed and no longer covered up. Management is able to properly reward good performers. The only person who really has to fear work measurement or be anxious·about it is the goof-off and the alibi artist. In my opinion, we have very few such employees."

Reasoning and Principle Involved

There's more to assuring that a new procedure or system will be a success than simply implementing it. Management must see to it that the project is fully explained and sold to the employees. In the final analysis, it's the first-line manager who, with the cooperation and support of his or her people, makes a new system work.

PROBLEM NUMBER 5

What to say to an employee who objects to management's considering making a change in a longstanding practice.

The Situation

It has been a longstanding practice in your department for employees to take coffee breaks when they want to. However, as the department has grown in size and work teams have increased in number, the practice has become increasingly a problem. When during a recent Production Department meeting, someone suggested that coffee breaks be limited to specific times of the day to avoid slowing or disrupting operations, management said that this might be done. Not surprisingly, news of this possible action got around the plant quickly. The morning after the meeting, Steve Porter, a packager in the finishing area came to your office to talk to you about it.

What You Should Say and Some Responses

"Good morning, Steve. How are you today?"

"Pretty good, I guess. Say, there's a rumor going around that I don't like."

"What's that, Steve?"

"Well, it's rumored that were going to be cheated out of being able to take coffee breaks when we want and will have to take them at a set time."

You smile and shake your head wonderingly. "News of a possible change sure travels fast around here. Yes, there's a good chance that specific times will be set for coffee breaks. But you would not be cheated out of anything. You'd get the same amount of time you always got."

"That may be. But it would amount to a unilateral change in working conditions, and that would violate the union–management contract."

"No, it wouldn't," you say. "If the change is made, you'll be getting no less than you have gotten in the past. Working conditions will stay the same. The current coffee break setup interferes too much with production operations. This didn't matter when the company was small, but now that it's larger, became more automated, and more people and equipment are involved, it's becoming a problem."

Steve refuses to accept your explanation. "That's a management problem, not the employees'. When a benefit or privilege is given for a number of years, it becomes standard practice and an obligation. You can't just take it away without the union's approval. It's a negotiable matter."

"Steve, like I said, nothing would be taken away. Management would be making a small change to improve operating efficiency, something it's entitled to do."

"I don't agree. If you change the coffee break system, I'm going to turn in a grievance."

Reasoning and Principle Involved

While there's no guarantee on how an arbitrator might rule when management's action doesn't eliminate a privilege but instead lends official status to it, the decision is likely to go against the union. It's management's responsibility to do everything it can to improve operating efficiency and to protect profit margins.

PROBLEM NUMBER 6

What to say to an employee who is habitually late to arrive at work.

The Situation

You were promoted to office manager of your company a few months ago. As of today, you feel that you got to know your people quite well. But you've noticed that Jack Cramer has usually been late arriving each morning. Since you know that Cramer has been a loyal and conscientious employee for many years, you wonder how he acquired this habit and has not corrected it. You finally get to the point where you decide to talk to him about it.

What You Should Say and Some Responses

"Say, Jack, I've been intending to talk to you for some time about your tardiness. I know you're aware that all employees are expected to be at their desks at 8:00 A.M., but you seldom are. Is there some reason you can't be here on time every day?"

"Yes, I suppose there is. My wife and I live out in the country. She has a job over at The Acme Company in Summerville. Ever since she took that job, I've always waited for her to leave home for work before I left. I wanted to be sure she got off OK. I guess it's just become a habit."

"I see. Well, I think we have to find an answer to this problem. At the moment, I see a couple of possibilities. We could make your official working hours start and end 15 minutes later than the other people in the office, but there are some disadvantages to that. It would be important for me to make sure that all the other employees who come in contact with you, or know about you, understand the new schedule and accept the reason for it as being valid only for you.

"Another disadvantage would be that some of the other employees might feel you're receiving special treatment. Then again, it's conceivable that other employees would also like to work different hours. We could get into a complex and difficult situation on that."

You wait to see if Jack has any comment or offers to make different arrangements at home, but he remains quiet.

"Jack, I feel that the overall needs of the company have been validly established as calling for the present hours, and that there should be no exceptions. I know you've been a loyal and conscientious employee for many years. Your contribution to the company's office operations is recognized and appreciated.

"But I don't feel we can make any exceptions in the schedule because this would probably lead to friction and poor morale."

Jack decides to go along with you. "Maybe I can get my wife to leave earlier in the morning. That would solve the problem. If not, I'll leave before her." Jack smiles, and then continues. "You know, I said that my leaving after her had simply become a habit. Our community has grown considerably in the last few years, and we have a lot more neighbors now. So I'm not so worried about leaving her alone at that hour in the morning. I'll be getting in here on time starting tomorrow."

"Thanks, Jack," you say as you leave him.

Reasoning and Principle Involved

Managers must always make a strong effort to preserve the uniformity of adhering to company policy when dealing with employee behavior. This can most easily be done by appealing to the employee's sense of pride and loyalty, and pointing out that what the company expects isn't really too hard to conform to.

PROBLEM NUMBER 7

What to say to a storeroom manager on how he should handle some major changes in procedures.

The Situation

Your company has embarked on an extensive project to cut costs and improve efficiency in the company's storeroom. Among your objectives are to reduce inventories, eliminate duplications and obsolete items, prevent frequent outages, and speed up operations through better arrangement of materials. Your storeroom manager, John Wagner, is an aggressive and enthusiastic person in his 30's. Although you are sure he will be eager to introduce and implement changes in procedure, you are dubious about how the storeroom people will accept the changes. You ask him to come to your office to discuss the problems he may encounter.

What You Should Say and Some Responses

"John, I assume you've read my report on how we intend to renovate the storeroom and update the operations. Do you have any suggestions on the project? We're still in the planning stage and will probably have several meetings with the Engineering Department before we finalize what we will do."

"It looks good to me. You and I have talked about some of these changes before, and I agree that the sooner we get started on them the better. Our storeroom costs are continuing to climb. The computer should enable us to cut out a lot of duplications and to better control our inventories."

"Have any of your people talked to you about the project?"

"No, at least not recently. Why do you ask?"

"I feel that some of your long service people might not welcome some of the changes we'd like to make. They may be set in their ways and resist these new procedures. You know, some of the employees in other departments of the company feared the computer when it was first brought in."

John nods. "I hadn't thought about that."

"It's natural to fear change. Change is seldom welcomed unless people demand it to relieve themselves of a burden or a discomfort. People fear change mostly because they don't know what to expect. Even minor or insignificant changes disturb habits and routines causing worry and stress. It takes time for new habits and routines to be formed, and some people need more time than others to get accustomed to something new."

"Is there something we can do to help the employees to adjust and to accept change more readily?" John asks.

"Yes, there is. In fact, there are several things you can do yourself as we get into the project. For example, change is sometimes more acceptable if it is managed without a lot of fanfare and publicity. Although it isn't always possible to make a change this way, the less adjustment that is required of people, the less apparent it is that you are making a change.

"As soon as we get our budget approved, you should tell your people what we're intending to do. The word is going to get out anyway. It's much easier to present truths in the beginning than it is to correct untruths and rumors later.

"It's a good idea also, to show confidence that the change will be a success. If other people sense that you have doubts about it, they will also have doubts, and the road ahead may then be rocky.

"While I don't think you'll be adding or laying off any people at least to start, try to maintain the status of individuals whenever possible. You can get into trouble if you build one person's status at the expense of another's. But recognize and respect resistance. Discuss an objection instead of flatly stating that everything has been decided.

"John, you may have to be very patient with one or two of your people. Allow time for a change to take effect. People cannot be expected to completely and enthusiastically accept a change immediately after they learn of it."

Reasoning and Principle Involved

There are many ways that management can sell change to employees. When managers develop a perceptiveness to people's feelings, they are much more likely to be successful having changes accepted without complaints or resistance.

PROBLEM NUMBER 8

What to say to a manager about how to sell a change by using a well-liked employee to push it.

The Situation

Management of your company recently decided to expend the use of the computer into additional departments of the company. Included were to be the estimating, planning and scheduling divisions of the Engineering Department. Since you were aware of the difficulties encountered by other departments in selling the computer to employees, you feel you should discuss the problem with Bart Stevens, Manager of the Engineering Department.

What You Should Say and Some Responses

"Bart, do you anticipate any serious problems when we start using the computer for estimating, planning and scheduling?"

"Yes, I do," Bart replies. "Aside from the obvious fear some of the technicians and clerks might have that they could lose their jobs, we're probably going to have a few people who will oppose the system no matter what we do to sell it and put it across."

"I agree with that," you say. "I've learned from experience that, at times, anticipation is a powerful tool for such situations. I was wondering how you were planning to handle such a problem."

"The way I see it, most of the people do a good job for the company, and they're the ones who will get the most benefit from the computer system. But some of the marginal workers might be against the system, figuring that management is trying to snow them just to get their cooperation."

"I can see your reasoning," you say. "But, as you pointed out, we've got a credibility gap to contend with. Since management has a lot at stake here, it's only natural we'd do what we can to push and sell the system."

You think a bit and then say, "Bart, what we need is a salesman who is not part of management."

"Are you saying we should get someone from outside the company to help us do a selling job?"

"Not outside—inside. I'm talking about someone right in your own department."

Bart scratches his head. "I don't follow you. Those are the very guys we are trying to sell."

"Right. If we could get them to convince each other, we'd have it made. Bart, what's the name of that extroverted guy who's always promoting some event or other, and serves as chairman of a couple of committees?"

"I think you mean Joe Wilder."

"Wilder, that's it. How would you characterize him, Bart?"

"Well, I'd say he's a politician and a real talker. He should be holding a public office job instead of working in a plant. He's friendly, sociable, and everyone likes him."

"How is he as a worker?"

"Above average. Wilder is a good, dependable employee."

"Fine! Now suppose you were to get him out on the department floor selling the computer to the machine operators and the fellows in the shop. Do you think it would help?"

"Yes sir!" Bart says. "Joe's a big man in the plant. When he opens his mouth, everybody listens. But why should he sell the computer for management? Unless he was really convinced that the system had a lot of advantages?"

You smile. "Of course, he'd first have to be convinced, even to the point where he was very enthusiastic. And that's where you come in. If you can do an outstanding selling job on Wilder, and maybe one of his buddies about the computer's value and usefulness, you could be creating some super salespersons."

"Are you saying we should use the strategies and promotional ideas we've been talking about on Wilder and one of his buddies in advance of the rest of the gang?"

"Right. And you can go even further. You might be able to offer him an incentive that would make him want to push the computer without having to be asked."

"What type of incentive?"

"You could get him closely and personally involved. Simply tipping him off in advance of the others would be a way of treating him specially. He'd be flattered, I'm sure, and when you explained the situation, you could ask him to keep it quiet."

"The 'situation' being most people's natural resistance to change," Bart comments.

"Exactly! Most people's, but not his. As a person with exceptional intelligence, acumen, and perceptiveness, you'd be selecting him to work with you in organizing the selling program and putting it across."

Bart nods enthusiastically. "I could sit down with him, let him in on what we're trying to do, and ask his advice on how we should go about it."

"Now you're cooking, Bart. If you could get Wilder who has the respect and admiration of the gang to work with you, he'd be personally involved in a very special way. It would give him a chance to get some recognition and management attention, and it would give him a stake in the computer's success he might work hard to protect."

Reasoning and Principle Involved

When managers acknowledge that there's more than one way to sell change, they should be able to come up with a selling technique to fit their particular situation. In addition, the more information managers can give people about a change, and the more ways they learn to do it, the easier it will be for them to sell the change.

INDEX